the
Spokane
River

# the Spokane River

*edited by*

## PAUL LINDHOLDT

A Samuel and Althea Stroum Book

UNIVERSITY OF WASHINGTON PRESS

*Seattle*

*The Spokane River* was supported by a grant from the
Samuel and Althea Stroum Endowed Book Fund.

Copyright © 2018 by the University of Washington Press
Printed and bound in the United States of America
Design by Katrina Noble
Composed in Bulmer, typeface designed by Morris Fuller Benton
24   23   22            6   5   4

Cover and interior photographs from the Washington State
Digital Archives: (Front cover) Spokane River at Post Falls,
Idaho, n.d., by Asahel Curtis. (Title page) Aerial view of
Spokane looking east to Idaho, 1950. (Part 1) Fisherman
along Spokane River, n.d., by F. Palmer. (Part 2) Mounted
party of Spokane Indians alongside Spokane River near
Fort Spokane, n.d. (Part 3) Spokane River dam, n.d.

Map by Raena Ballantyne DeMaris,
DeMaris Integrated GeoSpatial Solutions, LLC

UNIVERSITY OF WASHINGTON PRESS
www.washington.edu/uwpress

LIBRARY OF CONGRESS CATALOGING-IN-PUBLICATION DATA ON FILE

ISBN 978-0-295-74313-4 (pbk),
ISBN 978-0-295-74314-1 (ebook)

# Contents

## Encounters and Excursions

## Culture, History, Society

## Beneath the Surface

# Acknowledgments

Among the many people I would like to recognize, I begin with the citizens of Spokane. In the past decade, civic leaders and residents have come together to celebrate the Spokane River and make amends for those who so sorely mistreated it in the past. Many contributors to this book have been at the forefront of those celebrations and remediations. The Spokane Riverkeeper program at the Center for Justice deserves special recognition. Beatrice Lackaff was industrious in helping me select images to illustrate certain chapters. Joyce Vermillion indexed the book—then indexed it again after changes needed to be made. Members of the Spokane Tribe of Indians, including Margo Hill and Barry Moses, wrote key chapters and generated ideas that helped to sharpen the focus. Biologist David Boose of Gonzaga University read and commented on a full draft of the manuscript, as did historian Bill Youngs at Eastern Washington University and lawyer Rachael Paschal Osborn. Raena Ballantyne DeMaris enthusiastically agreed to create a map of the river. Karen Lindholdt gave her time to free me up to work on this project. My thanks go out to all of them.

Several foundations also got behind the book early on, allowing me and others the resources to edit, write, and pay for art and written contributions. The Northwest Institute for Advanced Study at Eastern Washington University gave me the gift of time through a Faculty Research Grant. The Community Building Foundation in Spokane liberally funded the writers and the work on the index. The Columbia Institute for Water Policy helped afford permissions and rights. The Smith-Barbieri Progressive Fund, a Spokane-based charitable organization, likewise provided sponsorship. The book has been a truly collaborative community process from the beginning.

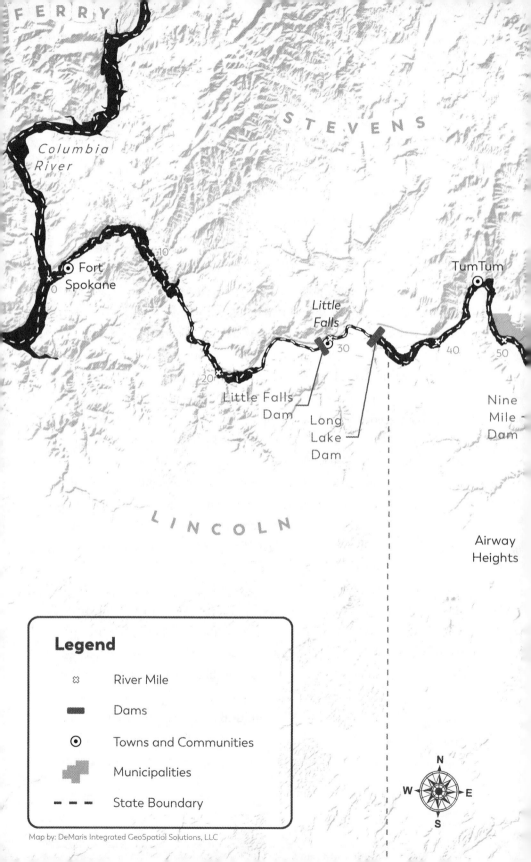

FERRY

STEVENS

Columbia
River

Fort
Spokane

10

0

20

Little
Falls

30

TumTum

40

50

Little Falls
Dam

Long
Lake
Dam

Nine
Mile
Dam

LINCOLN

Airway
Heights

## Legend

⊗ River Mile

▬ Dams

◉ Towns and Communities

▮ Municipalities

‑ ‑ ‑ State Boundary

N
W E
S

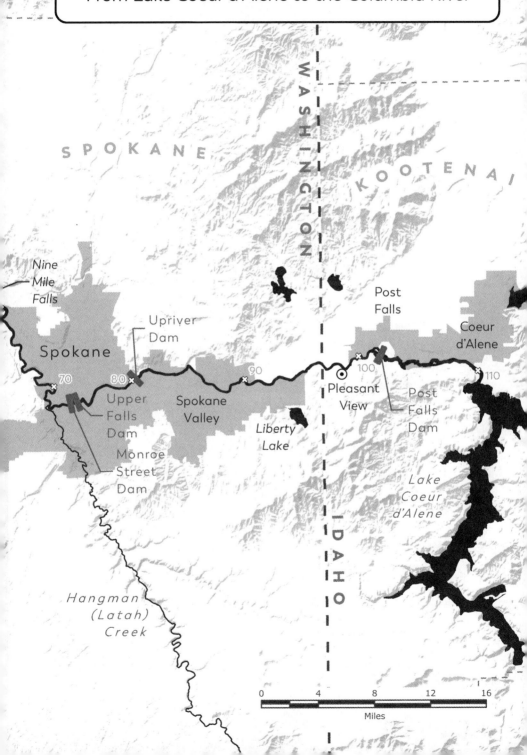

# The Spokane River
## From Lake Coeur d'Alene to the Columbia River

WASHINGTON

IDAHO

SPOKANE

KOOTENAI

Nine Mile Falls

Spokane

Upriver Dam

Upper Falls Dam

Monroe Street Dam

Spokane Valley

Liberty Lake

Post Falls

Coeur d'Alene

Pleasant View

Post Falls Dam

Lake Coeur d'Alene

Hangman (Latah) Creek

70

80

90

100

110

0    4    8    12    16
Miles

the
Spokane
River

# Introduction

PAUL LINDHOLDT

"NEAR NATURE, NEAR PERFECT," THE OFFICIAL SLOGAN OF THE CITY of Spokane, points to the Spokane River in particular. It is a bountiful trout stream, a recreational outlet for thousands of residents and tourists every year, a gathering place for Native Americans, and a site of competition over natural resources. Energy interests would like to squeeze more power from the river. Civic interests want to develop the shore with more parks and tourist attractions. Ecologists want to increase dam releases to enhance river health and restore native redband trout, whose populations have fallen. The recreation industry calls for more sites to launch and take out canoes, kayaks, and rafts. The Environmental Protection Agency and the Washington State Department of Ecology have weighed in on the need to clean up mine wastes washed downriver from northern Idaho and hazardous effluents discarded by industries in the cities along the river's course. A citizens' initiative has authorized funds to remodel Riverfront Park, the site of Expo '74, a makeover that offers promise for the river's health. We believe that all these diverse interests will welcome this book, in which we have aimed to survey the river's history impartially, describe its features affectionately, and address the perils that continue to beset it.

The Spokane River's basin drains an area of some 6,439 square miles (16,161 square kilometers), much of it in the mountains of Idaho. The only other book about this major tributary of the Columbia River is thirty years old and long out of print. It is high time for an updated account.

Among other things, this book honors the inhabited landscape the river runs through. This is not the primeval wilderness of legend but a cultivated landscape bearing the imprint of millennia of human presence. Historic (and prehistoric) patterns of habitation are easy to overlook, in part because some have been consciously obscured. In the 1850s, Col. George Wright hanged members of the Yakama and Spokane tribes and weakened their ability to fight by slaughtering hundreds of their horses. Today his name memorializes a fort, a cemetery, and an arterial road. Qualchan, the best-known of the chiefs Wright hanged, lends his name to a real-estate development, a golf course, and a foot race. On state maps, the stream where Qualchan died appears as Latah Creek (from the Nez Perce word for fish) but in the national registries it is known as Hangman. Federal cartographers will not let the state forget this treacherous bit of regional history. Evidence from salmon DNA recovered in nearby archaeological digs reveals that the Spokane River hosted "June hogs," salmon weighing as much as sixty pounds, fish that probably traveled clear into Idaho via Hangman Creek.

Other rivers I have known—the Skagit and the Columbia Rivers in Washington, the Snake in Idaho, the Youghiogheny in West Virginia—all seemed to me to run to sea at predictable rates. Not the Spokane. Our unpredictable local river foams, lulls, and recharges from invisible springs. Its volume ranges from 43,000 cubic feet per second (cfs), as in the spring of 2017, to less than 500 cfs in the late summer. The river water flows warm, then cold, then warm again along its course. Last summer, while kayaking between Lower Crossing and Plese Flats, I spotted a bundle of cottonwood leaves moving across the current. It made a sweeping turn and headed upstream. Was some hidden eddy doubling the river back upon itself? Was a fishing line being reeled from shore? Or was the bundle being moved by a beaver, its head and body hidden? I will never know for sure. I could not see below the surface glare. My best guess is that an animal had gnawed a branch off a toppled tree and was breasting the seasonal runoff to tote the fodder to its lodge. It was using the river as both a highway and a food source, much as indigenous people have done for thousands of years.

From the prospect of my hometown of Seattle, Spokane was little more than a hot spot studded with pine trees that blew pollen in the springtime and smelled good after a rain. Today the scent of needles in hot sun mixes with the faint vanilla odor of pine bark to blast me back to childhood vacations in eastern Washington with my father, the camping and fishing and hunting that drew us there, the meandering rivers. When Eastern Washington University offered me a job that brought me to Spokane in 1994, I found no book to read about the river that anchors the city and gave it the original name of Spokane Falls; that supported local aboriginal people and hosted thousands of others who gathered along the lower half of the river's 111 miles during salmon runs. They took their fair share of oceangoing protein. Presiding salmon chiefs distributed the catch and let other fish survive to spawn.

In recent years I have seen rafts of nutrient-fed vegetation clogging Lake Spokane above the Long Lake Dam, plumes of sediment muddying Hangman Creek, summer flows so low that many of the rapids at Barker Road had disappeared. These sights let me know the river needs attention and help. I have met people who know the river better than I do, whose relationships go back much further than mine, friends who have marshaled local knowledge and lore and write about it well. For this book, I have turned to those people: the paddlers, poets, and archaeologists; the entomologists and hydrologists; the historians and culture warriors; people who catch fish and people who write about fish; the local folks whose families have lived along this river and its tributaries for decades or for centuries.

No such book would be complete without the sanction of and input from the Spokane Tribe of Indians and from others who know the river well. Barry G. Moses was exceptionally helpful. Several chapters, including his, contain words and phrases in Salish. Careful readers will notice that the transcription style differs from chapter to chapter: *Nx Wl Wl tsuten* versus *nxʷlxʷlcutn*, for example, or a question mark used instead of a *ʔ*. We have retained the individual authors' choices of spelling, which serve as important historical and linguistic markers. These variations may reflect attempts made by elders to write for an English-speaking audience before the creation of a standardized writing system, for instance, or the inclusion of a Salish word in an English-language newspaper with little leeway for diacritical usage. In all cases, we believe the context is important.

Written material about the river itself was scant and scattered when I began. Much of the Native knowledge was preserved through oral tradition, but few fluent Salish speakers remained. The river lay locked in a dozen regional histories, among them *The Fair and the Falls*, the 1996 account of the city and the river by my colleague William Youngs. I realized the project would succeed only if I yielded to those who had longer and deeper intimacy with the river than I did. This collection of writings by twenty-eight different authors—a mix of the personal, creative, historical, scientific, and religious—touches on the multiple dimensions of our living river.

To reconstruct the history of human presence on the river, I turned to people from the Spokane Tribe of Indians and to colleagues at Eastern Washington University's Archaeological and Historical Services. The archaeologists attest to more than eight thousand years of Native presence, with the oldest civilization in present-day Washington State located at the confluence of Hangman Creek and the Spokane River. The archaeologists also bring into focus a range of artifacts and ancient lifeways. The organic river begins at Lake Coeur d'Alene (French for "heart of an awl"), named after the indigenous people and the acuteness of their skill at bartering with the French-Canadian fur traders in the early nineteenth century.

The Spokane River has inspired many forms of writing, research, and photography, from poems and personal essays to scientific discoveries. Just as the Euro-American founders of Spokane marveled at the river's falls and built the town around them, so the water up- and downstream from the city continues to center our lives today. Any royalties from the book will go to support the fine work undertaken by the Spokane Riverkeeper Program, including patrolling the river, public outreach, and scientific testing to monitor the river's health.

The book's opening section, "Encounters and Excursions," includes memoirs of swimming, canoeing, and fishing; accounts of pollution, rescues, and dangers; and meditations and commentaries on the river and its banks. Tod Marshall, the Washington State poet laureate, gives readers some regional history and free-spirited ways to enjoy the water. Tim Connor has been swimming Northwest waters for decades and focuses here on a stretch of the river whose recharge from the aquifer makes its flows particularly strong and cold. Becky Kramer, a staff writer for the *Spokesman-Review* newspaper, profiles the fisheries biologist Chris Donley, who grew up along its banks. Julie Titone, a seasoned paddler, takes us to the river's origins high in the mountains of Idaho. Few people know that the river holds enough native trout to buoy a year-round guide service and to have engaged the sociologist and fisherman Bob Bartlett for three decades. Nance Van Winckel finds poetry in the flotsam and the forces of the river's current. Businessman Chris Kopczynski offers a recollection of his childhood along the banks of Latah (Hangman) Creek, and the novelist Jess Walter concludes the section with some good clean fun satirizing wilderness evangelists in our grubby urban out-of-doors.

"Culture, History, Society" reaches back to a wide variety of ancestral pasts. Barry Moses and Margo Hill interview tribal family members and friends. They recover what we lost linguistically and ecologically with colonization and the building of dams on the Spokane. Bill Youngs resurrects a battle between the sport fishing and lumber interests from the city's earliest decades. William Stimson brings us to the mid-twentieth century, when citizens cooperated to fund a state-of-the-art sewage treatment plant to help clean up the sump that the river had become. Beatrice Lackaff lovingly recounts the genesis of People's Park in the early 1970s, when the banks of the Spokane River and Hangman Creek hosted a counterculture on the same site where Indians had gathered to catch and trade the salmon that ran up from the sea.

In the 1980s, other fans of the Spokane River collectively funded and built the Centennial Trail—a twelve-foot-wide, sixty-mile paved path that follows the river from Lake Coeur d'Alene in Idaho to Lake Spokane. Guadalupe Flores was involved and tells that story here. The Spokane Valley–Rathdrum Prairie Aquifer, which exchanges water with the river for those same sixty miles, entered the public consciousness in the 1990s, when the Burlington Northern railroad applied for permits to construct a huge refueling depot over the aquifer. John Roskelley, who was a Spokane County commissioner at that time, recalls the slick lobbying efforts that resulted in the half-million-gallon diesel holding tank being built and the spill that occurred in its first year of operation.

The second part of this book concludes with two poems by Sherman Alexie, one of the best-known Native American writers working today. Born on the Spokane Reservation, educated at Gonzaga University in Spokane and Washington State University in Pullman, Alexie has returned to the river often in his writings. In his 1998 film *Smoke Signals*, the most moving scene for many viewers is the conclusion, where Victor Joseph scatters his father's ashes into the river from one of the city footbridges. In a 2010 interview with Alexie and director Chris Eyre, we get a glimpse into the difficulties of filming on the Spokane River now that it has been constrained by industry. Eyre remembers: "We went out and scouted it, and the runoff was pretty great in the spring, and we thought, wow, these falls look beautiful. And we went back a week later, and they had turned the falls off at the dam, and the falls were dried up. We checked to make sure they would be on the day we were shooting; they were, or they got them turned on. We went back and got that shot. Luckily we'd realized that at some point they go off, and somebody governs that and not to show up on that day."

Shooting the movie cost $75,000 a day; cast and crew could not afford to second-guess the schedule of the dam releases. Corporate management of the river affects not only ecosystems—as we learn in several detailed chapters here—but also human systems and the arts. *Smoke Signals*, as "the second highest grossing independent film" of 1998 (according to Professor Joanna Hearne, who interviewed Eyre), is also "the only film ever written and directed by Native Americans that received national and international distribution."

The two Sherman Alexie poems included here strike notes of sorrow and anger at the dams, impassable to salmon, that have ended the massive runs of fish. Scholar Chad Wriglesworth analyzes these poems and the city's decision to carve one of them into stone in an art installation downtown.

The book's final section, "Beneath the Surface," focuses on the politics of the river and scientific research on its waters and ecosystem. Jack Nisbet takes a detailed look at the twelve years of coexistence between Natives and fur traders at Spokane House, the trading post founded in 1810 at the junction of the Spokane and Little Spokane Rivers. There, peaceable commerce and intermarriage prevailed. Biologist Allan Scholz blends history and ichthyology to analyze the environmental forces that have affected anadromous fish in the watershed. Also, in a rare interdisciplinary collaboration, aquatic entomologist Camille McNeely and geologist Carmen Nezat take readers beneath the river's surface to examine the effects of climate, water quality, mining, and water flow on the insect population.

Many experts have been willing to share their expertise, including Spokane County water-resource manager Stan Miller, who transports us underneath the Earth's crust to understand the hydrology that links the river and the aquifer. Lawyer Rachael Osborn focuses on the need for consistent instream flows to keep the ecosystem healthy and in balance. Seattle-area artist Don Fels traces PCB pollution in the river to an unlikely source: pigments manufactured in India and used in newspaper printing. The final chapters here imagine possible futures for the river. William Skylstad, bishop emeritus of the Roman Catholic Diocese of Spokane, submits his vision of a sustainable eco-theology, and three Spokane riverkeepers outline the history of their program and identify one of the major water-quality threats. Gonzaga University environmental studies professor Greg Gordon suggests ways to rewild the river, with minimal intervention, in the hope of promoting a more sustainable future.

The Native peoples and the river's current used to be one. That bond was severed after the energy industry clogged the river with dams. Many of the rapids and prolific fish runs swiftly disappeared. The indigenous people whose cultures relied on the free-flowing water stopped coming from afar for seasonal salmon gathering. Once an abundance of hydraulic wildness, the Spokane River grew tamer by the decade. But no human technology may forever halt a river current. Just as people from around the nation came together in North Dakota to try to protect the water there from an oil pipeline, so Northwest citizens are accomplishing the demolition or bypass of outworn dams. Time might reunite the Spokane River's rapids, fish, and people.

There is much cause for optimism. The Spokane Tribe of Indians has gained state and federal consent to build a casino in Airway Heights. The income from that enterprise will allow the reintroduction of salmon to the Columbia and the Spokane Rivers. The absence of fish ladders at the Grand Coulee and Little Falls Dams, however, remains a serious obstacle to salmon reintroduction. Those dams may eventually need to be abandoned once their reservoirs fill with silt or alternative energy sources supersede the hydroelectric power they provide.

People who have easy access to the river are more likely to recognize its value and act to enhance it. This theory grew out of a 1908 proposal by the Olmsted Brothers firm of landscape architects, which proposed paths and parks to connect people and the river. Few of the public access points they proposed were created, but one of them, Latah Park, might come to pass at last. A citizens' group is planning a pathway and interpretive signs. The path will follow a narrow swath of land upstream from the mouth of Hangman Creek to what is now Hangman Golf Course. Other citizens are working to curtail the passage of the trains that transport oil and coal beside the river and create the risk of catastrophic pollution in the event of an accident. There is also cause for hope that Washington and Idaho will come together to slow the depletion of the aquifer that slakes the thirst of several cities but on which the river's health depends.

The Spokane River, the spirit of this place, is worthy of our finest treatment. It is alive. This book is its biography—a testament to the energy and beauty it has generated for millennia.

# Encounters
# and Excursions

# Of Nudity and Violence, Waking and Water

TOD MARSHALL

> Creation is a great flood, forever flowing, in lovely and terrible
> waves. In everything, the shimmer of creation, and never the finality
> of the created.
>
> —D. H. LAWRENCE, *Mornings in Mexico*

I KNOW THAT THE CATCHIEST WAY TO START—FISHHOOK THROWN
into the reader's stream of consciousness—would be a detailed description
of naked bodies slipping through a cold, clear river—breasts and buttocks,
flanks and thighs, the shadowy basin on a bare ankle—but you'll have to trust
me; the nudity comes later. First, the graphic violence.

The Spokane River as we know it began with a flood, which means that, fig-
uratively, the city of Spokane, Washington, began with a flood, a violent wash
of water. To the east: Lake Missoula during the Glacial Age, three thousand
square miles, two thousand feet deep. All of it dammed naturally at what is
now the Idaho-Montana border on the Clark Fork River, a huge, icy cork that
kept back five hundred cubic miles of water. As the glaciers began to melt
about 750,000 years ago, geologists theorize, huge icebergs broke off into the
Missoula Basin; these made the water levels rise (imagine a bathtub ringed

by the Bitterroots and the Anaconda-Pintler Range, and the creatures that swam in those chilly depths) and overflow the frozen dam. This erosion ate rugged channels into the dam. Huge icebergs pinballed through the rivulets, breaking the blockage down to nothing in a matter of days.

No flood has been as destructive. The water flow has been estimated at four hundred million cubic feet per second (cfs). Consider the Amazon's meager flow of six million cfs; consider that four hundred million cfs is a greater moving volume than all the rivers currently flowing on this planet. Lake Missoula's release scarred the surface of the earth, its water lashing across the land, scouring, tearing, rending.

And then: scablands, basalt columns, deep ravines, the fertile depository of soil called the Palouse, and, the valley where my home, Spokane, Washington, would one day arise as a frontier city. In this changed, brutalized landscape, the great Lake Missoula's wash of water wasn't the first violence wrought upon the region—or the last.

In late summer, walking the many hiking trails along the river—trails that thread their way from the western edge of downtown deep into the suburbs and beyond, into the ponderosa forests and bare ravines that taper off into the high desert stretching across central Washington—you have to lift your feet to keep from kicking up clouds of dust. Leaves and bunchgrass are layered with a fine film that almost seems to cling to the plants; even the rare blackberry bushes offer fruit with a wine-like, earthy tinge. Although the temperature usually isn't as hot as Houston or anything at all like the southwestern US desert, the sun beats down for months with a relentless yellow heat. If it's August in Spokane, then maybe the last rain was in June; if it's September, then maybe the dull dryness has been eased by a shower or two—or perhaps summer has returned for one last flash of ninety-degree weather before October's chill. Regardless, on this walk, your shoes are dusty; the sun burns your neck; you can feel rivulets of sweat springing in your hair. Just north of where you walk, you can hear the distinct rhythm of moving water. Listen. Tell me that you're not interested in swimming, in taking a dip in the clear, cool current.

Where are you off to, lady? for I see you,
You splash in the water there, yet stay stock still in your room.

Dancing and laughing along the beach came the twenty-ninth
    bather,
The rest did not see her, but she saw them and loved them.

The beards of the young men glisten'd with wet, it ran from
    their long hair,
Little streams pass'd all over their bodies.

An unseen hand also pass'd over their bodies,
It descended tremblingly from their temples and ribs.

The young men float on their backs, their white bellies bulge
    to the sun, they do not ask who seizes fast to them,
They do not know who puffs and declines with pendant and
    bending arch,
They do not think whom they souse with spray.

WALT WHITMAN, "SONG OF MYSELF," SECTION 11

*Frontier mentality* means many different things to different people. For some, the word *frontier* evokes the adventurous spirit of Conestoga wagons and *Westward Ho!* expansionist attitudes—recast images of the Puritans' billowing sails. For others, that vision of opportunity is necessarily coupled to the politics of violent exploitation. Another definition probably articulates the profoundly American impulse to seek isolated space away from what Whitman called the "blab of the pave," a way back into the Thoreauvian woods where one can live the simple life (or cook up half-baked plans to overthrow the perishing republic). Still another narrative implies a wild, on-the-edge-of-civilization lawlessness in which ne'er-do-wells thrive. Aspects of many of these conceptions probably share ideological space in the story of the West. From brave Natty Bumppo, cavorting about James Fenimore Cooper's Catskills (look out for that twig!), to e. e. cummings's musing on the "defunct" Buffalo Bill, the isolated individual intent on wending his way through and inflicting his will upon this Western world is a recurring figure. This mythology also has a darker side, one that includes Ted Kaczynski (the Unabomber), the lonely world of the misanthrope and the fugitive, and various angry militias and their frequent messages of hate. Sometimes, to live and let live in the West is driven more by fear than laissez-faire. Being able to do your own thing, whether that's slaughter buffalo or preach anti-Semitism or just live a solitary life in the mountains, has been a major extension to the concept of being an American.

This characterization spawns both rugged entrepreneurs, intent on wreaking their change on the landscape, and nude bathers, men or women at home with their ideals and probably comfortable in their skin. Or so we might hope. But this emphasis affects one's view of the surrounding world. That is, when the individual and, by extension, the individual's needs become the focal point, then the individual's needs, desires, and vision become paramount, defining, delimiting. Further, if that vision is tied to a materialist culture, then things can go askew (dead buffalo, dead horses, dead soil, dead salmon). The results have frequently been ghastly. Unfortunately, in the West—and particularly in Spokane—the individualist bent has often emphasized exploitative utility.

Allow me to conjure the ghost of a Spokane founding father. Originally from Missouri, James Nettle Glover arrived in the Northwest in his twenties, settling in his mid-thirties in what would become Spokane. He was industrious, clever, and stubborn—enduring war with Native American tribes and a fire that destroyed much of Spokane's downtown. He was also a Romantic. When he first arrived in the region, Glover spent an entire night listening to the din of Spokane Falls, and he found himself moved. Toward rapture? By beauty? No. He decided that the puny, mule-driven sawmill on the river was wasting energy, cash, and possibilities, and so he bought the land and built a larger mill, which spawned larger mills and brought more people (and larger mills) and rail lines and miners and loggers and soldiers— and the rest is the beginning of Spokane's history.

What does it mean to listen to tumbling water and hear something useful?

Floods. The Missoula Flood transformed this region; the flood of settlers followed. In the twentieth century, this flood has reshaped many regions and biospheres; the last fifty years have seen the impact of industrial waste and suburban sprawl, the many great rivers of traffic flowing sluggishly into the surrounding valleys, the slow poisons of exhaust rising into the sky from the cars of consumers intent on the next bauble.

You're hot, so why not take a dip in the river? Why not walk to the river's edge, near the confluence of Latah (Hangman) Creek and the Spokane? The sand will be soft beneath your feet. The sheer sides of the ravine rise to meet the clear blue sky; the water chants and whistles and sings. Oh, why not shed those clothes and swim in the river? Look around. Others are naked. Several men, a few women, three or four frolicking children. Pull your shirt over your head, squirm out of those shorts; kick your underpants into the air—watch them hang against the sky like a silly kite. The sun on your butt feels good; the sun on your genitals and the inside of your thighs feels warm and soothing, light exploring skin that seldom directly senses this yellow heat. The sweat on your scalp trickles down between your shoulders. The water, the water, the water: why not embrace it in the only way you can, why not take a swim?

With regard to economics and industries, Spokane is not so different from many other Western towns. Smaller than Denver, bigger than Butte, about the same size as Boise: these cities and others owe their conception and growth to various extraction industries. The nineteenth and early twentieth centuries' emphasis on utility wreaked havoc on the planet; in the Pacific Northwest, the results range from fouled rivers and ugly clear-cuts to land so poisoned by radioactive waste that few can grasp the long-term implications. We have all read about, heard about, or seen firsthand the results of shortsighted, utilitarian management of resources. I need not dwell on such a holocaust or the reasons behind it.

Yet some specific instances may help us understand the profound implications of this corruption of vision. Think about dead horses. Col. George Wright of the US Cavalry was a respected and decorated soldier who had served the United States in conflicts from Florida to Canada, Maine to Washington. Before 1858, he had a reputation for resolving Native American conflicts in a much more reasonable manner than many of his compatriots, sometimes pleading for the lives of the Indians. This approach soon changed: whether the ideological or political climate of the region compelled the shift in his disposition is difficult to know. In 1858, he captured and hanged several important Indian chiefs and threatened the lives of hundreds of Native women and children. His burning of food supplies eventually led to starvation for some. And just east of what is now Spokane, coming upon the primary herd of eight hundred horses that constituted the Spokane Tribe's wealth, livelihood, and pride, he ordered the slaughter of seven hundred of the animals. The pile of bleached bones near the banks of the Spokane River was a hideous landmark for decades.

But think of one horse. An impossibly graceful creature. Consider the balance, the musculature at full gallop, the shimmer of each flexed tendon, extension of bone. Think of one horse and tell me that the blood of those animals and the ghosts of their bones aren't in the land, on the shoreline, inhabiting the current's threads and twists. Stand at the river near the

Washington and Idaho border—Horse Slaughter Camp—breathe in the summer air; think of one horse.

How easy to turn the wrongs done for the sake of use into a litany, a flood of crimes: the dams, the dumping of raw sewage into the river—the banning of which Spokane leaders resisted into the 1950s—the massive rail yards seeping poison, the Kaiser Aluminum Plant's toxic drip. Crimes against people as well as the environment: Qualchan and fifteen others swaying from gibbets at the hands of Col. George Wright in 1858, Chief Spokan Garry living out his days in a makeshift shantytown just west of the downtown waterfalls, the crowds of men who now gather every morning on the corner just off the freeway to panhandle because "ANYTHING HELPS." The list goes on and on. Lead, cadmium, arsenic, and zinc in the water and the fish. Poison and death, compromise and pain. The great flood of the nineteenth and twentieth centuries has not been kind to the river, the land, birds, fish, or beasts. As devastating as the great historical flood, the influx of humanity has been about extraction, a scourge aimed at the accumulation of wealth and the supposed progress of American society. "Death is the mother of beauty," Wallace Stevens wrote. Perhaps it would be worthwhile to look at how the opposite might be true, how beauty might mother death.

There have been, of course, wonderful ideas for the ethical treatment of the river and the surrounding land. For instance, in 1908 the Olmsted brothers proposed a park that would have protected from development nearly all of the land around the river. According to a 1913 report of the board of park commissioners, "Nothing is so firmly impressed on the mind of the visitor to Spokane as the great gorge into which the river falls near the center of the city." Such ambitions fell to the demands of the railways and other development, but in some ways the Olmsted plan seeded the great revitalization that changed the topography of downtown Spokane in the 1970s, realizing the original goal of the river as public park. Long before the World Exposition of 1974 and the transformation of the riverfront, the Riverside Park Company, a group of private citizens, donated all of the land on both sides of the river at its juncture with Latah Creek. This was the beginning of People's Park.

You're in the water, kicking around, sousing the sky with spray, but self-consciousness suddenly returns like Ahab stalking you from the *Pequod*. You wonder, "Ooh, what are they thinking about my body?" You remember a friend who once commented, "Some people shouldn't be naked." You wonder if a smart-aleck kid is talking about that white whale in the water. Or you worry about your thin shanks, your skinny ass, the sag of your scrotum. Or you notice that the man just forty yards away has a near pelt of fur on his back; the woman with her two children has pendulous dugs. You suddenly see that the man sitting near the beach has such a bloated gut that it nearly hangs over his genitals. You weigh and measure all of them; you weigh and measure yourself. The homeliest is not beautiful to you.

What does it mean when a poisoned river is the scenic center of a city?

What does it mean to look at a human body—morsel of divine dust—and be repulsed?

I want to suggest an echo in these questions. Any gawking tourist will laud the beauty of the falls—the rugged basalt cliffs, the saucy foam of the cascading water, the swallows circling in the scintillating mist. This privileging, though, isn't just a tourist perspective. Who hasn't encountered a "scene" in the natural world and thought, "Wow, that would make a good postcard. Where's my camera?" Who hasn't oohed and aahed at nature, at a glorious sunset, a vista of spiky mountains, the lush undergrowth beneath a grove of cedar trees? And of course, the Spokane Falls *are* powerful and glorious. As is the entire course of the river, any river, every intricate aspect of natural existence—the thorns and leaves, each stone and ripple, the articulated joints on a grasshopper's legs, the glassy shine of stars.

Somehow, we learn that seeing nature means gawking at isolated instances of the sublime—think of Old Faithful or sequoias or the mad traffic jams in Yellowstone when someone spots a wolf—and we don't consider the whole or even the particulars of what is before our eyes, whether the spectacle is a tumble of clear, clean water over rocks or a sickly foam of polluted spray marking a century of misuse. The superficial splash of water is enough to make us forget the poison, to gloss over the dreadful accumulation of trash on the basalt rocks, to ignore the vanquished salmon and struggling land.

Strange as this may sound, I think the same dynamic compels the proliferation of glossy photos spackled all over every supermarket magazine rack and throughout the aisles of Barnes and Noble. When beautiful bodies are displayed as commodities on the covers, the sublime glory of the body becomes equated with the "perfect body," and consequently the sheer delight of limb and vision and life, the life of any body, the movement of any limb, the glorious vision of the particular is irrevocably lost.

Decades ago, John Berger offered two different ways to depict the human body; borrowing from Kenneth Clark, he cast the difference between these depictions as the difference between being naked and being nude. Being naked is to be without clothes. Being nude is a stylized representation of the naked self that emphasizes the perception of the viewer; when one is nude, self-consciousness governs, and the body always acts in accordance with the desires of the onlooker. The beauty of the human body is thus reduced to its utility to the viewer. To put it another way, the body becomes an objectified spectacle. With the nude body, this dynamic becomes more pervasive because one is always both subject and object: always scrutinized, and always engaged in self-scrutiny. In our culture, we learn very early this measurement of how we look in the eyes of others, and its effects—from eating disorders to suicidal depression—are well documented.

River and earth, shrub and sky do not experience the violence of such self-consciousness. However, when our main interaction with the natural world is to view it as spectacle, then we perpetuate another sort of violence. This is a violence of reduction in scale that essentially enables us to pretend that the flow of a river, the arc of an osprey's flight, the dexterous leap of a frightened squirrel, and the scintillating spray of a waterfall are there as part of a useful diversion from the mechanical grind of our everyday lives. We reduce the beautiful to entertainment, and any ugliness, any blemishes, can be cropped out. Forget the litter; forget the poisons; forget context.

How we know the world shapes the ways in which we see the world and each other. In turn, these affect how we treat the world and how we treat each other. It's simple. A glacier flood tearing across hundreds of miles of stone and earth differs from a tide of people inflicting their desires on a land. The former is an event; the latter might be the result of a skewed epistemology, a way of seeing driven by cultural ideas of hierarchy, scale, and utility.

We must see the river anew. We must ask how we can walk into the world and yet not be in the world, be present. I am interested in a new kind of creative violence, one that blinds our learned and unsustainable ways of seeing, that breaks our "mind-forg'd manacles" (as Blake called them) and allows us to understand how we have been acculturated to see the world as ours to use, and use, and use. How can we learn to look at something—whether it is a person whose appearance radically differs from our own or a raucous river— and see it as us? "Je est un autre" (I is someone else), Arthur Rimbaud wrote. He wasn't talking about the natural world exactly, but he was talking about becoming a seer. In his declaration of polyphonic existence lies his recognition of our unique ability to see the strangeness in others and the strangeness in ourselves. To somehow respond to that strangeness with empathy, he gives us a route toward a creative violence that could allow us to see the Spokane River and the naked bather in a vision of embrace rather than judgment or use.

The water surrounding your body is clear. More precisely, it *is* your body. You can see the rocks of the river bottom. Maybe a rowdy jay lifts up from a nearby pine. Maybe a child splashes you. Your body is naked and with the naked water and with the naked sky: all are beautiful.

Next time you're hot, next time the world is sticky on your back like a wet shirt, why not shed those threads, toss that self-consciousness. Next time, why not take a swim?

Our vision of the world has always put the human species at the center of things. Whether compelled by the rugged individualist eking a life out of the desolate West or some biblical proclamation that the creatures of the earth are there for human use, this vision must be revised; we are a species among many others, and we must learn to see those other species as part of a complex and contiguous web of life. Our ability to transform the world toward our ends, whether through the slaughter of horses, the damming of rivers, or the construction of social hierarchies—a way of seeing to which we alone seem privy—should not license wanton abuse. A hierarchical vision hinders us from seeing the intricacy and grace that are in *every* moment of a river's course, every bud and branch and bug and bird, as well as every bald head and bloated belly. We shrink the world, violently bring it into accordance with an acculturated sense of what matters, and whittle a life-size panorama to the size of a single-image postcard.

Seven hundred and fifty thousand years ago, the Missoula Flood radically altered the landscape of the Northwest. In every waking moment, each of us has the opportunity to begin a similar sort of transformation. William Stafford implores "that awake people be awake." To be awake requires feeling the incredible energy of platelets tumbling through our bodies, their glorious power neither more nor less than that of a massive cataract. No more slumber: do not see the river as useful or spectacular, but instead feel that chilly current, those slick stones, wade in waist-deep, whisper to the river, and listen. Listen for more than the ghost of exploitation; listen for more than an empty beauty that may foster death. Listen for more than an elegy of pain, the horses' cries that bled into the current. Listen, listen to the water, and hope to hear that you are part of the reply.

# The River's Lasting Legacy

BECKY KRAMER

DON'T GO DOWN TO THE RIVER. GENERATIONS OF LOCAL KIDS HEARD that warning. Parents didn't want their children playing on the Spokane River's polluted banks. Chris Donley's dad was one of them. "I can remember it," said Donley, a Cheney native. "I was a teenager in the early 1980s, looking to burn up all of the gas and catch all the trout I could reach in less than a day's drive. But we weren't encouraged to fish the Spokane River."

Donley's dad had his reasons. Once the source of life-sustaining salmon runs for Native people, the river had become a foul place. Until the late 1950s, the city of Spokane pumped raw sewage directly into the river. Its slack waters were repositories for heavy metals and other industrial pollutants. Some stretches smelled so bad that homes were built far back on the bank. The sixty-pound chinooks—known as June hogs—had disappeared decades earlier. Dams built without fish ladders stopped the salmon runs. "In the hurry to make money and build houses, under the guise of economic development, we forgot about the river," said Donley, now a regional fisheries manager for the Washington Department of Fish and Wildlife in Spokane. "It was a slow but sure deterioration from neglect."

The river is cleaner now. And it's starting to regain a place in the local economy and lifestyles. People want to live on it, fish it, kayak and raft it. No longer a sewer, the river is the centerpiece of the Spokane Regional Convention and Visitors Bureau's campaign aimed at attracting tourists and keeping locals recreating at home. People feel protective of the river, too.

---

A prior version of this chapter was published in the *Spokesman-Review* in 2008. It is reprinted here courtesy of the newspaper.

In a 2007 Robinson Research survey, nearly 80 percent of respondents rated cleaning up or protecting the river as "very important." The survey queried 600 Spokane, Stevens, and Lincoln County residents. "As a culture, we're in the process of rediscovering this river," said Andy Dunau, executive director of the nonprofit Spokane River Forum, a clearinghouse for river-related issues. To re-engage people, he started organizing paddling expeditions in 2008 that covered the Spokane River's entire length. More than 750 people took part in the expeditions over five years before the Spokane River Forum phased out the trips, letting commercial outfitters take over. "After we've taken people down to the river, they start to appreciate it for the enormous, living resource it is," Dunau said. "I've never heard anyone question why taking care of it is important."

The river continues to need advocates. Despite the progress, steep challenges remain. As the population grows, more water is pumped from the Spokane Valley–Rathdrum Prairie Aquifer. During dry years, heavy pumping contributes to critically low summer flows in the river, and the conflict will only become more acute as the climate warms. Thirty years after efforts to curb phosphorus in the river began, algae blooms remain a problem in Long Lake, a Spokane River reservoir that's more commonly known now as Lake Spokane.

Upstream silver mines no longer dump tailings into the river's headwaters, and sewage treatment plants must meet stringent standards for discharging wastewater into the river. But the river still has pollution problems. Health advisories caution people to limit the number of fish they eat from the river to reduce their exposure to toxic chemicals. "If we really want to do right by the river, we have to think about the whole thing," Dunau said. "There's something mysterious about the river. It goes through all these different settings . . . but people only have experiences with different pieces of it."

Most of the region is connected to the Spokane River. Its watershed includes three Idaho counties—Kootenai, Bonner and Benewah—and parts of five Washington counties: Spokane, Stevens, Lincoln, Pend Oreille and Whitman. The watershed encompasses mountains and wheat fields, urban centers and rural areas. The river itself is relatively short—111 miles. But as it flows from Lake Coeur d'Alene to the Columbia River, it passes through at least six cities. Archeological evidence says people have lived along the Spokane River for thousands of years.

Pauline Flett, a native speaker of the Salish language, told Garrison Keillor a story of the river's origins during a 1998 taping of the radio show "A Prairie Home Companion" at the Spokane Opera House.

An earthquake ravaged the land, followed by a terrible flood. A boy and a girl took shelter on Mount Spokane. When the flood passed, they saw a flowing stream with beautiful waterfalls and rapids.

"What is crawling in the river? It's a salmon," the girl cried.

The discovery of salmon gave hope to the people, who became three bands: the Upper, Middle, and Lower Spokanes, based on where they lived along the river.

Today, about 600,000 people live within an hour's drive of the river. Many seldom see it. "It's a hidden river," said Judy Kaufman, an angler from Liberty Lake. "Unless you're going across a bridge or walking on the Centennial Trail, you don't really get to see it."

But that's starting to change.

At the newly redeveloped Huntington Park, you can hear the roar of the Spokane River, see its froth and feel its spray as the river rushes through the gorge below the Monroe Street Dam. Walking up a staircase parallel to the water creates the illusion of ascending into the heart of cascading waterfalls. In 2015, the city of Spokane and the Spokane Tribe dedicated the "Gathering Place" behind City Hall to connect Huntington Park with Riverfront Park. The public area also has a Salish name, honoring the salmon that were caught below the falls for centuries by the Spokanes and other tribes. "Snt'el'ʔemin'tn" means the place where salmon are prepared.

Spokane's civic architecture has begun to embrace the river as well. The Spokane Convention Center's new addition was built with glass walls and outdoor patios that showcase the river as it flows through downtown.

Familiarity with the river is essential to community activism, Dunau said. If people don't know the river, it's difficult for them to judge how plans for minimum stream flows or shoreline development or wastewater discharges will affect beaches, fishing holes, or scenic views.

"I think if the community recreated more on it they'd have more of a feeling for it—instead of just the complexities and that it's polluted and you can't eat the fish," Kaufman said.

Purging old images of the river from the community's collective memory will take time. Some memories still linger for Donley, the fish biologist.

"It's hard for me to get that image out of my memory of watching toilet paper float by."

# Swimming the Big Eddy

TIM CONNOR

THE SWIMMING HOLE I VISIT IN WEST SPOKANE IS CALLED THE BIG Eddy because of what happens when water gets ahead of itself.

You can witness the physics of this phenomenon in a bathtub. Cup your hands and shove the bathwater toward your island knees. Vortices appear in the wake, as fluid winks at gravity and tangos in all directions. In a free-flowing river, the result of these undulations is that a good fraction of the water is traveling counter to the main current. Amid such currents, it can be useful to know when and how to resist. Hubris is not ballast. Even a strong swimmer, once disoriented, can drown in a riptide.

I learned to swim at a very young age in a large, warm outdoor pool my dad managed in Panama. The pool in Spokane where I taught my daughter and son to swim was much smaller, and colder. As they gained confidence, we started to swim in local lakes and creeks before taking to the ocean on vacations in Hawaii. We also swam in Lake Coeur d'Alene, not far from its outlet to the Spokane River. Framed by evergreen ridges and distant peaks, the lake is a beautiful place for a leisurely summer swim in sublimely warm lake water.

Seven years ago, to save time and reduce my carbon footprint, I sought a place closer to home where I could swim in open, chorine-free water with good visibility. A friend suggested I try the Big Eddy. Only three miles from where I live, it's easy to reach by bicycle.

On most days I swim alone. When people chide me for this, I usually remind them that I'm actually at greater risk from distracted drivers while pedaling to a meeting than when I'm swimming in the river. Still, it's true that even after my son became a strong swimmer, I worried whenever I lost sight

Spokane River just upstream of the Big Eddy in west Spokane, September 2016. Photo courtesy of Tim Connor.

of his snorkel or his splash. Why one would accept such anxieties instead of just going to a local pool with lifeguards is not easy to explain. Not everyone will be persuaded.

For starters, it's a worthy, challenging stretch of water—with a remarkable backstory. The river flowing through Spokane was substantially remodeled by an extraordinary catastrophe in the very recent geologic past. The cover of a book-length US Geological Survey (USGS) report published in 1988 illustrates the rampage. It portrays what the fabled geologist J Harlan Bretz termed the "Spokane Flood." It shows a vast torrent of water, interspersed with great chunks of floating ice, overflowing the Spokane area and beginning to fan out over what is now eastern Washington. In the USGS illustration the floodwater is blue, though in reality it would have been coffee-colored, bearing tons of silt and rock beneath an armada of icebergs riding along the surface at highway speeds.

Nor was it one flood. At the end of the Pleistocene there were dozens of Spokane Flood events—perhaps as many as a hundred—each one caused by the ear-splitting breakup of a recurring glacial ice dam across the Clark Fork River, just seventy-five miles northeast of Spokane. The last outburst is thought to have occurred only thirteen thousand or so years ago, so it was likely witnessed by early North Americans. All of them would have been terrified, and most would have drowned.

The epic floods deposited a massive pile of gravel and cobbles—more than six hundred feet deep in some places—over some three hundred square miles. It is an extraordinarily porous deposit, holding roughly ten trillion gallons of groundwater. The vast layers of cobbles also altered the course of the ancestral Spokane River, diverting it from the Hillyard Trough in north Spokane to its present course through the downtown gorge and out through west Spokane.

The bowl of the Big Eddy forms where the modern river runs headlong into one of the massive mounds of cobbles. This magnificent obstruction forces the river sharply to the north and east before it resumes its prevailing course to the northwest. Heading down a trail to the rocky beach, I walk over oval chunks of granite and metamorphic rock in a layer more than a hundred feet deep. These stones, many far too heavy for me to lift, were excavated by ice in Canada, Montana, and Idaho, then washed up like so much driftwood as the late Pleistocene floods paused before vaulting over the high, basalt rimrock to the southwest.

In summer the Spokane River today is comfortably warm as it leaves Lake Coeur d'Alene and flows for twenty miles into the Spokane Valley. Few visitors are aware that the river is leaking huge volumes of water into the cobbles of the local aquifer. Ten miles east of Spokane, however, the interaction basically reverses. Strong injections of cold groundwater recharge the river. Where the river passes from Idaho into Washington, a mid-August swim is akin to snorkeling in the Bahamas. But just a few miles downstream, a half-hour dip can lead to the early stages of hypothermia.

The Big Eddy—some two miles upstream from where whitewater gallops between towering pillars of basalt at the geological feature called the

Bowl and Pitcher—is situated in what hydrologists call a "gaining reach" of the river. Two days before I wrote this paragraph, I took the plunge on a mid-June afternoon after a run of cool days with temperatures in the sixties. When I emerged after swimming a mile, my hands and upper forearms were the color of a Yukon Gold potato, with purplish streaks between my knuckles. My fingers were tingling. Otherwise I felt great. To say that a swim in cold water is invigorating only hints at the psychospiritual benefit such immersions can offer a wounded soul.

A couple summers ago I was wading ashore when a woman I didn't know called out to me with a question. "Ironman?" she asked playfully, obviously inquiring if I was in training for the triathlon series by that name.

"Tin Man," I answered.

My daughter is a poet. A year and a half ago she invited me to a literary festival at which she read a new piece she'd named "Backstroke." The poem begins with my teaching her to swim when she was young. Then the swimming and the swiftness of wild water unfold as metaphors for what it takes to endure heartbreaking experiences. The undertow of the poem is the awareness that a life in which we strive for truth, beauty, and affection can be treacherous. The possibility of a fully realized existence requires our vulnerability. If we find ourselves in over our heads, we had better know how to swim, and what and whom to swim toward.

What I know about heartbreak I'd prefer not to have learned. I can only compare it to another affliction I barely survived twenty years ago: strep pneumonia. After the fever broke and my lungs cleared, I regained my health in a matter of weeks. But losing someone you love involves seemingly interminable spools of grief and loneliness.

During my emotional convalescence, the river became a refuge for months on end. I actually discovered the Big Eddy not as a swimmer but as a birdwatcher. Catbirds, song sparrows, yellow warblers, and eastern kingbirds arrive along the banks by mid-spring. I almost always hear them before I see them as I tuck my bike into a riparian thicket of hawthorn, aspen, and late-blooming tansy. Directly across the river from where I dive in, a swarm of bank swallows streams in and out of nesting holes in a cliff while ospreys circle overhead, looking for their next meals in the river I'm about to enter. Nothing gets your attention quite like an osprey crashing into the water a few yards from where you're swimming.

When you're stuck in a vortex of despair, just about any sudden jolt to the senses can be therapeutic. I embraced the daily, icy plunge and began to accept it as a necessary passage to a place distant from my ordinary life, a realm that requires physicality and a much different form of awareness.

Best of all, I get to enter a wilderness whose richness begins along the shore and intensifies dramatically when I open my eyes underwater. It's a bit like stepping off a garden path into a rainforest.

Local conservation groups have pointed out a fragile population of native redband trout in the Spokane River. A few of those trout are skittish, but some allow me to swim at arm's length and admire them at close range. Especially in full sunlight, the redband is as colorful as a reef fish, with accents of bronze and jade framing its signature scarlet stripe. I have learned where and how they hunt, their mouths facing upstream as they hold their positions against swift currents laced with bubbles of air.

In the deeper pockets of the Big Eddy, thousands of northern whitefish also thrive. I first noticed them several years ago near the middle of the river, when I was gazing into the blackness of the channel. Shards of light below me—sunlight reflecting off dorsal scales—gave way to an enormous school of whitefish. I dove deeper, astonished, and at last I made out a vast shoal of shoe-length fish.

A couple years ago I had another shock as I was swimming upstream toward a chute of whitewater. In my peripheral vision, I glimpsed a fast-moving mass. My instinctive response, having snorkeled on ocean reefs where sharks hunt, was fear. The mass turned out to be a shimmering school of juvenile whitefish shifting direction in unison, like an oceanic bait ball of sardines.

That you can have experiences like these within the boundaries of a good-sized city is mind-blowing. And of course it took years of work. As the Spokane historian William Stimson has written, in 1935 the state health board declared the Spokane River to be "grossly polluted" by wholesale discharges of raw sewage. Even after the health department issued the warning, city voters, fearful of creeping socialism, rejected federal funding from the Works Progress Administration for primary sewage treatment. It took a generation to overcome such resistance so that Spokane could treat its sewage properly.

As other contributors to this book have noted, the river still has pollution problems that require close attention, but the public investment in and progress toward the Spokane River's recovery have been remarkable. A river that was once neglected and oozing with sewage now flows with water that, except after big storms that bring large runoffs from urban streets, is safe to swim in—so long as you can handle the currents and avoid the rocks.

For worse and then for better, human impact on the river has been every bit as profound as that of the late Pleistocene floods that shaped its present course. As a consequence, the river became Spokane's living emblem at the time of the 1974 World's Fair and has remained so ever since. Even Spokanites who rarely put their toes or kayaks in the water still have a powerful emotional connection to the river, simply for its aesthetic presence in their lives.

This quiet connection really matters. In a cultural and political sense, public aspirations for a cleaner environment make all the difference to bringing about change. People in Spokane have come to expect a clean river, and these growing expectations have made it possible to take the necessary steps that were needed to rescue the river from willful neglect. Only a deep shift in public values could have allowed a growing number of anglers, rafters, kayakers, and swimmers to intimately experience the beauty and sanctuary the Spokane River now offers.

Beyond the economic value a revitalized river adds to property values, whitewater outfitters, fly shops, and the like, it's impossible to quantify this evolution. You have to weigh it by other means and marvel at the contrast between the material ambitions and the mists, birdsong, and white-capped rapids in the gorge below. Suffice it to say that swimming alongside a redband trout burnished in filtered sunlight makes me feel as wealthy as I could ever hope to become.

# River Lessons

JULIE TITONE

AS A JOURNALIST, I LEARNED ABOUT THE SPOKANE RIVER FROM
scientists. As a canoeist, I learned from the river about life. What to do when
you're riding a wave. That following the leader isn't always a good idea. That
waterfalls and kisses were meant for each other. That voices carrying over
water in the dark create a perfect requiem.

The Spokane is unlike most Western rivers—it's a river segment, really.
Its 111-mile course begins not in a creek fed by mountain snow but in Lake
Coeur d'Alene, a 25-mile-long natural lake kept unnaturally high in the
summer by the Post Falls Dam. Six more dams block and shape the west-
bound Spokane before it flows into a Columbia River reservoir created by
the Grand Coulee Dam.

Lake Coeur d'Alene is fed by the St. Joe and Coeur d'Alene Rivers. Both
begin high and wild in north Idaho's mountains. The ideal boat to navigate
either river would start as a whitewater kayak or raft, morph into a whitewater canoe, and then transform, for easy steering and quick progress, into
a lake canoe or sea kayak. Once, while reporting on a historical remnant of
the timber industry, I was a passenger on the slowest, most meditative craft
of all: a tugboat moving at one mile an hour on the St. Joe River. The logs it
pulled were bound for one of the steam-puffing sawmills at the convergence
of Lake Coeur d'Alene and the Spokane River, sawmills that my four-year-
old son called cloud factories.

Where the rapids of the St. Joe and Coeur d'Alene taper off, both rivers
take on the burden of industrial history. Logging-related sediment clogs their
tributaries. Runoff from historic mines contaminates the water and shores.

The Coeur d'Alene River carries an especially heavy burden of metals. Lead, which settles out, is the biggest human health hazard. Zinc, which stays in the water, is most toxic to fish but also suppresses algae, helping to keep the water clear. Because the waterways are so beautiful, the average boater is oblivious to the pollution.

The Spokane River is also fed by the vast Spokane Valley–Rathdrum Prairie Aquifer, itself a swift underground river that begins at the southern end of Lake Pend Oreille. This regional water supply is worthy of global envy. Mapped, it looks like a paisley design with a fat end that fans out under the prairie and a thinner end that curls southwest along the Spokane River.

According to Native American legend, a duck that was hunted on Lake Pend Oreille later popped up pierced by an arrow in the Spokane River. I thought of that duck the first time I popped up in the river, beside a capsized canoe. As I sputtered, I could not have recalled the safe consumption limit for waterborne PCBs, which are yet another industrial legacy. But I remembered the impaled duck. Such is the power of story. Like the Interior Salish tribes since time immemorial, we members of the paddling tribe have our own stories of the river.

Between Lake Coeur d'Alene and Post Falls, Idaho, the current moves slowly. This is a reservoir, created when the river backs up behind Post Falls Dam. It is where the local rowing club practices, launching its multi-oared shells from a church camp just after dawn. I joined the rowers one summer out of curiosity. I liked the synchronicity of the sport. I liked watching mallards glide through mirror-smooth water. I liked the tug of the oars against rarely used back muscles. But I quickly concluded, likely to the relief of my teammates, that rowing is not a sport for a gal with short arms and legs.

Soon after, I bought a used fuchsia sea kayak. It allowed me to witness the transformation of this stretch of shoreline. Once a place of sawmills and well-worn cabins, by the 1980s it boasted some of the most expensive real estate in Idaho. For a while I could escape the new construction by tucking my pink boat into a small inlet called Black Bay and looking skyward at the ponderosa pines. Then, in 1995, a 28,469-square-foot mansion was built there. That monstrosity dwarfs the tiny bay. Idaho's lack of shoreline regulations—allowing those terraced stone walls to abut the water—add environmental insult to aesthetic injury.

I lived not far from Q'emiln Park, just upstream of the dam. This park is a convenient place to launch a canoe or kayak if you can deal with the waves and noise of powerboats, something we paddlers do grudgingly. This part of the river was the scene of a bad parenting moment for me. I had allowed my son, then about twelve, to paddle my kayak. With slender arms poking out of his life vest, Jake wasn't big enough to handle the seventeen-foot boat. And though I was canoeing alongside to keep an eye on him, I had overestimated my ability to help him if he tipped over. Which he did. To my immense relief, the fright on his face dissolved into a grin when folks in one of those noisy powerboats rescued him. They gave him a ride and towed the kayak to shore. Score one for good Samaritans who burn fossil fuels. "Mom," he told me for years, "I like boats with motors."

The Post Falls Dam is actually a hydroelectric project composed of three dams, one across each of the constricted channels of the Spokane River. The pioneer Frederick Post built a wooden dam there to divert water to his sawmill. A century later, while reporting for a news story, I toured the historic brick powerhouse that blocks the middle channel. Two things about that visit stick with me. First, the light that poured cathedral-like through the high windows of the powerhouse. Second, a conversation I had with a power company employee. After explaining the efficient new turbines, he told me about the flotsam that gets trapped at the dam. Frisbees, pieces of dock, dead animals. "I haven't seen a body come through," he said. "When that happens, it's my last day." Most bodies in the Spokane River turn up across the state line in Washington, where homicides and ill-advised swims regularly make Spokane headlines.

On the Idaho side, the most dangerous part of the river is just downstream of the dam. Chain-link fences and hazard signs don't always deter people from wanting a close view of the small gorge and its leaping waters. One April, when the river was raging, a vivacious acquaintance of mine, who spent decades exploring rivers far and wide, chose this place to end her life. Neither fear nor scenic beauty is a match for the demon depression.

So far, I have wished to live and paddle for another day. In the interest of survival and fun, I took classes from the Spokane Canoe and Kayak Club. The Spokane River provides the perfect canoeing classroom. It's handy—practically in the backyard of half a million people. And its waters range from class I (easy-peasy, obstacle free) to class III (big waves, advanced skills and nerves required).

My friend Louise Watson and I showed up one summer morning for a paddling class at Post Falls' Corbin Park. Bill Brooks, a former air force survival instructor with the authoritative voice to match, was going to show us the basics of ferrying. "Just do what I do!" he commanded with a smile, so we followed Bill back and forth, shore to shore. We worked our way upstream toward a small rapid that dissolved into a strong current. We sat in quiet water and watched Bill paddle across the eddy line and into that current. Dutifully, Louise and I followed him. Our boat capsized the second the bow hit the fast water.

Promptly rescued, we scurried for dry clothes, our teeth chattering. That was when I thought about that legendary arrow-stricken duck, wondering if it had popped up anywhere near this spot. I also thought about wetsuits and pledged that my wardrobe soon would include one. Bill told us that he had sliced through the eddy line at a bad angle, so we had been mistaken to follow his lead. He was a strong enough paddler to compensate for the error. We were not.

For years, Corbin Park served as launch site for the Spokane River Classic. Like Spokane's storied Bloomsday Run, the river race featured world-class athletes in front and enthusiasts of every skill level behind. The racers crossed the Idaho-Washington line and bounced or torpedoed through the rapids toward the take-out at Plante's Ferry Park in the Spokane Valley. I took part in the Classic several times, most memorably when I served as bow paddler in Stan Mrzygod's wood canoe. Such a boat is the offspring of a fine piece of furniture coupled with a musical instrument. Waves thumping their rhythm upon a cedar bow—that is a bucket-list sound.

The race is no longer held. Instead, the Spokane Canoe and Kayak Club is investing in the future by hosting a paddle, splash, and play event for kids. Maybe they'll grow up to play in the Spokane River rapids.

The first bit of whitewater past the state line is an isolated play hole created by a slab of concrete. It's called Dead Dog, so named by kayakers who encountered a carcass there. The size and very existence of rapids depend on river flow, of course. The US Geological Survey gauge in Spokane shows historic minimum and maximum flows as 2,420 and 46,200 cubic feet per second. Incidentally, that is the oldest continuously operated USGS gauge in Washington, having started its observations in 1891.

The Upper Spokane, or simply the Upper, is what local paddlers call the twenty miles of river between the Idaho-Washington state line and Spokane's city limits. This is where, during that sweet late-spring convergence of long days and adequate stream flow, whitewater enthusiasts get together to cavort in waves at the end of the workday.

The best rapids are between Barker and Sullivan Roads. Sullivan Rapids is the biggest. Its long wave train was rollicking more than enough to intimidate Louise and me as we headed toward it for the first time during our canoeing class.

Lean downstream, we were told. Don't stop paddling! And if you get really nervous, back-paddle to slow your momentum—which we did, start to finish. The braking maneuver worked so well that, having gotten through the whitewater, I felt disappointed. We'd taken the fun out of the roller-coaster ride. River lesson: go for it.

I've since gone through many class II rapids and also, when paddling tandem with an expert, some class III whitewater. But I've only canoe-surfed a few times. The first time was on the Upper Spokane. From the stern, Brian Burns told me where and how to plant my paddle as he maneuvered the boat from still water into a standing wave. I paddled madly against the current, wondering if we'd really defy physics and sit on top of the froth. Then Brian said: "Julie, look up." We had achieved our goal, and he didn't want me to miss the moment. We were balanced on the wave. While his paddle held us in place, I could ease up, inhale the pine-scented air, even admire the nearby boulders and the water pouring around them. When I find myself working too hard, not stopping to smell the roses or pines, I think of that moment.

That I ever reached my skill level of chicken-intermediate canoeist is due to the patient instruction of friends like Brian. ("Draw left, Julie. No, your other left.") Sometimes I've served as an instructor's aide during canoe classes, reinforcing the lessons and serving as moral support. Hey, if a short woman with little depth perception or coordination can run rivers, anybody can!

Once, during a class on the Upper Spokane, I stood calf-deep in water between willows and a canoe containing two newbie students: a middle-aged man in the stern and his wife in the bow. He was telling her what to do. His tone was obnoxious, and his advice was bad. Did I lean over to her and say, "You know, that paddle will reach the back of the boat"? Or did I just imagine telling her to give him a whack?

Between the Upper and Lower Spokane River there are three dams—Upriver, Upper Falls, and Monroe Street. Paddlers enjoy this stretch of water along with everyone else in Washington's second-largest city: from a building, a park, a tourist gondola, the Centennial Trail, or the steps of the Opera House on July 4, when fireworks bursting above are reflected in the water.

From the optimal river viewpoint on a bridge above Spokane Falls in the heart of the city, the water thunders, courses, exults its way around a staircase of rock in the spring. To stand above that, and feel somehow part of the river, is one of the Northwest's great experiences.

I can't be the only boater who has looked down on Spokane Falls in its less rambunctious moments and imagined a route down that basalt staircase that would allow a paddler to emerge unscathed and triumphant. Nor am I the only woman to be kissed in the mist that rises from the falls—a benediction that I imagined would ensure romantic bliss. Rivers inspire not just legends but fantasies, too.

The Lower Spokane begins at Peaceful Valley, a historical working-class neighborhood. Longtime residents and their well-heeled neighbors look out, or down, on a quiet stretch of river that seems oblivious to the urban bustle just upstream. The current from Spokane Falls quickly grabs paddlers who put in here.

Canoeists approach the Sandifur Memorial Bridge downstream of Peaceful Valley on the Lower Spokane River, October 2013. Photo by Julie Titone.

My memories of the lower river are set in a frame of golden yellow leaves. It's a stretch perfect for late summer and autumn outings, when water levels in the upper river have petered out. You pass the location of a hoped-for whitewater park, where kayakers could go to hone their skills in waves created by carefully placed boulders. You pass the confluence of Hangman Creek, a major tributary that flows under Interstate 90 and also goes by the politically correct name of Latah Creek.

In this stretch of river, I've practiced surfing and eddy turns, photographed fly fishers, and done yoga stretches on the pebbled shore. I've also been schooled, again, in humility. I watched as a canoe just downstream flipped for no apparent reason. "How did that happen?" I asked a friend paddling nearby. Not ninety seconds later, my well-scratched solo boat hit the same subsurface rock, and I was in the drink. As the saying goes, "If you're a boater, you're a swimmer."

Paddlers can take out at the T. J. Meenach Bridge, known to legions of runners as part of the annual Bloomsday route. Or they can stay on the water and follow the S-curve of river that flows toward Riverside State Park.

Just upstream of the park is Spokane's sewage-treatment plant. Boaters jokingly call its outfall Tootsie Roll Falls. The cleaned-up sewer water smells distinctly musty but not bad. Mostly the river just smells alive and sublime. It may have something to do with those dancing negative ions so notably present at rapids and waterfalls. Another distinctive fragrance I remember on the Spokane was on the upper stretch, near Sullivan Road. It smelled like doughnuts as I paddled below the exhaust fans of Krispy Kreme.

Paddlers who go as far as the sewage-treatment plant usually intend to tackle the river's biggest whitewater. The towering Bowl and Pitcher rock formation compresses the river into class III rapids and snags fallen trees during the spring runoff. If the water is high, even the most skilled paddler can get Maytagged—circulated in a giant foaming hole.

Riverside Park visitors who look down from a viewpoint and footbridge can easily observe paddlers pass through the Bowl and Pitcher. I've only paddled through that spot at low water. The one time I did it solo, I was praying that no one was watching. I got turned around and floated through backward. I'm not sure which of my emotions was stronger, accomplishment or embarrassment.

Beyond the Bowl and Pitcher is an obstacle course of rocks and rapids known as the Devil's Toenail. After that, the river keeps winding through Riverside Park, where ponderosas stand like shoreline sentinels. Paddlers may hear pop-pop-popping from the Spokane Gun Club.

The current slows down after a few miles, as Nine Mile Dam backs up the river. For that reason, canoe trips usually end at the Plese Flats day use area. But one especially memorable river outing for me began at Plese Flats.

It was August 2013. We gathered that evening with Vic Castleberry to honor the memory of his wife, Robbi, who had died unexpectedly. Robbi was a warm, wry conservationist who navigated politics with the same skill and determination she showed when canoeing whitewater. The Spokane River will never have a stauncher advocate.

We paddled west into the sunset, toward a park picnic spot. My photographs show a basket of flowers under a canoe thwart, tables piled with food, wine being poured for a toast, water dimpled by rising fish. My favorite shot is overexposed but somehow perfectly ethereal. On the left, grass and willows bend from shore; on the right, the setting sun silhouettes a kayak and a canoe. Vic is in the bow of the canoe. Another paddler I've always looked up to, the artist Bob Snider, is in the stern. It was Bob who convinced me to buy my sleek sea kayak, which I was paddling that evening, rather than a lighter but slower model. "You want to keep up with the guys, don't you?" he had asked. That still makes me laugh.

We cruised back to Plese Flats in the dark, guided by the occasional light on shore and by each other's familiar voices. The basket of flowers was emptied. Sunflowers, tiger lilies, and carnations floated away. Robbi's presence was real.

Sometimes, I thought, reality beats legends and fantasies all to hell.

# Two Fly-Fishing Love Stories

BOB BARTLETT

I AM AFRICAN AMERICAN, A LOVER OF RIVERS, AND A LONGTIME FLY fisherman. My story comes from fishing many rivers throughout my life, most recently the Spokane. For nearly thirty years—not long by some standards—I have lived near it, fished it, and played along its banks. My people have been river and mountain people for as long as anyone can remember. I was raised "country," where black folks spent what little free time they had hunting and fishing out of necessity more than sport. I was born and raised in the same mountains and on the same river as my father, his father, and his father's father. As Langston Hughes wrote, I have known rivers.

New Creek, pronounced *crick*, is a small mountain stream at the foot of rolling mountains in the eastern panhandle of West Virginia. It meets the Potomac River on the north end of Keyser, my hometown. New Creek is full of sacred family stories. My father, his father, and his father's father lived on the banks of that river, and so did I until another war called me away. My father taught me to fish for food on New Creek, and we kept and ate everything we caught. In those days we used a casting reel, a pole, and live bait like night crawlers, crawfish, and grasshoppers. Once our limit was caught, it was time to go home. I never wanted to stop fishing, though, and I still don't.

As a teenager I learned that fish caught in the lip were much easier to release than those that swallowed the bait and hook, and so my live-bait fishing gave way to a fly rod and artificial lures—surface poppers with rubber legs, hooks tied with feathers and some thread. My love of rivers and fly-fishing has never wavered. One of my favorite poems as a young man was, and still is, "The Negro Speaks of Rivers." In Langston Hughes's verse, there is a reverence for black folks and rivers, a reverence instilled in me long before I was born.

## My Father

Pop could catch a fish out of a garden hose—he was that good. He was one of the best fishermen and one of the hardest-working men I have ever known. Pop worked in a dry cleaner's for over forty years and then bought the business when he was in his early sixties. But Saturday afternoons and Sundays he reserved for fishing.

Pop was born with a small hole in his heart but somehow grew out of it. In World War II, he passed his military physical and served as a combat medic in a racially segregated army. At the age of eighty-eight, he had a massive heart attack, the kind that would have straight-up killed most people. I made the six-hour flight from Spokane back East in time to find him unconscious in intensive care. Never had I seen Pop down for longer than an eight count, so this was serious. Within forty-eight hours he returned from the dead, but he suffered a second heart attack while still in recovery. His doctor and nurses offered no explanation, took no responsibility, and gave him little chance of survival.

Five days later we brought him home, twenty-three miles south of the hospital, across the Potomac River Bridge that divides West Virginia from Maryland. At his request, "Do Not Resuscitate" orders were posted all over the house. The next day, before the hospice nurse arrived, Pop motioned me close: "Son, let's go for a ride."

Pop wanted to go to New Creek to spend what little precious time he had left on earth. We headed down the hill to the creek. A few miles upstream, I parked under a large weeping willow on a familiar bend, a spot we had fished many times. We sat with only the occasional call of cardinals and shorebirds sounding all around us. Pop finally broke the human silence: "Take me home." It was the last time we would visit New Creek and the places along it that he loved so much. Pop's health gradually worsened. His heart gave up for the last time shortly after I returned to Spokane. Every time I feel the urge to fish, which is often, I miss him even more than I did that year he died.

Since the 1970s, I have lived in the West, and never far from a river. It's twelve minutes from my garage to the Spokane River. For me, it has been a match made in heaven. At first glance it has many of the same qualities of other Western rivers that I have fished, without the wilderness setting and the rattlesnakes. It is an urban fishery with a paved trail along the banks for miles and miles in either direction. From a distance it looks "fishy," clean. Urban amenities like restaurants and sports bars are conveniently nearby. But Pop warned me long ago: "Son, looks can be deceiving, and every love interest has potentially deadly secrets."

The Spokane is home to fish like the protected redband rainbow, the westslope cutthroat, and the brown trout, all of them susceptible to deception by dry flies and streamers. Each section of the river has its own unique characteristics and plenty of secrets. The upper river begins at the Idaho state line in the Spokane Valley and ends at Upriver Dam near the town of Millwood. That section tends to be the warmest and to hold the highest population of bass and other species with scales. The middle river begins below Upriver Dam and stretches downstream to Riverfront Park. It is the shortest, it has the least public access, and it is the only section open to fishing year-round. The lower section starts below the Monroe Street falls and flows into Long Lake. That stretch, from the falls to the Spokane Gun Club, reportedly has the highest population of trout per mile.

Fishing on the upper and lower sections is tightly regulated to protect the redband. During the season in that stretch, all wild trout need to be released, and hooks with barbs are prohibited. Illustrated signs appear along the river in multiple languages, informing people of the redband's protected status. Signs also warn against eating too many fish to limit exposure to toxic heavy metals, the residue of decades of mining upstream in Idaho.

## Fish Food

Fish everywhere feed on the natural foods available. Insect numbers, diversity, and size vary based on the river bottom, water temperature, and water quality. Grasshoppers, beetles, ants, and even the clumsy occasional mouse that fall into the water become links in the fish food chain. To fly fishers, waterborne bugs add to a river's reputation and status. The Spokane is known for its caddisfly hatches and for its bottom-clinging bugs like stoneflies, salmonflies, tricos, blue-winged olives, and pale morning duns. Clouds of adult bugs can be seen swarming above the river and along the riverbank at times. However, there is a learning curve to fishing the Spokane.

The river looks inviting from above, but a closer examination from its shores reveals its dangers, its potential for spurring a visit to the hospital or morgue. Among the secrets of the Spokane is its bottom of round and slippery rocks, with shifting boulders the size of small cars. Metal-studded wading boots and a wading staff are a must, but even these are not guaranteed to keep you vertical. Wading and fishing are difficult and dangerous in spots. Pop was right: every love interest has potentially deadly secrets. Fishing from a drift boat is a much safer bet.

My first time on the river, I was impressed with the clouds of swarming adult caddis. There was no wind that day, and fish were rising near the middle of the river. My confidence soared. Poised on the river's edge, I tied on one of the adult caddis patterns in my fly box that matched the size and the color of the real bug. When my studless, felt-soled wading boot broke the clean river surface, I looked skyward and thanked Pop. Then both my feet slipped, and I discovered the river's hazardous bottom. My confidence took a dip, and my body almost followed.

Once within casting range of the rising fish, I managed to fool a couple of small ones, but countless others refused the adult imitation. Its size and color were perfect, but its life stage was wrong. I made another mental note. I planned my next river outing, equipped with metal-studded boots and in less of a rush. I knew there were bigger fish. The best daytime tactic I learned was to use a floating line and two flies in tandem: a big, floating bug imitation on top and a weighted bug imitation drifting below it. A sinking line with a big, weighted buggy streamer fished close to the bottom also proved to be a good tactic.

## Natural Predators

Ospreys and eagles patrol the river during the day. Aerial predators send most fish into hiding. With that fact in mind, I called my fishing buddy Dan and planned a night trip. I learned about night fishing on similar rivers back in Colorado. Big fish can be furious night feeders. You need a full moon and some really big dry flies. We scouted a stretch of river during the day, aware that we were adding to our risks in an already tricky environment by going after nightfall. My twelve-year-old son, John, joined us. His orders were to go for help if Dan and I went missing in the dark. John carried the only flashlight.

It was late summer. With our flies already tied on, we crossed the paved Centennial Trail and approached the water. Dan moved a little way upstream, and we both entered with caution. A few more cautious steps further in, now knee-deep, I made my first cast into the abyss. Nothing at first, but the third cast fooled a fish.

From its splashy, aggressive take, I could tell it was big. Keeping tension on the line, I began retracing my steps in the dark. Fish and river bottoms both have the advantage at night. John hadn't ventured far from where I posted him with the flashlight. Dan appeared at my side as I slid the fish into the shallows at the river's edge, to hear my son yell, "Dad, look at those eyes. They look like cat eyes!"

It was big, all right, an eighteen-incher. The trout's pupils were fully dilated, typical for a night feeder. The barbless fly was firmly stuck in his lip. I removed it, thanked the fish, and turned it toward deep water. A sacred memory was created. I hope Ol' Cat Eyes lived a long life in the Spokane River.

## Sean Visintainer

Sean looks young, both for his age (thirty-three) and for his experience as a professional fishing guide and business owner. Born and raised in the Spokane Valley, at age twenty-three he purchased the Silver Bow Fly Shop and remains the sole proprietor. I am one of the shop's many regulars, and we have been friends for almost ten years. While the shop is Sean's business, fly fishing is his passion. He has fished the Spokane River far more than most people, both for business and for pleasure. His staff of guides now log many days hosting clients in pursuit of local wild trout from drift boats.

The Silver Bow is located in a very unlikely spot: an industrial park pinched between two construction companies. It has the outward appearance of a river cabin, with an inviting wood exterior and wood-railed front porch often adorned with drying waders and wading shoes. Customers are welcomed by a resident golden retriever, sometimes two.

A black chalkboard sign near the door lists the latest fishing report and river conditions. The sign above the door reads "Silver Bow Fly Shop—Making Fish Nervous Since 1988." Sean was waiting for me in the upstairs loft where he and his staff teach fly-tying classes and hold river seminars. It was a cool overcast day in February, perfect for casting big purple streamers.

Sean started fishing at the age of nine in local lakes and ponds, using spin tackle and sitting in a float tube. Occasionally he fished the Lower Spokane River. He explains, "I had this inner desire, a calling to fish. Fly fishing began at twelve after I read *The Fly Fishing Encyclopedia*. I'm self-taught." While attending community college, Sean got to know the owner of the Silver Bow shop and remembers, "I knew early that I wanted to own a fly shop, and I became the fourth owner of this place. It's a labor of love."

I asked Sean what he sees when he looks at the Spokane River. "I see a unique urban fishing experience. *Urban* is almost a term I don't like to use because when you're on it, you don't feel like you're in an urban setting. The river goes right through this major city, yet it has beautiful scenery and beautiful wild trout. It's awesome. I used to warn clients that today we could hook some trout and see some deer, some marmots, some bald eagles, and maybe some half-naked swimmers. You never know. One of my guides actually found a dead body."

## Catchin' Frank the Tank

Sean told me:

> One evening me and a couple of my guides were drifting the upper section of the river when one of the guides hooked this beautiful brown trout. He got it to the boat. We took pictures, estimated its length at nineteen inches. and released it. Two years later, while fishing the same stretch of river, my other good friend Bob hooked and brought to the boat this healthy, fat brownie. I took the customary picture and released it. "Wait," I said. That fish looked familiar. I later compared the second picture with the first.
>
> After comparing the spots on the gill plate, we quickly determined that it was the same fish we caught before. Amazing! But wait: an even more amazing thing happened later that summer. While drifting through the same spot, a friend of mine unknowingly caught that exact fish on nearly the exact fly. He took the customary picture and released the brownie. Later he showed me the picture, and sure enough it was the same fish, now caught three times! We named him Frank the Tank.

Sean sees the river through multiple lenses simultaneously: as a business owner and as a steward of the river. He is hopeful. "I've seen days where the Spokane River would rival any river in the West. I no longer guide on the Spokane. My guides are booked almost daily during the summer months. I still manage several personal float and fish trips per year just for fun."

He observes, "A great thing has been happening over the past one–two years. I have seen a mass movement to improve the river. Those involved are both anglers and nonanglers, conservation groups like the Spokane River-keepers, the Spokane River Forum—on whose board I sit—and the Spokane chapter of Trout Unlimited, to name a few. The City of Spokane has taken a bigger interest in the river lately. A lot of positive things are happening."

Sean elaborates:

> I'd like to see two more things happen: better river access, and better spawning habitat for the redband. Because of the dams and the fluctuating flows made to create irrigation and power, we will have to make the river better artificially. From a professional standpoint, the fish in the Spokane River are doing well, but we need to do more to improve the river quality and the fish population. Currently Silver Bow is the biggest licensed operation on the river. We have certain clients who return every year just to stay downtown and fish the Spokane River. We recommend the Spokane to everyone who visits the shop, and we caution them that there are easier places to catch wild trout on foot, but no place as close as this one.

Sean and his staff have a vested interest in the river that goes beyond their business interest. He loves the river like many of us do, and especially the wild trout. The Spokane River continues to have a bad reputation. It is known for its toxic, slippery bottom, dangerous swift runs, and hidden currents. Its banks are often crime scenes, and every summer the river claims its share of careless users. But its reputation is getting better, thanks to people like Sean and other anglers and nonanglers. It holds a lot of secrets, and we continue to fish the Spokane, always in pursuit of another Ol' Cat Eyes or Frank the Tank.

River stories have a way of drawing us close, connecting us to the past and the present, providing a lens to the future. The life and health of the Spokane River and the wild trout that live in it are in the hands of the story keepers, those who can speak for it and those who love it—secrets, hazards, and all.

# Latah Creek

CHRIS KOPCZYNSKI

"THAT'S A MONSTER, LARRY." MY DAD GAZED IN WONDER AT THE animal pulled from Latah Creek just one mile from where the creek flows into the Spokane River.

Horrified, I also stared at the huge black mass of fur being dangled by its hind legs. It dripped a pool of water on the concrete floor inside the doorway of my dad's cabinet shop. A head and two paws hung from the ball of fur. A flat black tail fell over its belly.

"This is a big beaver, Chris." Larry spoke to me, but I was so intimidated I could only stare. The creature was bigger than me. I was five years old and just learning about the stillness of death. I possessed no vocabulary to respond. I was not sure I was even breathing.

"Caught him just up the creek, Kop, and this one's worth some money." Everyone called my dad "Kop," even my mother.

"Yes, sir, this might be the largest one in the valley, Kop. Fifty or sixty pounds, and just look at the fur. I got two smaller ones in the back of my pickup. I'll be taking them up to Pacific Hide and Fur to sell."

My dad admired the fur and puffed on his pipe. "Well, Larry, those beaver pelts will be wrapped around some lady in New York City in the next couple of months."

Larry walked out the door, flopped the dead beaver in the back of his pickup, and drove up the Inland Empire Highway. Larry Rupp was twenty-six years old, lean, fit, athletic, sporting a crew cut and biceps chiseled by eight years of military service. The first four years after high school, he served in the army. Hungry to see more of the world, he quit the army and signed up with the navy for four more. Part of his duty included a tour in

Hiroshima in the spring of 1946, on cleanup duty after the atomic bomb leveled the city. Now he trapped beaver and worked construction where he had grown up, along Latah Creek. In 1953, the creek abounded in beaver, pheasants, muskrats, and coyotes.

My dad had purchased five lots on the bank of the creek for a hundred dollars each in 1950. The lots were cheap because they were "reclaimed" land, built in the historical floodplain. Thousands of cubic yards of concrete rubble that bristled with rebar had been trucked down from buildings destroyed by the great Spokane fire of August 4, 1889. The Army Corps of Engineers directed that the waste be dumped along the shores of Latah Creek. That same Army Corps channelized the creek, destroying the meanders, the islands, and the natural channel formations to build a steep bank and manmade levee from Inland Empire Highway to the 11th Street Bridge.

On his new streamside property, with my assistance, my dad built a forty-by fifty-foot Quonset hut, without insulation, to serve as home base for our family cabinetry and home-construction business. A mile downstream from the shop, Latah Creek flowed into the Spokane River. That confluence was named People's Park when Expo '74, the first environmental world's fair, brought thousands of visitors who needed a place to camp.

After seeing Larry Rupp's beaver, I was bitten by the adventure bug and wondered what other creatures made their homes along the creek. I roamed its banks without supervision, downstream or upstream as the mood took me. Just outside our shop stretched the Chestnut Street three-arch bridge. Hunting for the plentiful bull snakes and frogs one day, I spotted two older boys wading in the pool under the middle arch of the bridge. The oldest boy was wearing a white T-shirt, a red ball cap, and shorts. Hunched over with his face an inch from the water, he submerged his arms in the pool past his elbows and waded as if he were stalking something.

"Just a couple more feet and I got 'im," he yelled to his friend on the bank. His partner held a burlap bag that wiggled. The big boy suddenly dove under the water, head and all. When he surfaced, yelling, he had lost his ball cap. "I got him!" He waded backward toward me on the bank, and

I saw a horrible snapping creature. He pinched behind its claws with his thumb and index finger.

I had never seen anything so hideous, but my curiosity won out and I stood my ground. The mudbug was some six inches long, its eyes protruding, its six antennae flailing. The boy waded right up to me, thrust the creature at my face, and yelled "Gotcha!" I stumbled, tripping and falling on the mud, crawling to get away.

"It's a crayfish, kid! Lots of 'em in the water, and man, are they good eatin'." He threw his prize into the burlap sack, and they were off.

"Mom! I saw monsters in the creek today! They look like bugs, but they live underwater!"

Every day I brought home new tales of the creek. The beavers were marvelous engineers. Where one beaver pond ended, other beavers built their dams and huts. With the help of nature books, my mother helped me identify, one by one, the creatures I was seeing: marmots, muskrats, snakes, ducks, squirrels, pheasants, deer mice, and bull snakes. The water held trout, suckerfish, and carp. Kingfishers, warblers, mergansers, ducks, and magpies darted through the skies. Blue herons, eagles, ospreys, falcons, and geese cast larger shadows.

"What is that awful smell in the creek, Mom?" After every rainstorm a stench arose.

"That's sewage, Christopher. That's why we never eat the fish you catch from the creek."

Dad gruffly contradicted her. "The creek purifies itself every two and a half miles."

My mom snapped back, "Now, Kop, don't you tell him that. You know that cannot be true. It's irresponsible care for the water that causes the awful smell, and you know it."

There was a common belief that nothing harmed the creek. As Spokane began to grow in the late 1800s, the city sited a dump one block from Latah Creek on Seventh Avenue and Coeur d'Alene Street. Every piece of trash leached into Latah Creek. Next to the dump, a twelve-thousand-square-foot wooden vinegar factory was built in 1890 and flourished until 1959. The area farmers produced cider, malt, white wine, pickles, and vinegar. It gave the valley its name, Vinegar Flats.

Latah Creek flows into the Spokane River, and until 1957 the invisible menace of raw sewage flowed into the Spokane River as well. Not until the 1980s was the Latah Valley tied into the city sewer system. But it wasn't just raw sewage. Larro Feed, Paint, and Hardware across the street from our family shop dumped paints, solvents, and dirty rags next to the creek.

As a teenager, I thought I knew everything worth knowing about life, and I was eager to join the workforce and conquer the world. My dad had other ideas. He was the twelfth of thirteen brothers and sisters who grew up during the Great Depression, and his education ended in high school. He wanted his children to go to college and earn a degree.

I couldn't see the value in more education, but I agreed just to please him. After my first year of college, I came home empowered with knowledge. It was my turn to school him.

"Hey, Dad, remember those huge round granite boulders we found while excavating the cabinet shop? They're not native to the area like basalt. They're granite from the Purcell batholith six hundred miles to the north near the Bugaboo Mountains. An ice sheet carried them to Sandpoint, and then they rolled downriver in the great Ice Age floods. Those were the largest floods in the history of the known world. Rolling made the boulders round before they got to the shop."

"Really? You can tell all that by just looking at that rock?" My dad marveled at my new authority.

"Speaking of rocks, the cliffs on the creek are the top layer of the Miocene basalt flows, twelve thousand feet thick. Our shop and the creek sit right on top of an earthquake fault line called the Latah Strike-Slip Fault. Someday, the earth is going to shake." I had my Dad's entire interest and attention, and I continued with my lecture.

"Now, look at this rock." I held a piece of shale with a fossil of a brachiopod embedded in a piece of limestone. I'd found it at ten thousand feet on the face of Mount Stanley in British Columbia. "This animal lived three hundred million years ago, fossilized on top of the mountain. There were other fossils of fish and small crawfish too, just like we find in the creek, only these animals died over three hundred million years ago." My father nodded in astonishment.

> And get this, Dad, Latah means *fish* in Nez Perce. Huge chinook, sockeye, chum, pink and silver salmon used to travel hundreds of miles up the Columbia, the Spokane, and Latah past our property to spawn in the creek. The Nez Perce built a fishing weir at the mouth where it flows into the Spokane River. They trapped a thousand salmon a day for thirty days every fall. Our shop is built right over one of the Spokane Indian fishing camps. But here is another astounding fact: the largest mastodons ever discovered used to roam up and down this creek bed. The Coplen family homesteaders found their bones on their land in a bog at Tekoa. More mastodon bones showed up near Rosalia, and those are the largest mastodon skeletons in the world. They became the main attraction at the Field Museum of Chicago and in the Museum of Natural History in New York.

Following my college education, I also told my dad about the other changes to our land. Two years before the Civil War, the name Latah was changed to Hangman Creek on federal maps after the Yakama chief Qualchan and other warriors were hanged upstream some twenty miles from our shop. In 1911, the construction of the Little Falls Dam killed the steelhead and salmon runs forever.

Larry Rupp, with his daughter Karen, trapped beaver and muskrat until 1968, when there were no more. In the 1970s, the construction of Highway 195 changed the hydrology of the creek forever. It channeled the stream's twists and turns; it trashed vegetation and animal habitat. Upstream, forests were logged, roads built, farms plowed clear to the edge of the creek. Fecal coliform bacteria from livestock, leakage from septic tanks, chemicals from industry, and lack of shade damaged the creek. Standards for temperature,

Latah (Hangman) Creek, a major tributary of the Spokane River. Photo courtesy of Chris Kopczynski.

pH, and bacteria were often violated. The result was that Latah Creek had too little oxygen to support its ecosystem.

But much life survives, and people grow wiser about wild water as more knowledge becomes available. The salmon might never return, but we have many other flourishing species. In 2015 a beaver built a dam on the creek behind the shop, the first I have witnessed in forty-seven years.

For six decades Dad and I used Latah Creek to help us solve the world's problems at the kitchen table. Dad conceded that the Earth's resources were finite, not constantly self-renewing, as he had once thought. I conceded that the value of education was infinite, just like he said.

When my father was eighty-five years old, weakened by arthritis, Parkinson's and Alzheimer's, he came to my office with my mother's help. Long before, I had taken over the family business and sat where he used to sit. He held out a wrapped package. "I want you to have this, Chris."

"Can I unwrap it now?"

"Yes," he breathed.

I unwrapped the paper to find a painting signed by Tom Holt, a famous local artist.

When he was eighty-nine, a month before he died, I was having breakfast with my father, and I said, "I love you, Dad. Thank you for all your sacrifice to give us a college education." From his wheelchair, unable to speak, barely able to move, he extended his right arm across the table. His palm unfolded slowly, displaying a huge right hand callused from a lifetime of construction, and fingers the size and color of barbecued bratwursts. He clenched his fist, raised his thumb in the air and smiled, his eyes alive with kindness.

The painting my dad gave me hangs above my office desk. It depicts the banks of Latah Creek on a beautiful summer day, with the cool, blue water gurgling through the valley. Basalt cliffs rise above the creek. Ponderosa pines, quaking aspens, cottonwoods, and alders line the banks. It shows no cabinet shop, no Chestnut Street Bridge, no homes, no streets—just the stream and memories of what we learned together about, and from, the water he loved so much.

# When the River Comes toward Me

NANCE VAN WINCKEL

## When the River Comes toward Me

it comes with whatever it's
sucked up on the way. Iron
stairs. Ice chests. Stove pipes.
Rocking chairs. It won't let me
make it kind or cool. Won't let me
resweeten it with my three great aunts'
enormous breasts floating before them
as they call me into chest-high currents.

A renegade in March, by June
the river receives pardon—for cows
carried off. Car roofs and tree roots.
Its black toothless gums grind past.

Anything anyone's erected here, the river
one day takes down. Boils in its ice.

Voices call in High Dutch
from the low country, and No, no way
I'm wading out there. Only my aunts could

From *Pacific Walkers* (University of Washington Press, 2013).

balance in the water like that
with those unsinkable, inscrutable
spheres of milk and marble. Any one
could crumble a building.

When the river comes at me,
it's filling fast: ladders sofas swing sets.
Chisels pencils hacksaws.
Black hats black leashes black dogs.

Don't make me look
or look away. The women laugh
the water's laugh, forgetting me
each time the fox steps down
and sips at the ripples
with his fine red mouth.

# The Urban Outdoors

JESS WALTER

SOMEONE ONCE CALLED GOLF A GOOD WALK SPOILED. BUT I'LL TELL you what really spoils a good walk: man scat. Big. Human. Turds. I can't tell you how many times I've been walking along the river only to find that someone has loafed on the trail.

"This is my number-one outdoors issue," I told the editors of *Out There Monthly* when they first contacted me about writing this column. (Full disclosure: initially, I returned their call because I misheard the magazine's name and thought I was being publicly linked with Tom Cruise again.) As I explained to the editors, I consider myself an "urban outdoorsman," a man whose entire relationship with nature takes place within the city. I am king of the white-trash frontier.

So I have rafted the mighty Spokane towing an inner tube of beer. I have fished beneath bridges for bottom-feeders so loaded with heavy metals that you weigh them with a Geiger counter. I have sledded the great peaks of Manito Park and watched drunken rock climbers scale the brick faces of those handful of old buildings that we haven't turned into Diamond lots. This is what I want to write about, I told the editors, the outdoor opportunities and issues right here in the bespoiled heart of our city. And the biggest issue I see right now is this public display of defecation, the trail of turds. I have lived on the river most of my life. I've taken thousands of walks along our great urban stream and have seen man scat roughly, oh, every single freaking time.

---

This chapter was originally published as two short essays in *Out There Monthly* in 2006. They are reprinted here courtesy of the magazine.

For years, I did what anyone does when I saw trail dung. I ran away. But hunters don't run when they come across deer droppings. Conservationists and biologists don't run from bear scat. They study it. They poke at it with sticks, take it back to the lab to dissect and analyze. There is no better way to learn about something than to study its shit.

So, in my desire to understand why people crap on trails, I began crouching alongside the offending stool like those trackers hired by posses in old Westerns. (It's usually a stoic Indian played by Ricardo Montalban, who holds up a broken twig and then calmly announces that three men and a mule passed by nine hours ago, that one of the men was wearing dance tights and that the mule was clinically depressed.)

Here's what I've learned by studying path poop:

1. The people who do this are either horribly backed up or this is a breed of shitting giants. (I mistook one of these things for a fumbled football and in a fit of muscle memory, nearly pounced on it.)
2. Too many Fritos, not enough salad.
3. Trail dumpers exclusively drink malt liquor. There are always malt liquor cans nearby. If I were in the malt liquor industry, I'd stop marketing to rap fans and go for the lucrative outdoor shitter market.

My brother and I were making preparations for our annual State of the Spokane River Float (this mostly involves getting my brother out of his home-detention ankle bracelet) when a Montana "friend" made a snarky comment about our beloved river. "Do you actually go in that water?" he sniffed, like a French wine snob over a box of Gallo. "Isn't that, like, one of the most polluted rivers in the country?"

Damn you Montanans and your crystalline streams and poetic fly fishermen. Maybe if Ted Turner bought up our whole state for emu farming, then our river would be undeveloped and gin-clear, too. (A side note: do you ever notice how many Montanans live here and pine for the Big Empty? So here's a question: if Montana is so freaking perfect, why don't any of you live there?)

So I said, "Sorry goat boy, but we have an urban river and if you think we're going to apologize for the fact that our river foams like a poured Guinness and has more heavy metal than a 1988 record store, then you need to go back to Flathead Lake, rent a studio apartment for $1850 a month and get a job cleaning the back hair out of Sylvester Stallone's hot tub."

The truth is, the Spokane River gets a little cleaner every year—at least every year that the city doesn't dump raw sewage into it. Although it's counterintuitive, I think the recent and proposed development along the river canyon downtown could bode well for the river's long-term health. Right now you're more likely to see rusted Oly cans than fish, but if there's one thing rich people hate, it's litter in their front yards, so they're at least going to keep the banks clean.

My brother and I got a good look at those banks on our annual State of the River float. We put in below his house in Peaceful Valley and finally flopped out of the water beneath the T. J. Meenach Bridge, near my house. It was one of those 160-degree days and so the riverbank was packed with people standing up to the threads of their cutoffs, drinking cans of Keystone and huffing glue. Some days, floating the river is like being in a parade in the Ozarks. Yet even the toothless mountain people laugh at us.

My brother and I make the same mistake every year during the State of the River float. We do a hurried count and then buy a "two-person" raft, which translated, means "one-person" unless you're talking about two persons who have a level of intimacy that, frankly, my brother and I simply don't have. ("I wish I could quit you," I whispered as we snuggled in the raft like two fingers in a glove hole.)

It really is a stunning river, alternately calm and roiling, and you can find yourself in stretches that defy description. We were in one of those places, shaded by leaning firs, our raft barely above water level, my brother and I wedged into it like Scandinavians in a two-man luge, when we happened to float by a drunk guy holding a forty in one hand and his George W. in the other (perhaps figuring his piss just ends up in the river anyway, he was skipping the middleman). He pointed at us with his big beer. "Rub-a-dub-dub," he said, "two men in a tub."

It was at that point my brother said, "Hey, your oar keeps poking me in the back."

"That," I said, "is not my oar."

# Culture,
# History,
# Society

# What Is the Name of Our River?

stem̓ łuʔ skʷesc łuʔ qe ntx̣ʷetkʷʔ

BARRY G. MOSES (SULUSTU)

THE TRADITIONAL STORIES OF THE SPOKANE PEOPLE SPEAK reverently of the river, from its creation to the salmon in its waters that once gave life to the people. Despite its importance, the original Spokane name of the river has been shrouded in conflict. It is no small irony that many of the modern descendants of the Spokane people no longer recall the name of our sacred river. This chapter traces the various names of the Spokane River using historical records produced by early settlers, traditional Spokane stories, data from neighboring tribes, and oral history.

## A Long-Ago Legend

Pauline Flett has dedicated her life to the preservation of the Spokane language. As a tribal elder and fluent speaker, she has worked tirelessly for decades to document and promote the language. With the linguist Barry Carlson, she coauthored a Spokane dictionary. She has transcribed hundreds of pages of elder interviews, created curricula, and taught Spokane-language classes at Eastern Washington University. The Spokane language owes Pauline a tremendous debt of gratitude. In 1998, Pauline spoke at the Spokane Opera House on the public radio program *A Prairie Home Companion*, hosted by Garrison Keillor, retelling a traditional Spokane creation story that she titled "A Long-Ago Legend."

According to the legend, many centuries ago, a terrible earthquake destroyed the Spokane country. The earth opened and swallowed people, animals, houses, and trees. Thunder and lightning came next, followed by a massive flood. Every living soul perished, except for a boy and a girl who took refuge on the summit of Mount Spokane. From the safety of the mountain, the two young people witnessed the creation of the Spokane River. I have provided my own translation of Pauline's story:

hec nsoʕ̓ʷ łuʔ sewłkʷ (the water drained away)
u wíʔičis č̓ išút u hec mʕʷop (and they saw below a flowing stream)
hoy u wíʔičis ye qʷamqʷmt sⱦipmétkʷ (then they saw a beautiful waterfall)
u łuʔ sƛ̓xetkʷ (and the fast water, the rapids).

The Spokane River emerged from the destruction and gave relief to the survivors. Salmon appeared in the water and sustained the young boy and girl, who became the ancestors of the three bands of the Spokane people.

Pauline's retelling of the "Long-Ago Legend" placed the Spokane River at the heart of creation and at the origin of the Spokane people. From the beginning, Spokane identity was linked to the river, the falls, and the salmon. But what was the name of the river? The story did not say.

## My Personal Relationship with the River

When I first learned of this project, I wanted to write a purely academic paper on the name of the Spokane River. However, I soon realized that I could not avoid personalizing the story. The people who know the Spokane language and traditions, the people from whom I would have to seek information, are my relatives and close friends. In a similar way, my own work has revolved around researching and maintaining traditional knowledge. I could not write this piece as though I were an outside observer. I am part of the story, a descendant of Spokane ancestors. I am reclaiming the language, culture, geography, and place-names of those who went before.

My effort to identify a precontact name for the Spokane River relied on four basic sources, many of whose narratives overlap. First, I consulted historical papers, such as the journals of Lewis and Clark and the writings of the explorer David Thompson. Second, I consulted my collection of old tribal stories, although it is incomplete. Third, I called on tribal elders and specialists from the Spokane tribal language program. Finally, I consulted language experts from other tribes. The answers arrived in their own time. People often did not know the name of the river when I first asked. Only later did they return with an answer.

## The Historical Record

### SKEET-SO-MISH, RIVER OF THE COEUR D'ALENE PEOPLE

Meriwether Lewis and William Clark gave perhaps the first written description of the Spokane River. The Corps of Discovery never entered Spokane territory, but they passed about 150 miles to the south, and in 1806 they received three men from "a nation called the Skeets-so-mish." The visitors reported to Lewis and Clark that their homeland spanned an important waterway, beginning at an intermountain lake and draining into a large river. The river of the Skeet-so-mish then passed a major waterfall and emptied into the Columbia.

Prior to European contact, the Coeur d'Alene people called themselves the Schitsu'umsh, meaning "the discovered people" or "those who are found here." Undoubtedly the Schitsu'umsh people were the Skeet-so-mish mentioned by Lewis and Clark. Moreover, the description of the territory given by the explorers, along with their hand-drawn map, clearly shows that a river they identified as the Coeur d'Alene River was the Spokane River.

### SKEETSHOO

Perhaps influenced by the name given to the river by Lewis and Clark, several early sources referred to the Spokane River as the Skeetshoo River, an English approximation of the Spokane word for the Coeur d'Alene Tribe, *sčícwi?*.

In 1809, under the auspices of the North West Company, David Thompson built Kullyspell House, in present-day north Idaho. Thompson recorded several important visits from the Schitsu'umsh or the Coeur d'Alene. During that time, the Schitsu'umsh likely influenced Thompson's understanding of regional topography and place names. Only a year later, Jaco Finley (or Finlay, or Findlay) built Spokane House near the confluence of the Spokane and Little Spokane Rivers. Finley chose a location close to the primary camp of the Middle Spokane people, "a spot where the Indians were accustomed to gather in large numbers to dry their fish."

Thompson applied the name Skeetshoo to the Spokane River when he visited the area in June 1811. He wrote in his journal that his team had crossed a stream that flowed "into the Skeetshoo River." The next day, he encountered Finley and a camp of about forty Spokane families. Thompson also created a map that showed the Skeetshoo (Spokane) River flowing from Skeetshoo (Coeur d'Alene) Lake and passing Spokane House.

The association between the Spokane River and the Coeur d'Alene territory was preserved in the English language. The Washington territorial governor, Isaac Stevens, referred to the Spokane River as the Coeur d'Alene River in his correspondence. One historian wrote, "When Governor Stevens speaks of visiting the falls of the Coeur d'Alene River, he refers to the Spokane Falls, around which the present city of Spokane is located." Likewise, Stevens designated the Little Spokane River as the Spokane.

## Traditional Stories

The historical record represents an outsider's perspective. Lewis and Clark never visited the Spokane country, and David Thompson apparently received much of his information from the Coeur d'Alene people. Their writings produced valuable historical data, but nowhere did they record a name that the Spokane assigned to the river. To find our own designation for the Spokane River, I extended my search to include our traditional stories.

### COYOTE BRINGS SALMON

Many of our stories mentioned the river, but only one specified a name. "Coyote Brings Salmon" was a traditional story that mentioned the Spokane

River, along with its relationship to the Coeur d'Alene people. Coyote was chasing the salmon up the Columbia River, and everywhere he went, he exchanged fish for a bride. The story mentioned the river almost in passing: "łu? spílye? nc̓?ilš łu? n spoqín ntx̣ʷetx̣ʷ łu? č sc̓icwi? s̓túlix̣ʷs" (Coyote went up the Spokane River to the Coeur d'Alene country). According to the narrative, the Coeur d'Alene refused to give him a wife, so he took his revenge by creating the Spokane Falls to block the salmon from going farther upstream. The author of this story is unknown, but a related version was retold by Sherman Alexie and titled "The Place Where the Ghosts of Salmon Jump." Alexie's poetic retelling of the story is engraved in a spiral formation on a path overlooking Spokane Falls.

The story of Coyote bringing salmon to the Spokane country likely predated European contact, but the term *spoqín ntx̣ʷetkʷ* (Spokane River) seemed anachronistic. Prior to contact, the Spokane people referred to themselves by the names of their specific locations on the river: the sntu?t?úlix̣ʷ (Upper Spokane), the snx̣ʷméne? (Middle Spokane), and the scqescíłni (Lower Spokane). The general term *spoqín* (Spokane as a tribal designation) did not appear until after the establishment of the Spokane Indian Reservation in 1881. It is possible that the story was translated into English at some point in the past and then retranslated into Spokane as the language revitalization movement gained momentum. Ultimately, it is not incorrect to refer to the Spokane River as spoqín ntx̣ʷetkʷ; I simply thought we might find an older name.

## The Teaching of Elders

GIVER OF LIFE

Margo Hill is a Spokane tribal member who graduated with a law degree from Gonzaga University and now teaches at Eastern Washington University. Margo remembered that her grandmother Sadie Boyd once spoke of the river in our language. Sadie was a respected tribal elder and storyteller who lived for more than a hundred years; she died in 1986. Margo wrote that her grandmother called the river Nx Wl Wl tsuten, a name she translated as

"The river gives us our way of life." Margo wrote the name phonetically and informally, but modern Salish writers would spell this word *nxʷlxʷlcutn*.

Sadie's name for the river surprised me. I have only ever encountered this word in a Christian context, in a Salish-language hymn written in the late 1800s by Jesuit missionaries that included the line "x̣est yesu kʷ in xʷlxʷlcutn" (Good Jesus, you are my savior). Linguistically, both Sadie Boyd's translation and the Jesuit translation are correct. The word *xʷlxʷlcutn* can signify both a giver of life and a savior.

My uncle, Pat Moses, recalled a similar name. Some years ago, a group of elders, teachers, and students from the various local tribes gathered once a month to discuss common language questions. He remembered that someone had offered a name for the Spokane River during one of those meetings: nxʷixʷyétkʷ. He explained the meaning of the name and said, "The river is the giver of life. It gives us food and fish."

Several weeks after my uncle, Pat Moses, told me about the Spokane River as the giver of life, he recalled another name. He said the people sometimes referred to the river as nqqeʔtétkʷ, the Narrow Water, or the Narrow River. This name contrasted the Spokane River with the Columbia River, known as nkʷtnetkʷ, the Big Water, or Big River.

Robert Wyncoop is my friend and a fellow teacher of the Spokane language. Late in my investigations of the river name, he sent me a text message stating that in the city of Spokane, he once saw a collection of place-names attached to a large map. The Spokane River was labeled nťteʔétkʷ, or Little Hits on the Water. The origin of that name was unclear.

### Our Kalispel Neighbors

Neighboring tribes, such as the Kalispel and the Coeur d'Alene, shared cultural, linguistic, and geographical ties with the Spokane, and the tribes often assigned similar or cognate names to prominent locations in our traditional territories. For example, the Kalispel referred to Mount Spokane as čq̓ʷoⱡsmn, while the Spokane referred to it as čq̓ʷuⱡsm. Despite minor dialectical differences, both terms suggest the shared cultural practice of obtaining willow bark (q̓ʷoƚs in the Kalispel language, or q̓ʷuƚs in the Spokane language) from the slopes of the mountain. If our people shared place-names, it seemed logical to ask the Kalispel about the Spokane River.

J. R. Bluff is the director of a program dedicated to revitalizing the Kalispel language. When he heard my question, he said he did not know of any traditional name for the Spokane River, but he told me a story about the Pend Oreille River that might shed some light on the issue. He said that many years ago the Kalispel people did not have a separate name for the Pend Oreille River: it was so vital to their culture and survival that they simply referred to it as ntx̣ʷetkʷ, the river. They had no need for any other designation unless they interacted with people from other tribes, in which case they referred to their river as qlispe? ntx̣ʷetkʷs, or the Kalispels' River. That account made me wonder if a similar naming practice existed among the Spokane people.

As I expected, a Spokane language manual confirmed that *ntx̣ʷetkʷ* is a general term referring to any river, but it can also function as a relational term referring to the most important river in the vicinity. In other words, to a person on the reservation, *ntx̣ʷetkʷ* specifically means the Spokane River, but to a person closer to the Columbia River, it means the Columbia.

Like the Kalispel, the Spokane people had little need to specify the name of the river. But what did we call the river when we spoke of the outside world or when we interacted with other tribes? To answer that question, I once again consulted our Kalispel neighbors.

Stan Bluff is the former chairman of the Kalispel Tribe. Today he is a respected elder and cultural adviser in his community. He is also one of the few remaining fluent speakers of the Kalispel language. Stan said that many years ago, perhaps in the 1930s, his parents sometimes traveled to Spokane from Cusick by wagon. They camped near the top of the Division Street hill, near the present-day intersection of Division Street and Bridgeport Avenue, which was then outside the city limits. The women and children stayed in camp while the men went into the city to conduct their business. In those days, his parents referred to both the city and the Spokane River as sx̣etkʷ, the place of fast water.

The story surprised me. Based on my own knowledge of the language, I knew that sx̣etkʷ is the traditional name of the falls that now lie at the heart of the city of Spokane, but I had never heard this name applied to the entire river. I expressed my surprise to Stan, and I asked if he was sure that his parents referred to the river, not just the falls, by this name. He replied, "Yes. Before the dams, the whole river was fast." At least two other sources confirm that the people called the whole river sx̣etkʷ, and not just the falls.

On a high bluff overlooking Long Lake Dam, the Avista Corporation erected a cultural marker that retells a traditional Spokane story. The marker reads, in part: "Long ago, according to a story told by Spokane tribal elders, a mischievous character named ppatiʔqs (doodlebug) lived beside sx̣etkʷ, the Spokane River." The story recalled the origin of various plant foods of the Spokane people—white camas, brown camas, wild carrots, and wild onions—and confirmed that "Fast Water" was one of the river names.

My aunt Iva Eli and other tribal elders discussed the question and also thought they remembered hearing people long ago refer to the whole river as sx̣etkʷ.

When I learned that the name sx̣etkʷ applied to the whole river, my awareness expanded. I came to understand that the spirit of the river is more powerful than I had ever imagined. Except for the fast waters of the falls, I have only ever known a river domesticated by hydroelectric dams and pacified into a series of artificial lakes. The water ultimately surrendered to the force of concrete and steel, but a reflection of its strength has survived in our language.

Johnny Arlee is a Flathead tribal member who works as a language specialist for the Kalispel Tribe. When I posed my question to him, he immediately responded, "The river was called sčicuwiʔ or sčicuwitkʷ—the waters of the found people." Like David Thompson, Johnny associated the Spokane River with the Coeur d'Alene. The Kalispel tribal language curriculum also identified the Spokane River as sčicuwitkʷ and the Little Spokane River as nxʷmnetkʷ—the Steelhead River.

In the end, the diversity of river names resembles a roll call of geographic designations: ntx̣ᵂetkᵂ, spoqín ntx̣ᵂetkᵂ, sÅx̣etkᵂ, nxᵂlxᵂlcutn, nxᵂixᵂyetkᵂ, nqqeʔtétkᵂ, Skeet-so-mish, Skeetshoo, sčicẇiʔ, sčicẇitkᵂ. Each name shows the complex history and varied relationships between the Spokane people, the river, and our neighboring tribes. As the perspective of the observer changes, the Spokane River may be the River, the Spokanes' River, the Fast Water, the Life Giver, the Life River, the Narrow Water, Little Hits on the Water, or even the Coeur d'Alene River. Each name reflects a different aspect of the spirit of the river.

# Nature and Industry in Early Spokane

*The Lumber versus Trout Debate*

J. WILLIAM T. YOUNGS

IN 1882, SPOKANE ENGAGED IN ITS FIRST ENVIRONMENTAL DEBATE. That year, an editorial in the *Spokane Times* complained that sawdust from the town's lumber mills was killing fish. The paper claimed that the Spokane River was known "as one of the finest on the coast for sportsmen to visit." Bringing fishermen to the falls enriched local hotels and merchants—"and what benefits them," the *Times* declared, "benefits the entire country." All that mutual benefit might soon end, however, according the paper: "It is the fish-destroying sawdust that is threatening to rob the sportsmen of his pleasure by depopulating the river of its finny tribe. The sawdust from the mill in this city is daily given to the current, and sure death is thus dealt out to thousands of handsome trout that should otherwise gladden the hearts of rightful captors."

When the trout versus lumber dispute erupted, the debate was but the latest expression of Spokane's ambivalence about the uses of the falls. The town builder James Glover had shown that double-mindedness when he first arrived at Spokane Falls on horseback in 1873. On his way toward the falls, he passed by a high basalt bluff along the river. "The prevalence of this rock," he noted in his reminiscences, "was one of the things that struck me forcibly as I neared the falls. I used to wonder what I was going to do with such heaps and mountains of basalt. But in later years I understood what the Almighty had put it there for." And what would that divine purpose be?

As Glover was pondering God's purpose in providing so much rock near Spokane Falls, other Americans were beginning to appreciate and preserve the country's natural wonders. John Muir, America's premier environmentalist, was making his home in Yosemite Valley at about the time Glover wandered into Spokane. Just as Glover questioned the utility of Spokane's basalt, Muir pondered the value of rattlesnakes: Why had God put them on the earth? Muir answered his own question: God had put rattlers here for their own sake. The snakes were "good for themselves," Muir wrote in *Our National Parks*, "and we need not begrudge them their share of life."

Given his own appreciation of nature, one waits for James Glover to say that "the Almighty" created basalt for its beauty. But Glover's response was typical of the Age of Industry. He answered the riddle of the basalt this way: "In after years I understood what the Almighty had put it there for. Almost all of it, except a cliff here and there, has been used in the construction of basements." Ironically, using basalt for basements is now the leading cause of radon poisoning. Radon remediation is big business today.

Glover brought that practical turn of mind to his first encounter with the falls themselves. When he arrived, there were already several squatters living by the falls, but in 1873 there was no town. Glover spent his first night in a roofless log cabin. It was located, he later recalled, "on Front, between Mill and Howard." Lying on the dirt floor, rolled up in his blankets, he listened to the "roar" of Spokane Falls and then fell into "a comfortable and restful night's slumber." The next morning he rushed from the cabin to see the falls, and sat beside them, drenched by their spray while "gazing, wondering, and admiring."

After his soaking by the falls, Glover joined the squatters for breakfast, telling them he "wanted to see more of the wonderful river." He learned that about a mile upstream he could find a boat hitched to a post. Well, it was not exactly a boat, the squatter said: it was "a makeshift of a skiff, a pine log ten or twelve feet long, hollowed out a little so that two people can ride in it if they sit very still." With the thunder of the falls in his ears, Glover crossed the Spokane River in this precarious log canoe and spent the morning walking downstream to the lower falls.

The river must have been magnificent that day. The spring runoff would have sent water surging past the rocks and islands. "I was enchanted—overwhelmed—with the beauty and grandeur of everything I saw," wrote Glover. "It lay just as nature had made it, with nothing to mar its virgin glory." Glover was experiencing sensations common to the early settlers of the West: the twin passions of wonder and avarice. Forty-four years later, when he wrote his memoir, Glover struggled to find words to describe the potent mixture of emotions that he felt on that first day in Spokane. "I liked the beautiful, clear stream of water," he recalled. "I liked the falls, with their foundation of basaltic rock that would remain forever. . . . I never have been able to express the force with which this country impressed my mind at the time I first saw it." Yet while awestruck by the falls, Glover also experienced a different but equally powerful sensation: acquisitiveness. Having seen the river's beauty, he made a fateful choice: "I determined that I would possess it."

Other early visitors to Spokane Falls were also impressed with both their beauty and their utility. In 1877 a well-traveled couple, Robert and Carrie Strahorn, arrived in Spokane and recognized immediately the extraordinary beauty of the falls. Robert Strahorn was employed by the Union Pacific Railroad to explore and publicize the West. He had initially refused to take the job unless his wife could come along on what turned out to be a multiyear, fifteen-thousand-mile journey by stagecoach. They arrived in Spokane Falls shortly after having visited Yellowstone, the world's first national park. Though Carrie Strahorn was accustomed to scenic marvels, she was not so jaded as to miss the unique beauty of Spokane Falls. For that matter, who among us even today would not be spellbound if, for example, a trail in Yellowstone led us to a setting like Spokane Falls? In her travelogue, *Fifteen Thousand Miles by Stage* (published in 1911), Carrie Strahorn wrote enthusiastically about Spokane's "wonderful falls with the magnificent valley, its rich bunchgrass carpet then yellow as gold in its autumn garb." Her husband also appreciated "the majesty of the situation," but he emphasized the practical value of the setting. True to his calling as a railroad promoter, Robert Strahorn declared, "Here will be the greatest inland city of the whole Northwest."

SPOKANE FALLS, WASHINGTON TERRITORY, BEFORE THE GREAT FIRE.

Woodcut of Spokane Falls, *Harper's Weekly*, vol. 33, 1889

Given its beauty, Spokane Falls might arguably have been preserved as a park. But it was missing the one feature needed to ensure the preservation of a beautiful landscape: uselessness. In his book *National Parks: The American Experience*, the historian Alfred Runte argues that parks have tended to be established only on "useless lands." Natural beauties that could be turned to profit were invariably exploited. The huge trees that once encircled Puget Sound were beautiful, but today they are gone, cut into lumber for building San Francisco, Seattle, and other cities. Yellowstone's forests and geysers, by contrast, were remote and without practical value, so Yellowstone could become a park. In the same way, Yosemite Valley offered little for the logger or farmer, so why not make it into a park?

Spokane Falls lacked the defense of uselessness, but when the lumber versus trout debate began in 1882, the town still retained much of its frontier character. A sport-fishing business flourished by the falls. The *Spokane*

*Times* declared: "Its fame has called to our midst some of the most prominent sporting men in Oregon and on Puget Sound." In 1882, a healthy river meant healthy fish, and healthy fish brought recreation to fishermen and profits to the businessmen who catered to their needs. The *Times* asked, "Why should one man [the mill owner] become rich by depriving others of their rightful source of profit and pleasure, and by defying the law?"

Spokanites were not alone at the time in recognizing the cost of industry to the environment. Robert Barnwell Roosevelt, Theodore Roosevelt's uncle, led a group of fishing enthusiasts in the New York Association for the Protection of Game. Among his concerns was the pollution of the Hudson River. As a Democratic congressman from New York, he originated a bill in 1871 to create the United States Commission of Fish and Fisheries, a forerunner to today's US Fish and Wildlife Service, to explore the reason for the decline of fish in coastal and inland waters. The commission published influential annual reports and, in 1884, an important work, *Fisheries and Fisheries Industries of the United States.*

As citizens of the United States and other countries became more aware of river pollution, scientists explored the relationship between fish and sawdust. Governments legislated fish protection. In 1903 a Canadian, Archibald Patterson Knight, wrote a tract titled *Sawdust and Fish Life*, summarizing a half century of that research in Canada and the United States. While noting that the results were inconclusive—the dangers of sawdust to fish depended on various factors—Knight also noted that many American states had by that time passed laws against throwing sawdust into rivers.

For a time in Spokane, the "finny tribe" and their "rightful captors" prospered, but "progress" was not on their side. At Spokane Falls in 1882, you would have seen the same riverscape that the Indians had known long before James Glover came to Spokane. Returning to the same spot just ten years later, you would have seen a new world. Bridges spanned the river and connected islets to the shore. Railroad tracks ran right beside the falls. Flumes diverted the water to flour mills, sawmills, and a hydroelectric plant. Trees had been felled to make way for buildings. Fill dirt eliminated one of the river channels. Piles of lumber lay along the shore, and the floor of one sawmill extended from the south bank of the river to Havermale Island, hiding the southern channel.

In 1890 the law in Spokane was on the side of the fishermen, but when the question of sawdust and fish was raised again later that year, the press solidly backed the mill owners. When the local Rod and Gun Club was campaigning in 1890 against the growing impact of sawdust on the local trout population, the *Spokane Falls Review* claimed that the club was fighting for something "impracticable—that is, to maintain the old-time reputation of the Spokane River as a trout stream." At the time, however, the law did favor the sportsmen. "The largest industry in the city," the Spokane Mill Company, employing four hundred people, had been effectively shut down because the only way to dispose of sawdust was in the river, and such dumping "would mean the subjugation of their employees to repeated arrests."

The *Review* and many of its readers, however, now sided with the mills. One correspondent dismissed the Rod and Gun Club as a "boil, wart, excrescence, ingrowing great toe nail, or cinder in the eye." He claimed that the tail end of a mill race is the best possible place to catch a trout. Even the Rod and Gun Club objected only to sawdust, not to other kinds of pollution. In a letter to the *Review*, the club president, Henry A. Herrick, declared, "It is proper and right to make use of the streams of the state as natural sewers of the cities of the country, and this use of streams does not seriously interfere with the fishing interests, as much of the matter deposited in the river from the sewage is available to the fish as food."

The Rod and Gun Club's stance would hardly qualify as enlightened environmentalism in the modern world. You want to treat the river as a sewer? No problem! The "lumber versus trout" debate foreshadows later environmental conflicts, such as the debate over the protection of the spotted owl that would divide Northwesterners a century later. But in 1890 the *Spokane Falls Review* probably spoke for most of its readers when it asserted the inevitability of industrial progress:

> The Spokane is not a large river, and the erection upon its banks
> of a large city, and the consequent utilization of the stream as a

natural sewer, is just as certain to drive away the trout as the sun is to rise in the morning. The trout is a fish, and he avoids the great cities as man avoids the region of pestilence. . . . He cannot pass in comfort from the Columbia to Spokane Falls, because already the river has been polluted below this city to a degree that renders it unfit for drinking. This contamination will necessarily increase with the growth of the city and the development of manufacturing enterprises.

Just as James Glover had concluded that the Almighty intended the magnificent basalt columns along the river to be ground down for use as basements, other Spokanites could view the river itself as a *natural* sewer. In such ways, utility trumped beauty in early Spokane.

Some eighty years later, another generation of Spokanites celebrated nature in the first-ever environmental world's fair, Expo '74. With the rediscovery then of the original beauty of the falls, the city turned back the clock while opening a new chapter in Spokane River history. During the ceremony marking the opening of the fair, almost two thousand trout were released to swim in the sawdust-free river.

# The River Gives Us Our Way of Life

MARGO HILL

FEW PEOPLE UNDERSTAND THAT THE SPOKANE RIVER AND TRIBUTARIES were once among the most abundant salmon fisheries in the Northwest. The river's summer chinook salmon (kings) commonly weighed fifty to eighty pounds. My grandmother said, "The salmon hung from the horn of the saddle and stretched toward the ground." Tribes from across the West knew of the summer fishing camps at Spokane Falls. Some estimates put the number of salmon running in the watershed at a million annually, three hundred thousand of them harvested by the Spokane tribal people and the neighboring tribes.

Our people, the Interior Salish, engaged in subsistence patterns and maintained close relations with the ancestral homeland and culture, following seasonal food sources throughout the region and along the river. When the tribal people were restricted to the reservation and lost the use and control of these traditional places, it became difficult to maintain this connection. It is a continuing tribal hope that we will one day regain access to those places. Traditionally, we lived along the riverbanks, traveled in canoes, and used sophisticated fishing techniques to provide about half our food. We fished from canoes and even speared fish from horseback. We built weirs, nets, and baskets to snare the salmon, trout, and other fish. Then we dried them in the sun or by a fire to preserve them for the winter. We still observe ceremonies in honor of the first foods: berries, roots, salmon, deer, and elk. We thank the Creator for these gifts.

The Salish-speaking Spokan (Spo qe n i) have traditionally been divided into the Lower Spokane (Scqecioni), the Middle Spokane (Sntu t ulixi, Snx w meney, "salmon-trout people"), and Upper Spokane peoples. According to historians, these three bands exercised exclusive control over fishing and camps along the Spokane River, although they shared some prairie lands south of the river for harvesting roots and some hills north of the river for gathering berries and hunting game. Tribal people lived and thrived at the falls of the Spokane River and harvested fish communally. The tribal groups followed a division of labor and an organized protocol. "The women of various tribes basically controlled negotiations among themselves for food—whether hunted/fished by men but later processed by women (such as dried deer meat or fish, including dried eel), and all materials women made, such as tule mats, bags, and tanned deer hides. Men traded horses and weapons." So wrote the anthropologist John Ross of Eastern Washington University in 2011. Spokane and Coeur d'Alene people also traded as far east as Montana, exchanging fish for buffalo-hide robes.

A mutual dependence on trading helped to maintain peaceful relations between Spokane and Plains people. Some historians say there was such an abundance of fish that the Spokane people allowed neighboring tribes to fish the Spokane territory. The area known as Little Falls was a major trading site for the Coeur d'Alene, Colville, Nez Perce, Sanpoil, Nespelem, and Palouse tribes, who congregated primarily to exchange goods and fish. Spokane people traded with Blackfeet for horses and hides, meeting partway to ease the journeys. Western Plains groups wanted trade items such as wood bows and arrows, buckskin clothing, dried salmon, and eels from the Spokane.

The Spokane Indian people never took these gifts from the Creator for granted. I remember my great-grandmother praying and giving thanks. At all our gatherings, we give thanks. Whether it is a simple meal or a ceremony or winter dance, we always begin by acknowledging the gifts from the Creator and praying over them. Ross wrote, "A non-Indian observer may not understand how these people were able to flourish in an environment seasonally limited in key resources. One could not help but be impressed, even humbled, when older women, prior to digging roots, would acknowledge their physical needs, and, before any harvest, invariably first pray to various spiritual powers for the rich harvest." When my kids and I traveled to dig roots off the reservation at Coffee Pot Lake, we always stopped to pray. Sometimes when we said our prayers we would knot a handkerchief and leave it with our prayers. Ross observed of our tribal traditions that "they saw the 'providence' of nature as a complex combination of sacred beliefs and rituals acknowledging a special relationship with various powers and with an environment upon which they were totally dependent." Today, providence still means the protective care of God, or nature as a spiritual power. It means spiritual care.

Tribal people had place-names for locations along the Spokane River occupied by a particular group during the fall fishing season or the winter. We named specific locations in relation to Coyote stories that explained natural events, which have been corroborated by geological evidence. One famous story from the Colville Confederated Tribes is "How Coyote Diverted the Columbia River." The Columbia River once flowed through the Grand Coulee riverbed. Tribal legends say Coyote was responsible for turning the water toward the river's present channel. These stories correlate with topographical features such as rock peaks. Our people also had special spots for deer hunting and campsites they occupied during the fall fishing season.

### Grand Coulee Dam

From time immemorial the salmon traveled up to the tributaries of the Spokane River to spawn. The tributaries were famous not only for their chinook salmon runs but also for two steelhead runs, a small coho run, and a huge population of cutthroat trout. Fish were smoked, dried, and traded. The Spokane River was the economic engine of the northwest. But that era came to an end when construction of the Little Falls Dam blocked the upper three-quarters of the Spokane River in 1910–11. Then the Grand Coulee Dam blocked the Columbia and the rest of the Spokane River in 1939. Both dams were constructed without fish ladders. The Columbia and Spokane

Rivers became the energy powerhouses of the Northwest, sacrificing the fish to provide other services and products.

When I was traveling to the Colville Tribe's powwow in Nespelem, I stopped with my kids for the laser light show at the Grand Coulee Dam. I started to speak up to say that the statements they made were wrong! I was saying things out loud, and my kids were getting embarrassed that the suyapees (white people) could hear me. The laser light show brags of the engineering feats of constructing the dam, a so-called manmade wonder of the world. In the soundtrack, the river speaks to the dam: "You did what I could not do. You provided the missing link. Irrigation. You made the desert bloom."

But what was so wrong about a river that flowed free and swam with millions of salmon? I told my children that maybe the desert was not supposed to bloom. When engineering changes the ecosystem, it is not always good for natural systems. It is not good for the river, for the fish, or for Indian people.

The laser light show has now changed, no longer pretending to let the river speak. It begins with a voice-over: "The Bureau of Reclamation and the Bonneville Power Administration proudly present 'One River, Many Voices.'" It tells the story of Grand Coulee—its geological beginnings and the story of Coyote. Then it tells the story of immigrants—farmers, orchardists, and ranchers—and how, in response to dry conditions in the West, Congress and President Theodore Roosevelt created the Bureau of Reclamation in 1902. The purpose of the BOR is to provide water to the arid West. Congress approved the Grand Coulee Dam in 1935, and it was completed in 1942, creating the reservoir called Franklin D. Roosevelt Lake. Dryland farmers discovered their need for irrigation after the dam was built. It is the largest electric power–producing facility in the United States. Power generated for farms and towns was meant to expand the economy and feed a nation.

But the creation of bounty for some took away the bounty of others. Salmon, steelhead, and lamprey can no longer swim to Kettle Falls in the upper Columbia or to Little Falls in the Spokane River, traditional gathering spots where the tribes harvested fish. Mel Tonasket, a Colville Tribal Council member, said, "Salmon were our trading commodity and our major food supply. When they stopped the salmon from coming up past Coulee Dam to our fishing sites, it disrupted our whole system." Homes, livelihoods, and fifty-six thousand acres of land were inundated by the construction of the Grand Coulee Dam. Colville and Spokane people had to move their houses or tear them down before the flooding of the lands. The Colville and Spokane tribes—mourning the loss of that source of vitality, natural balance, and cultural significance—have gathered for the Ceremony of Tears since 1940.

## Our Way of Life

The Spokane Indians of the Interior Salish people inhabited northeastern Washington from the city of Spokane to the Canadian border. The traditional lifestyle of the Spokane people related closely to the seasonal rounds and the Spokane River. We called the river Nx Wl Wl tsuten, or "river gives us our way of life." The name Spokane is believed to mean "children of the sun," but there are different pronunciations and interpretations of the name.

My great-grandmother Sadie Boyd was born at the confluence of the Spokane and Columbia Rivers and was raised in a teepee near Davenport; she was one of the longest-living Spokane Indian women when she died in 1986. She had to move from the Spokane Indian Reservation to the city of Spokane so that she could feed her children. A land that had once been so plentiful for Native Americans was now a place of suffering, a city named after a people now forgotten. In Salish we say *tupiye* for great-grandmother. My tupiye sewed and did beadwork to support her children. She told of going to the Catholic school that we now call Gonzaga to ask for leftover food at the kitchen doorstep. They gave her scraps of vegetables, meat, and fruit. Every other day she drove with her horse team and buggy and made the rounds of meat markets that gave her scraps. This is how she kept her young children from starving. She spoke of our history, of Chief Spokan Garry and how the Spokane people did not want for anything before the suyapees came. (In English, the word means "upside-down face," which is what we called the trappers who had less hair on their heads than on their chins.) The Spokane River had provided food and a way of life for my great-grandmother and her family, but they could no longer rely on it.

## Spokan Garry

The great leader of the Spokane Tribe was Chief Spokan Garry, the son of Chief Illeum Spokanee, considered one of the best and brightest tribal leaders in the Northwest. Garry was born in 1811 and was selected by white civil leaders, along with Kootenai Pelly, to be educated in European ways at the Red River Mission in Winnipeg, Manitoba. Garry became fluent in English, French, and many Salish dialects. My great-grandmother married Thomas Garry, the adopted son of Spokan Garry, and she spoke of how important his influence was. Garry created the first school in the Northwest, a large lodgepole and tule-mat structure near present-day Drumheller Springs. He taught his people to speak English and read the Bible. He enjoyed much respect. He was married and lived with some suyapee comforts, such as coffee and sugar. He always rode a white horse. Isaac Stevens, the first governor of the newly created Washington Territory, acknowledged Garry as a leader and went to his house to meet with him. That acknowledgment and meeting now both seem ironic. Stevens was appointed to negotiate the treaties in this region, but he failed to make a treaty with the Spokane Tribe.

Times were changing fast, and Indians were being accused of stealing from whites and killed on the spot. Yet the accusations of white men raping Indian women or stealing from Indians were never investigated, let alone prosecuted. War broke out in 1855, and although the combined forces of the Spokane, Yakama, Colville, and Coeur d'Alene peoples initially defeated the United States, more troops were sent. Col. George Wright's troops had superior weapons, long-range rifles, and new types of bullets that had devastating effects. Garry's own farm was simply taken over by a settler, Howard B. Doak, who claimed it while Garry was fishing at Kettle Falls. Garry was then in his late seventies. The white man burned Garry's log house to the ground. Although Garry had served the government as a negotiator, translator, and Christian teacher, officials did nothing to help Garry keep his home. Chief Spokan Garry learned that he could not trust the suyapees, and he never again spoke the language of the white man. He lived out his final days in a teepee in what is now named Indian Canyon, on land owned by a friend.

The Spokanes traveled to the different fishing sites along the river to harvest fish. We harvested it, prepared it, and even bundled it into bales like hay to trade. It was devastating when the dams stopped the fish runs. Tribal leaders and grandmothers asked, "What about the salmon? How will we feed our children?" They were promised electricity and government rations. When the first wagonload of government rations finally arrived on the reservation, it was late winter. The Native people were starving. When they cut open the salt pork, it was filled with maggots. But their children were hungry. They had no choice. They scraped out the maggots, boiled the salt pork, and fed it to their kids.

Once, the Spokane Indian people had so much food that they could share it with neighboring tribes: they invited other tribes to come and fish along the banks of the Spokane River. The river was so plentiful, running with the salmon that made the people strong. The river bank was lined with racks of drying fish. Later the people were reduced to begging for scraps. Grand-mothers like Sadie Boyd continued to do what they knew. After hitching her team of horses to the wagon, Sadie would load up her children and travel to fish markets. She dried the fish she got. The meat scraps she smoked, and the bones she dried to make soup.

I've listened to the stories of those who have traveled before me. My great-grandmother and other ancestors set an example of how to work hard, survive, and never give up. They lived off the river and land and provided for their families. Today we have lost our traditional opportunities for lead-ership as well as our way of life. Now my son will never be chosen to sing the Indian song that calls the salmon run unless salmon can be restored somehow to the Spokane River. For many generations our people have lost their way. We are not only traveling the paths of the reservation: we are also finding roads to the city—just as my great-grandmother moved back to Spokane, which was the land of our ancestors, seeking ways to support her children and grandchildren.

## Stories from My People

The river that gives us life has been so degraded and changed from its natural course that it can hardly be considered that same "giver of life" we revered. When the US Cavalry battled the combined forces of the Spokane, Coeur d'Alene, and Colville peoples, Indian leaders were hanged, and their teepees and food caches were burned to the ground. Some seven hundred horses were slaughtered and left beside and in the river. The river ran red with their blood. Indian hostages were marched to Walla Walla, and the Indians were forced onto reservations. Today, tribes still live with the devastating consequences of the actions of the white man. Today we do not battle the US Cavalry: instead we battle the white man's corporations. The United States military is not killing us; we are dying from contamination left by mining companies unfettered by federal laws. They are contaminating our rivers, our groundwater, and our land.

Up in Canada there is a company named Teck Cominco Metals, Ltd., that operated a lead and zinc smelter in Trail, British Columbia, from 1896 to 1996. The slag went right into the Columbia River. The Colville Tribe asked for the river to be listed as a Superfund site to make it eligible for federal funds for environmental cleanup. The Department of the Interior and the US Environmental Protection Agency long neglected to fulfill their trust obligations to the Colville Tribes or to the Spokane Tribe. Today, lawsuits by the Colville Tribes and the State of Washington against Teck continue, and yet the Columbia River along the Colville reservation connected to the Spokane River is still not listed as a Superfund site. The legal issue here, I know as a lawyer, is whether the Comprehensive Environmental Response, Compensation, and Liability Act (CERCLA) applies outside the United

States. Enacted in 1980, CERCLA is a US federal law that established the Superfund to clean up sites contaminated with hazardous substances and pollutants. For decades we have been awaiting an answer to that legal question.

The Spokane River is also polluted by sewage from the city of Spokane and several other treatment plants, and by thousands of tons of zinc, cadmium, and arsenic that Coeur d'Alene mining operations used to dump into the upstream rivers. Our people remember the Spokane as a free-flowing river. Now engineers control it. Grand Coulee Dam, Long Lake Dam, and Little Falls Dam block our river.

The Columbia and the Spokane River are part of one whole. The Columbia benefits farmers—irrigators primarily—and the Army Corps of Engineers. Both rivers benefit corporations: those that sell electricity and those that rely on subsidized electricity to make their profits. Today the Spokane River drains into Franklin D. Roosevelt Lake, behind the Grand Coulee Dam, and the reservoir stores industrial contaminants along with water. The Nx Wl Wl tsuten, "giver of life," is now called the Columbia Basin Project by white engineers.

Tribal people still attempt to follow the routes of their ancestors. Even today, elders like Jim Sijohn tell us, "We fish the places where our grandparents took us." In the olden days, along the Spokane River, near Blue Creek, there was what Indians referred to as the CCC camp. The Civilian Conservation Corps was a public work-relief program that operated from 1933 to 1942. It was a major part of President Franklin D. Roosevelt's New Deal, providing jobs related to conservation projects and development of natural resources on rural lands owned by federal, state, and local governments. The tribal men earned about thirty dollars a month, of which twenty-five dollars was sent home to their families. The camp was located near a traditional spiritual spot where Spokane tribal people would go to sweat and pray. They would "finish off" (immerse in the water) in Blue Creek. People came from all over to go to medicine dances at this sacred location. Now a uranium mine contaminates this spot, and our tribal members can no longer bathe there.

The hydrogeologist Fred Kirschner has tried to explain to our tribal elders that there are lots of moving parts when it comes to the river ecosystem. One of those moving parts is the contamination from industry, mining, and urban pollution that taints the river water and everything that lives in it and near it, becoming concentrated in the bodies of living things. This affects all species of fish, including rainbow trout and kokanee salmon (an Okanagan term for landlocked lake populations of sockeye salmon).

The pollutants find their way into the bodies of the people who eat these fish. Tribal peoples traditionally ate up to two pounds of fish a day. The fact that we made stews and soups out of eels, which have even higher tissue and gut concentrations of contaminants, made them more harmful for us. My great-grandmother Sadie Boyd used to eat fish-head soup. I would walk into her house and check to see what was cooking on the stove. Quite often I saw salmon eyes staring back at me.

After World War II and the Korean War, there was large-scale industrial production in the region. Upriver from Spokane we had Kaiser Aluminum; farther up were the mining companies in the Silver Valley of Idaho. Before 1981 it was legal to discharge contaminants into the Spokane River, and many companies took advantage of the opportunity. Elders recalled that the Spokane River ran milky back then. The Spokane tribal elder Vi Seymour recalled how the wolverine disappeared after the waters began to be polluted and the Grand Coulee Dam was built. Vi recalled, "The fish we caught were edible and good in the 1940s. We smoked the fish, and now I tell my kids not to fish and swim in the river." She remembered a time "when our men were away at war and we would go out to pick berries. The river was clear, and we swam in the river. Now the water quality is so bad—it has changed from long ago. You can see places on the river where there is black sand. The Indian people didn't know what it was—black sand—but they didn't like it. So the tribal people would go inland to the lakes." As it turned out, that black sand was polluted residue from the Teck smelter.

Vi Seymour also told me, "We used to camp and fish at Blue Creek in the 1930s and 1940s. We would fish for steelhead. Margo's grandma said salmon came up all the way to Idaho before Grand Coulee. We would camp and gather our berries and roots along the river—it was our sanctuary. We would rest at these places on our way to the big salmon runs at Kettle Falls! We had a salmon chief, and everyone was given salmon in the same amount. We used to gather shellfish and mussels, too." Today we can still see crayfish in the rivers, but no more mussels.

Buzz Gutierrez talked about his mother, Sally Moses. She said, "We're not going to eat this fish." The Moses family had taken fish from the Spokane and Columbia Rivers for as long as anyone could remember. "We would smoke it, can it, and dry the fish that had migrated up from Coulee," she said. "Fishing was our livelihood—our life blood." Buzz also heard Swanatee or Bigfoot stories from his selah, or grandpa, when they went hunting. Buzz remembered being told. "They said Swanatee would come down and steal the fish from the Indians in the 1880s when they were harvesting and fishing. Every weekend our families would go fishing. Sometimes we'd pass the Germania Mine—in the 1930s we'd grab blankets and towels and go down to the rocks along the Spokane River. We'd travel to the Columbia River and fish for rainbow and whitefish. We'd camp at Blue Creek or McCoy Lake and then travel over what is now Peters Road. We'd can the fish and deer meat. Our grandmothers and mothers had root cellars" instead of freezers. Buzz also told about being with Bill Matt Sr. and the Moses sisters at Starvation Flats, digging roots with their petsa, or root digger. One day the boys accidentally rolled into red ants.

We talk about the Columbia River and the Spokane River as one river, because the fish swim from river to river. Our Spokane Indian people would fish at Blue Creek. Then, beginning in the 1950s, our tribal elders Ignace and Salena Pascal told us, "You can't eat them." The fish had worms. The river could no longer provide us with healthy food. Now we tell our kids we can fish, but we cannot eat too much. Buzz is more cautious. "I tell my grandkids they can't eat any fish. Last May I was down on the river fishing with my grandkids. We are so conscious of the pollution that we release most of the fish we catch and take only a few home to eat." Buzz said of the river as a kid, "It was our store." The Indians didn't have grocery stores. "We fished for rainbow trout and eastern brook trout."

Today contamination in the Columbia and Spokane River continues, but it is not as bad. Teck Cominco put in a new smelter that pollutes less than the old one. In 1992 it shut down a fertilizer plant that was processing batteries, computer waste, and electronics, whose waste went right into the Columbia. Scientists say that the water today is much cleaner. It is hard for my tribal elders to accept this, but they listen.

Under the Clean Water Act, tribes can set their own water-quality standards for the river. Even though the Spokane Tribe now has standards for the Spokane River, it is still contaminated, and mercury and other toxins are still present in fish tissue. The scientists explain that the contaminants are absorbed from the water by the plankton—the microscopic organisms drifting or floating in the water—and then by the fish that we are used to eating.

When I was working in the Spokane tribal attorney's office, I found a quote by Alex Sherwood, the Spokane tribal chairman, in a 1973 legal file. Alex said, "I find myself talking to the river. I might ask, 'River, do you remember how it used to be? The game, the fish, the pure water, the roar of the falls? You fed and took care of our people then. For thousands of years, we walked your banks and used your waters. You would always answer when our chiefs called to you with their prayer to the River Spirit.' Sometimes I stand and shout, 'River! Do you remember us?'"

# How Spokane, Once a Pollution Denier, Became a Model for the Nation

WILLIAM STIMSON

SPOKANE'S 1974 ENVIRONMENTAL EXPOSITION WAS MOSTLY WORDS and dreams. It did not explain exactly how "Tomorrow's Fresh New Environment"—Expo '74's theme—was supposed to materialize. Six miles downriver from the Expo site that summer, however, there was a convincing exhibition of how the environment gets cleaned. Engineers and laborers were working furiously to meet a federal deadline to turn the thirty-acre site of Spokane's antiquated sewage treatment plant into a $45 million labyrinth of gigantic tanks, tunnels, and chemical labs capable of processing 77 million gallons of sewage every day. One of the first expressions of the stringent new standards created by the federal Clean Water Act of 1972, the plant would become a model for the rest of the nation.

The most interesting thing about this exhibition of enlightened environmentalism is that it was taking place in a city that had once been what today would be called a river-pollution denier. For half a century, Spokane had adamantly refused to clean up its river.

The Spokane example proves that merely providing information—the Expo approach—is not a solution. An early mayor of Spokane, Charles M. Fassett, who served from 1917 to 1919, gave that a thorough try. A progressive in the Teddy Roosevelt mold, Fassett campaigned relentlessly for cleaning up the environment. "If filthy conditions exist in any part of your city, it is a direct menace to your life, and the lives of the members of your family, regardless of how careful you are of your own premises." As an example, he pointed to the heaps of trash accumulating in Spokane backyards, along country roads, and floating down the river. The reason that many people were putting garbage anyplace but the city dump, Fassett argued, was that it cost money to put it in the dump, and it was free to dispose of almost anywhere else. That problem persists to this day in parks near the dump. Fassett suggested dropping the steep fees at the dump to encourage people to take their garbage there. Of course, that would mean general taxes would go up. "Let them go!" Fassett said. "So long as we get our dollar's worth."

It was no accident that about this time in the city's history, taxpayer associations became an important part of Spokane politics. These self-appointed committees, usually comprised of businesspeople, hired keen-eyed executive directors whose only job was to monitor local government spending. From around 1914 on, any proposed expenditure by Spokane local government was scrutinized and criticized by organizations whose main purpose was to keep taxes low.

The city's major newspaper, the *Spokesman-Review*, became a leader in this movement. It had led crusades against many public menaces, from public drunkenness to corruption in City Hall, and now it added government spending to its list. An editorial published on March 29, 1914, declared: "The prodigality of legislative bodies, from Congress down, presents a situation that calls for serious investigation." For the next fifty years, regular editorials with titles like "The Taxpayers Must Have Relief," "No High Tax Official Is True to the People," and "Curbing Waste at Washington and Olympia" informed Spokanites that they were overtaxed. It came as no surprise that the newspaper dismissed Fassett's plan for free garbage disposal as asking too much of the taxpayer. Nor was anyone surprised when a frustrated Mayor Fassett resigned from the City Commission and took a job teaching at a university.

By the early 1920s, nevertheless, a lot of people were beginning to see that something had to be done about the Spokane River. It was a disgusting mess and an embarrassment to a city that bore its name. Among those who took note was the director of the Washington State Department of Health. In 1931, he issued an order to Spokane to stop using the river as its sewer.

As it happened, the time was right to build a sewage treatment plant. As part of the New Deal, the federal government offered to underwrite the whole labor cost of digging the needed sewer "interceptors" as a means of employing some four thousand out-of-work laborers. The city's contribution to the project would be to build and maintain a treatment plant, estimated to cost $20,000 per year. The public utilities commissioner, Alonzo Colburn, said that would cost local taxpayers about $1.75 per household per year. "This whole sewer and sewage disposal proposition looks so simple that I cannot understand why anybody would oppose it," Colburn said.

But taxpayer associations did oppose it. The *Spokesman-Review* quoted Lester M. Livengood, the manager and counsel of the Taxpayers' Economy League of Spokane County, as calling on citizens to vote against the measure. "It is true," Livengood told the newspaper, "that a pathetic story is told of a dead fish seen in the river. . . . But it is also true that the sewage of the city of Chicago is discharged into the Mississippi river, which flows by the city of St. Louis, whose citizens use the water for drinking purposes after it has been treated."

The sewage treatment plant went on a special election ballot in November 1933, and the *Spokesman-Review* chose Livengood, its longtime ally in the fight against taxes, to explain the choice for its readers. In a series of newspaper articles, Livengood assumed a posture of neutrality, casting his articles in question-and-answer form:

Question: Assuming the bacterial and nuisance pollution of the river to be as stated in the 1933 Greely report on sewage disposal, has the degree of this pollution tended to increase seriously year by year in recent years?

Answer: No. The city engineer has for years made a monthly bacterial count of the river water below the sewer outlets and this year has made the counts twice a month. This count, while it shows a seasonal variation, does not show any serious progressive bacteria increase year by year.

The scientific-sounding language obscured the simple conclusion of studies by the city engineer, two outside consultants, and the State Department of Health that the Spokane River was grossly polluted and had been for a long time.

Although a majority of the voters were in favor of the bond issue of 1933, it failed because the special election attracted so few voters. Under pressure from the state Department of Health, the city put the treatment plant on ballots again in 1936, 1938, and 1940. In all these elections, the citizens' leading source of information, the *Spokesman-Review*, attacked the measure as a government plot, with headlines like "Unending Sewer Expense Roils" (December 4, 1935); "$2 Tax on Spokane Homeowners Stirs Revolt" (March 8, 1936); "Sewage Plan Cry Is Louder" (September 27, 1938); and "Sewer Water Trick Exposed" (March 4, 1940).

World War II pushed the matter of water pollution aside for five years, but as soon as the war was over, Jack Taylor, director of the state's Pollution Control Commission, led a delegation to Spokane to confront the city commissioners. In a conference in November 1945, Taylor told them the city had a legal and moral obligation to eliminate the health hazard of a river full of sewage. The state, he added, had just passed a bond issue for river projects and was willing to pay much of the bill. But under state laws the city had to launch a sewage-treatment program immediately.

This meeting was attended by three of the five Spokane city commissioners and a dozen Spokanites representing the Chamber of Commerce and the local medical society, among others. The city's Chicago-based sewer-system consultant claimed that, although it would of course be preferable to do a more thorough job of sewage treatment, simple "primary treatment" would clean up the river adequately to end biological threats. The Health Commission's advising biologist, Nathan Fasten of the University of Washington, was quick to point out that what is considered a clean river in the East is one that meets minimal health standards, but in the West, "clean" means suitable for activities like swimming and fishing.

But the commissioners insisted on the cheapest possible approach. The response of one city commissioner made it clear why: "It is better to be satisfied with half to three-quarters of a loaf than none at all." In other words, the citizens of Spokane might reject the measure if the city asked for a $5 million plant and sophisticated treatment rather than a $4 million plant and minimal treatment. In the end, state officials agreed to the cheaper route as a means of getting Spokane started on the cleanup of the river. But state officials warned that more steps would have to be taken in the future.

The city commissioners seem to have underestimated the desire of Spokane citizens to reclaim the river. Once the state and the city struck their deal, the Spokane Chamber of Commerce, the Washington Water Power Company (now Avista Utilities), and the Spokane County Medical Society led a campaign to pass the 1946 bond issue and get the river cleaned up. Representatives of 190 local businesses signed a petition supporting the measure. This time, even the *Spokesman-Review* signed on and urged people to vote. The measure drew a huge off-year turnout of thirty-five thousand, of whom thirty-four thousand voted to approve the bonds. It was one of the most popular bond issues in Spokane history.

Even so, the measure never produced a sewage-treatment plant. Because the postwar boom in building had raised the prices of concrete, steel, and labor, the lowball estimates offered by the commissioners were useless. To most outsiders the solution seemed obvious. If businesses and homebuilders had to pay more for construction, the city would too. An engineer in the Spokane office of the state Department of Health summed up the situation in a memo to his bosses in Olympia: "Due to general advance in costs, the city is now short a few hundred thousand necessary to complete the project. However, the people of Spokane have expressed their desire for the project by a wide margin and remaining finances can easily be raised by revenue bonds."

The commissioners, however, refused to ask voters for more money. They rejected the bids and went back to the City Hall routine. The Health Department tried putting pressure on the city. A June 29, 1950, article in the *Spokane Chronicle* reported: "City commissioners once more today were urged to clean up the Spokane river by early completion of the city's $3.5 million-plus sewage disposal project. ... The council patiently listened to City Clerk Alex Brown read the letter and then ordered it placed on file with the rest of the state pollution control letters."

One strategy the commissioners did try was to trim back the already minimal sewage-treatment plant plan they had ordered from their Chicago engineering consultant. When the director of the Department of Health heard of this, he wrote to the Chicago consultant: "We understand that upon receiving your estimated cost of the proposed plant the city Commission apparently felt that the cost was excessive and instructed you to search for means of reducing the cost a very considerable amount. The fact that construction costs have risen does not reduce the responsibility of the city of Spokane to provide adequate sewage treatment."

Five more years passed. By the mid-1950s even the *Spokesman-Review* was calling for action. In an editorial titled "How Much More Delay in Cleanup of the River?," the newspaper complained, "It has taken the city all the years since 1946 to get the main trunk lines of the new sewage system laid and the disposal plant itself is still in the blueprint stage."

While the commissioners dodged these pressures from above, they were feeling more coming from below. In 1958, the heads of all the engineering departments at City Hall signed a recommendation that urged the commissioners to add a tax to the water bill to finance the completion of the sewage-treatment plant. "The public Sewer System is faced with a tremendous construction investment. We must catch up on the backlog of needed improvements, overcome the inroads of deterioration and obsolescence, and expand facilities to meet future demands." This "tremendous construction investment," which the commissioners must face "courageously," would add about ninety cents a month to an average homeowner's utility bill. The commissioners never took the step.

Charles Fassett, the former Spokane mayor who had tried to move the city to remedy its environmental problems decades earlier, explained in a journal article what was going on. Fassett wrote that in a government where all possibilities for innovation are cut off by a fear of taxes, government workers soon conclude it is safe only to "say nothing, do nothing, be nothing."

The agony of the commissioners ended in 1960 when a group of business leaders organized an initiative to change Spokane's form of government to a city-manager system. Six of the seven new council members were business-people—none of them particularly interested in governing per se, but all of them keen to see action on a list of Spokane's urban problems. Most of all, they wanted a revived city business district. They also knew that Spokane needed a new city hall, a new public safety building, and a working sewage-treatment plant. They hired an experienced city manager and told him to see that these things got done.

This change set a new course for Spokane city government. The city hardly became spendthrift, but from then the performance of local government was measured by action, not low taxes. The difference is epitomized by the career of a city employee who became one of the major figures in Spokane's Expo-era renaissance.

Glen A. Yake, a lifelong Spokanite, learned his engineering-management skills as a twenty-four-year-old commander of an army company of combat engineers in wartime France and Germany. After the war he went to Washington State College on the GI Bill to earn his engineering degree. He briefly tried the more remunerative path of private-sector engineering but found he preferred tackling the giant problems of engineering a whole city. Yake started work with the city in 1954 and was one of the frustrated engineering managers who signed the plea to the commissioners to "courageously" enact a tax to finish the sewage-treatment plant.

Under the new form of city government, he was appointed city engineer, and as such he found himself in charge of almost everything the city did, other than police, fire, and park services. In the 1960s and 1970s, Yake was responsible for the city's role in renovating the downtown area, for obtaining railroad land for the future Riverfront Park, and for developing the Expo grounds into a city park. He also supervised the construction of the new $45 million sewage-treatment plant.

One of Yake's young engineers, George Miller, worked on the planning of the plant. Asked how it could have been finished so quickly after decades of delay, Miller replied: "Because Glen was in charge of it. He was the smartest man I ever knew."

Yake was also a good delegator. Miller remembered that Yake once called him in and said, "George, the city needs a police academy, and I want you to build it." Miller agreed and asked his boss how much money he would have and what budget it would come from. Yake smiled back at him and said, "That's the kind of thing I hired you to figure out."

Yake had little patience for bureaucracy. In the middle of the furious action in the city preparing for Expo '74, he sometimes advised the City Council members that they really ought to approve the measure before them because the action already had been taken. He could operate like that because he had the full backing of the city manager and the entire Spokane City Council. In a few years in the mid-1970s, downtown Spokane was renovated, the railroad yards became a park, and the state-of-the-art sewage-treatment plant that Yake supervised was finished on time and named one of the top ten engineering projects of 1977 by the American Society of Civil Engineers.

How did Spokane finally become worthy of its claim to be an environmental leader, three years after Expo '74? Determined bureaucrats in the state's Department of Health pressured the city relentlessly: the story is told in four large boxes of memos, plans, and directives now stored in the state archives. In the 1960s federal officials and legislators—including Washington State's own senator, Henry M. Jackson—labored for thousands of hours to write an unprecedented plan to clean the waters of a whole nation. Finally, the city of Spokane reconstituted its government from an organization afraid of action to one capable of implementing rigorous new federal standards.

With all due respect to President Ronald Reagan, government was not the problem in Spokane. Sewage was the problem: government proved to be the solution.

# People's Park, Summer 1974

BEATRICE LACKAFF

AN AUGUST AFTERNOON FINDS A DOZEN OR MORE PEOPLE ENJOYING
the cool pools and streams that braid across the sand flats at the confluence
of Hangman Creek and the Spokane River. Some people are building a stone
dam, a black Lab is barking, kids are digging in the sandy bank, and a boy
with a net is trying to catch tiny fish. People have been enjoying summer
at Hangman Creek for more than eight thousand years, but one of those
summers was unique: the summer of 1974.

The sandy peninsula is a site where Native peoples gathered for millennia
to communally harvest the abundant salmon, share fairly with everyone, and
sustain the fishery for all to come. But that peace and bounty changed fast.
In the nineteenth century, the ancient culture was overwhelmed by a brash
new population of white people who thought they knew everything. Soon
the native peoples could not gather on the peninsula anymore. There was
little point in being there anyway: the migration of salmon had stopped.

In 1974, people from around the world converged in a mainstream American city whose name most global citizens had never heard and couldn't
pronounce: Spokane, Washington. They came to attend Expo '74, the
World's Fair. Of all the global visitors, none was more alien to the local folks
than the counterculture of mostly middle-class young Americans whom
America called hippies. That summer, hippies visited Spokane and lived
in a little transient, communal village on the sandy shores at the mouth of
Hangman Creek.

The city of Spokane perches on the banks of its inspiration, the falls of the
Spokane River. By the 1960s the river was pretty much a cesspool, the falls
obscured by bridges and train tracks. The city's economy was sluggish, and

the downtown core was leaking retail sales to trendy malls in the suburbs. Business leaders were alarmed. The citizenry was not very involved with city affairs, except in voting down funding for improvements.

Many people living in the poorer neighborhoods below the falls surely loved the river. Old newspaper accounts tell of poor people living in shanty-town shacks crafted of driftwood, cardboard, and odd bits of lumber. The shantytown arose on the north bank of the Spokane River, just west of the Monroe Street Bridge. That informal community began in the early 1900s and persisted until the city purged the ramshackle little neighborhood by fire in 1946. On the opposite bank of the river, just below the falls, the Peaceful Valley neighborhood occupied traditional Spokane Indian fishing and gathering grounds. A lively but low-income neighborhood in earlier decades, it is gentrifying today. Residents planted large gardens to feed themselves; they kept goats and chickens, fished the river, and gathered firewood. The West Grove Addition neighborhood extended under the High Bridge train trestle on a peninsula between Hangman Creek and the Spokane River, which became the site of People's Park during the summer of 1974. Those homes went up around 1910 and made a quiet neighborhood until, as the Spokane editor and writer Martin Maloney recalls, "everyone got evicted and all the houses were torn down."

By the late sixties, a little counterculture was developing in Peaceful Valley. Their business district was not far from home. The *Spokane Natural*, an alternative newspaper founded by Russ Nobbs and Martin Maloney, was located by West 4th Avenue and the railroad tracks. The EMF and the I Am (Christian) coffee shops, the Odd Shop thrift store, and a head shop named the Flower Pot clustered around Main Avenue and Division Street. In certain quarters of Peaceful Valley, LSD and marijuana were fairly common. The EMF Coffee House—the name standing for "Electric Mother Fucker," according to the musician and luthier Buzz Vineyard—was festooned with psychedelic posters, hosted live music, and created a relaxed and homey atmosphere.

Local business sponsored public events and celebrations. The *Spokane Natural* held benefit concerts in High Bridge Park. Rainier Beer hosted

"Freshtivals," free concerts that drew thousands of kids. Young people gathered by a monumental old steam engine while diesels still rumbled overhead, pulling trains across the High Bridge train trestle. In August 1969, the same month that Woodstock took place, the *Spokane Natural* described the final free concert in High Bridge Park, which featured the musicians John Currier, Buzz Vineyard, John Werr, Ted Bellusci, Barbara Owens singing Italian operetta, and the bands Tender Green and Cold Power. A thousand people came out for the music and enjoyed "a fantastic jam session" when Tender Green left their equipment out for all to use.

Spokane not only had homegrown hippies but also boasted its own chapter of the Yippies: the Youth International Party, passionately against war and for free speech, a political arm of the counterculture. Antiauthoritarian anarchists, they eschewed guns and violence, preferring to express their opinions through pranks and street theater. Spokane's Yippies aligned themselves with Jerry Rubin's strain of anarchy and with a jocular Marxism—that of Groucho, Chico, Harpo, and Karl. They published an occasional newsletter, organized protests, and networked with the national Yippies. Two Spokane high school friends, Rik Smith and Douge Davis, led the group of eight or so. Their headquarters was a small room with a file cabinet, across from an old casket factory in Peaceful Valley. Smith and Davis were inspired to start the group when they learned about the 1909 Wobbly free-speech fights in the heart of downtown Spokane. (The Wobblies are the Industrial Workers of the World, a labor union founded in 1905.) Rik and Douge dedicated themselves to continuing Spokane's struggle for truth and justice.

At the same time, a few blocks east on Riverside Avenue, Spokane Unlimited, a group of downtown businesspeople, hired King Cole, an urban planner from California, to do something, anything, to revitalize Spokane's downtown. Cole soon began to rally citizen groups, including labor unions, service groups, churches, youth groups, and garden clubs. He invited them to participate in the Association for a Better Community (ABC). With grassroots vision and energy, the ABC took on city improvement projects, such as the Japanese Tea Garden. Before long, the ABC was working with Spokane Unlimited and local government. Here was a vital confluence—citizens engaging with leadership to improve their city. But now that the wheels were moving, where were they headed, and what route should they take?

The downtown business district was built on the banks of the Spokane River where the river falls down a spectacular cataract. It became clear to both ABC and Spokane Unlimited that because the river is the heart of the city, Spokane would have to reclaim its waterway in order to reclaim its economy and vitality. Money, park plans, feasibility studies, and negotiations with railroad companies were all in the works—but how to bring them together? Someone suggested a crazy idea to Cole, and he liked it. So did other people, including the formidable Bureau of International Expositions in Paris. Spokane would host a World's Fair with the theme "Protecting Our Environment." It would be the first environmental World's Fair.

Spokane was the smallest, most remote, and most obscure town ever to host a World's Fair. There were other impediments to success: Spokane didn't have the money. The people wouldn't support a bond measure to fund preparations for the fair. And by 1970, the Spokane River that flowed around the proposed Expo site was grossly polluted.

In 1971, Expo backers proposed a $5.7 million city bond issue to pay for removing the railroad tracks over the falls and spiff up Havermale Island. Fifty-seven percent of voters were in favor of the measure, short of the 60 percent required for passage. Expo backers and opponents regrouped. As the window of opportunity to qualify as a host site began to close, and after passionate debates and rallies by both sides, a previously unpopular business and occupation tax was passed by a brave City Council, and the money to continue with Expo preparations became available.

In the coffee shops of Peaceful Valley, members of the counterculture grew cynical about the coming exposition. The Expo (dubbed "Exploit '74") was considered a corporate scheme to enhance downtown landowners' property values at taxpayers' expense and an opportunity for greenwashing by evil corporations. The Yippies hatched their own crazy idea. Since the world was coming to Spokane for the Expo anyway, why not put on a *real* environmental fair? They would host a counter-fair! They would show the world how to live close to the land, grow their own food, and create community.

In 1972, Rik Smith attended a national Yippie conference in Iowa, where the Yippies decided that their 1973 major event would be a free concert and "Smoke-In" in Washington, DC. The major event of 1974, they decided, would be a counter-fair in Spokane. The Spokane Yippies began their preparations with enthusiasm. While the Expo project simmered on a back burner, they planned a local smoke-in featuring free music and pot to echo the national event. They got the permit to hold a concert on May 26 at High Bridge Park, arranged for bands to play, plastered posters all over town, bought a lot of cigarette papers to roll joints, and got to work.

In those volatile times, the Spokane Police were determined that on their watch there would be no rude, embarrassing, or potentially violent Yippie protests—especially with the whole world invited to Spokane for Expo '74. They kept a close eye on Rik Smith and Douge Davis. As Smith's FBI file grew, he and the local police enjoyed an outwardly cordial relationship. The police occasionally dropped in to chat with Rik and remind him that he'd better not stir up trouble.

The music at the smoke-in had no sooner started than the police burst on the scene and a melee erupted. Ignoring the pot smokers, police grabbed a man drinking a beer, handcuffed him, and put him in the back of a police car. The crowd rallied to protect the prisoner, surrounding the car while someone opened the car door. The man darted away in handcuffs—looking rather like a chicken, one might imagine—and people in the crowd began throwing rocks, injuring several policemen. Rik Smith and four others were arrested and charged with disturbing the peace. By the next morning, their friends had bailed them out.

The front-page story about the incident in the *Spokesman-Review* on May 27, 1973, revealed no connection to hippies, Yippies, or the evil weed. However, Expo and city leaders, the police, and the FBI were vigilant to avert further disruptions from Spokane's small band of activists, who were in fact working to bring large numbers of their ilk from all over the country to Spokane for the counter-fair. A committee was formed to decide how to handle the incursion of young activists. Meanwhile, Rik and Douge were not above attending City Council meetings and mixing demands for free food and marijuana with ominous warnings that the behavior of the youthful hordes could get out of control unless they had a space of their own where they could gather during the fair.

In March, with the Expo only a couple months away, Rik and Douge, poking along beside the Spokane River in an old Volkswagen, found themselves passing under the now-silent and abandoned High Bridge, entering feral parkland that only a few years before had been the West Grove neighborhood. The area felt wild and secluded. It was also roomy enough for camping, gardening, community kitchens, and meeting spaces. Visitors could swim and play on the beach at the confluence of Hangman Creek with the Spokane. "This is ours!" Douge and Rik agreed, toasting the site with a beer. They continued to attend meetings of the Park Board and the City Council to propose a youth campground on the peninsula. "Every time we'd go in, we'd basically make threats. We were nice, but we still made the threats." After all, "we couldn't control anything if it's just out in the streets."

In March 1974, the Spokane City Council voted 6–1 to approve some $70,000 "to provide water and bathrooms for a 'low budget visitor's camp.'" Arguments for hospitality and forestalling trouble persuaded the council. Bill Fearn, representing the city, "explained that the proposed site was intended for young people—many with limited funds—to throw down a sleeping bag." Councilor Jack Winston, casting the only negative vote, dourly warned, "It seems to me there is going to be plenty of sex down there." The Yippies named the peninsula People's Park, after the park in Berkeley, California, where in 1970 one person died and others were injured by police as they rallied to protect a park that had been informally created on neglected land.

By 1974, the national Yippies had changed their minds and decided they would not be coming to Spokane for the counter-fair after all. Rik Smith told the Spokane historian Bill Youngs, "That just kind of left us hanging out here. We were real disturbed by it." But the planned summer gathering in Spokane was gaining momentum anyway. Stories appeared in underground papers. People from across the country began trickling in to help set things up. Rik and his wife met a lot of friendly strangers at the airport, and new

Walking under High Bridge in the summer of 1974. Photo courtesy of Alan Hitchens.

arrivals often slept on their floor. The city installed toilets and running water and managed traffic at the campground. But it takes more than toilets and running water to create a functioning village out of a growing crowd of young campers.

Chuck Windsong of Missoula, Montana, an early member of the Rainbow Family counterculture group, told me he was living in Eugene when friends showed him a letter in a Spokane newspaper appealing for help. Hippies were everywhere, it said, sleeping in doorways and panhandling. The letter asked for advice on what to do. "Heck, we know what to do! If they can camp, they won't need to be on the street panhandling." Chuck wrote a letter back containing detailed plans and received an invitation to come to Spokane and implement his ideas.

Chuck said that the Rainbow Family began with veterans disillusioned by the Vietnam War, spurred to create their own brand of activism after the

Kent State massacre in 1969. The Family had been "gathering hippies" at festivals and sharing the skills for communal living that they had learned in the military so that voluntarily homeless kids could survive. The Rainbow Family taught about slit-trench latrines, sanitation, community kitchens, and getting everybody to help out to leave a site in good condition. They believed in the power of community, respect for the environment, and the principle that everyone is family and must share.

Chuck and his friend Dominic hitchhiked to Spokane to help out. When they arrived they found People's Park all sectioned off for them. The city had installed a faucet, so they planted the garden right next to it. People swam and played in the creek and river. With Rainbow Family guidance, a communal village of transients developed. One of Chuck's friends manned the community kitchen, and Chuck worked in the garden. "That was a fine garden, and beautiful with flowers," he recalls. "Every day was an exciting adventure. There were people freaking out because they were bipolar and were off their meds, and they went to this Calm Center." There was a clinic. "We had bandages, there were broken legs and arms, all kind of things happened. Children were being made, and children being born."

"We had pretty good relations with the cops. They'd bring people in from the street and we'd take care of them. Pot was not a big deal, just a part of life. Nobody smoked in front of the cops—it was just Rainbow rules being implemented. We got respect from the community for what we were doing. The churches were very helpful, donating food for the community kitchen, and the city treated us well too." Rainbow Rules mostly boiled down to the everyday application of common sense.

The village boasted a marketplace for handmade crafts and a council circle where people gathered to discuss problems. When the issue of nudity offending the "straight people" came up, the group decided it was the gawkers' problem, not theirs. My neighbor Rose lived across the river high on the bluff above the confluence. She said, "All these naked people would swim over. I was never afraid of them; they were very nice. But you never know, so I didn't talk to them very much."

People were smoking lots of pot, and psychedelic mushrooms and LSD were readily available. Harder drugs like heroin or meth, and even excessive alcohol, were generally considered counter to the hippie journey. That journey was varied and meandering, tending to favor spiritual values over material ones. The common understanding was that we are fundamentally all one, an expression of nature and spirit. The path was unmarked except by peace and love, and the challenge lay in figuring out how to follow it.

Many of the good citizens of Spokane knew and cared nothing about the hippie philosophy. Instead, they fixated on the drugs and nudity. Daisy, a young mother of four at the time, remembered, "Good people didn't go to People's Park—there were probably drugs and nudity—it was a gathering for certain strata of people, not of our circle." My friend Byron told me, "Oh, I thought it might be a fun place to go and watch the boobies flop," but he never got around to it.

David Brown worked for Spokane City Parks in nearby Browne's Addition. "People from the park would come up all the time and hang out. I would talk to them. There was quite a variety, most between maybe fifteen and twenty-five years old. But there were people in their thirties or forties, and some with their kids. They were from out of town, a lot from California. A lot of them were high. They were very amiable, extremely friendly, no negative vibe. No way did I think it was unsafe to be with them—they were a mellow group, gentle and kind, just traveling around." But young David never challenged his grizzled park-crew companions when they referred to "those damn hippies."

Another confluence of cultures occurred when local high school kids went down to People's Park to buy pot, which proved to be a memorable experience for some. Steve, a seventeen-year-old high school student at the time, recalls agreeing with his buddies, "It won't be hard to score some drugs. Let's go to People's Park." They encountered all kinds of naked people, some on acid. The boys went to the information booth, where a woman inside turned to them, her breasts visible through her "totally unbuttoned shirt," and sweetly inquired, "Were you guys looking to buy some weed?"

Steve recalls thinking, "This is awesome! She tells us this guy to look for. My friends are too paranoid, so I go and find this guy who lives in a cardboard box! Or, two boxes kind of put together. We go inside—and it's a fucking museum in there! There are Indian rugs on the floor, leather-bound books— it was so cool—like some English drawing room! And it was all, like, inside that box!"

More than five thousand people, mostly from out of town, stayed at People's Park during Expo '74. Upstream, the World's Fair was a great success, with more than 5.1 million visitors. Spokane charmed the world with its well-run expo, local folks' warmth and hospitality, and the beauty of its riverfront and falls. Riverfront Park, the former railroad hub turned Expo site, remains Spokane's pride and joy.

Looking back on the community camping experience along the Spokane River during Expo '74, we realize it was a remarkably successful example of like-minded strangers living cooperatively together—with support from the city and parts of the community and a mutual understanding with city police. Bad things no doubt happened there, but for the most part a gentle and peaceful group of people created a functional little village for a time. Many lived a kind of dream that summer, swimming in the creek and hanging out in People's Park. As Chuck Windsong remembers, "It was awesome, that summer, one of my best."

Decades after Expo '74, an aura of the illicit still lingers amid the tall ponderosa pines, the willows, the lilacs, and the apple trees of People's Park. A visitor risks encountering everything from nude volleyball to gay liaisons. Overeager police in the 1980s busted the nude sunbathers on the remote sandy beach on Hangman Creek. They were arrested for "lewd behavior," but they hotly challenged the claim that there was anything lewd about discreet nude swimming and sunbathing, and the court ultimately vindicated them.

Fishermen and undaunted others still stroll through the untended trees and grasses so close to the urban hubbub, reveling in the relative solitude that the park's unsavory reputation affords. One end of the Sandifur

Memorial Footbridge over the Spokane River was located at the entrance to People's Park in 2004, the other end near the Kendall Yards urban village. Since the bridge was built, more and more families, casual hikers, dog walkers, and disc golfers have been coming to enjoy nature and the quiet of the park, bounded on three sides by the Spokane River and Hangman Creek.

With its dazzling pavilions from countries around the world, Expo '74 created a confluence of cultures. Yet while Spokane and the rest of the world flocked to the Expo, Spokanites generally avoided the counterculture in People's Park. Few recognized that the hippies were trying to figure out how to live sustainably. Many of their practices—eating healthy food, recycling, conserving energy, avoiding pollution and war, and placing a higher value on nature and people than on money—seemed threatening at the time, even communist. In the future, those practices are likely to be viewed as essential to human survival, or at least to a decent quality of life.

In early spring you can see winter's grip release Hangman Creek so that it flows full and brown with Palouse silt into the white-capped green turbulence of the Spokane River. At first the creek and the river water are clearly separate, two unequal ribbons of color flowing side by side, but not far downstream, the two begin to flow together and merge into one.

I never visited Spokane until well after Expo '74. I drew much of the information here from *The Fair and the Falls: Spokane's Expo '74; Transforming an American Environment*, by J. William T. Youngs. I also interviewed all the people I could find who spent time in People's Park during the Expo—people like Bob Gallagher, musician and proprietor of the 4,000 Holes used record store, who reflected on the counterculture and People's Park. "For a long time afterward," he told me, "I was highly disappointed that peace and love didn't do it, didn't change anything. But now I see that good things, like peace and love, just take time."

# The Spokane River Centennial Trail

GUADALUPE FLORES

THE SPOKANE RIVER CENTENNIAL TRAIL IS A TWELVE-FOOT-WIDE, thirty-nine-mile paved path beginning at the Washington–Idaho border, where it connects with the twenty-one-mile Idaho Centennial Trail. Washington's portion parallels the Spokane River through downtown Spokane and ends at Lake Spokane. As a multipurpose recreational trail, it preserves open space, encourages nonmotorized transportation, educates the public, and enhances wildlife habitat.

Only thirty years after James Glover's 1878 founding of the city he named Spokane Falls, local citizens sought to preserve the area's natural beauty, which was being rapidly degraded by railroad lines and hydroelectric dams. In 1907 Aubrey L. White, the first president of the Spokane Parks Board, dreamed of parks located within fifteen minutes of every home. His dream was expressed in the 1908 Olmsted Brothers plan, which proposed to reserve land in many places along the Spokane River for parks and recreation. In his 1988 history of the river, John Fahey wrote, "If the Olmsted design had been carried out, parks and parkways would follow the river along its entire length within the city." Commercial growth squelched the elaborate plan for many years, but during Expo '74 the river once again became the chief attraction of the city, and the exposition site was preserved as Riverfront Park.

Today, the park and the river remain downtown Spokane's outstanding natural features. The Centennial Trail extends the focus on the river and

A prior version of this chapter was written for the Friends of the Centennial Trail, whose board of directors has granted permission to reprint it here.

pays homage to the Olmsted Brothers plan. The trail borders the river from its source at Lake Coeur d'Alene through rural, urban, and natural settings to beyond the historic Spokane House at Nine Mile Falls. The trail represents the community's commitment to preserve the area's rich cultural, historical, and natural beauties, and it enhances the quality of life sought by citizens of the inland Northwest. It is a grassroots story of fulfilling Spokane's dream to preserve the river corridor for public recreation. A lasting legacy of community progress, it is both a monument to the past and an endowment for the future.

As early as 1971, Sam Angove, the Spokane County Parks director, envisioned a bike trail along the Spokane River. But the idea was realized only when a group of Spokane Valley citizens rallied around. In 1984, the Spokane Valley Chamber of Commerce formed a Parks and Recreation Committee to explore recreational possibilities along the river. When committee members realized their common interest in a trail, they created a volunteer group, the Committee of Six, to further the idea.

In 1986 this group proposed a 10.5-mile recreational trail in the valley, naming it the Centennial Trail to coincide with Washington State's centenary in 1989. Expanded and renamed the Centennial Trail Steering Committee, the group proposed a much grander project: a multipurpose recreational trail connecting the confluence of the Spokane and Little Spokane Rivers with the shores of Lake Coeur d'Alene, spanning over sixty miles. A land swap between the Inland Empire Paper Company and Washington State Parks added more than ten scenic miles of riverfront between Millwood in the Spokane Valley and the state line. By placing the land under state parks ownership, the committee could explore federal and state funding options.

Getting locals involved was one of the first steps in planning the trail. In April 1986, a citizens' petition urged the Spokane County commissioners to support the bike trail. The commissioners endorsed the idea, but other parties required much more persuasion. On the Centennial Trail Master Plan, Idaho's governor, Cecil Andrus, was quoted as saying, "In our lifetime Spokane and Coeur d'Alene will be one City, fully developed. If we don't provide for open spaces and recreation on the river now, it won't happen."

Denny Ashlock summed up the vision in a public position statement: "Not since Expo '74 has the Greater Spokane community had a project that would provide such a major improvement to the quality of life. The Centennial Trail will return to the people miles of the river bank that can be used for a multitude of recreational activities." The Centennial Trail by design became a four-way project involving the state, county, and city, with the committee of citizens as the liaison.

Construction of the Washington portion of the trail was planned in two phases. Phase 1 would run east from Riverfront Park in downtown Spokane through a variety of urban, suburban, and rural landscapes to Idaho. Phase 2 would run west from Riverfront Park downstream through mostly forested environs. Anticipating rising costs for design and engineering and money for land acquisition, the total estimated cost of the trail was $13.3 million. As a result of Representative Tom Foley's hard work and persuasive powers, the House Interior Appropriations Subcommittee approved $3.6 million to begin construction on Washington's trail and $1.35 million for Idaho's portion in fiscal year 1989. Over two years, the Washington portion of the trail received federal funds of $7.2 million, and the twenty-one mile section in Idaho was allotted $2.4 million.

Federal money was awarded on the condition that the community raise a matching amount. The required amount of local contributions in Washington was $6.1 million, of which $3 million was still needed after the land trade. This amount was provided by state, local, and private sources. Most of the $3 million in local matching funds came from donations and in-kind provision of various amenities, such as benches and trailheads. Local contributions provided citizens with a chance to be part of the vision of the trail and to take pride in making it come true.

Starting with a Centennial Trail promotional video by Dean Moorehouse and KXLY-TV, presentations and trade shows were staged to support local fundraising and involvement. In 1988, Moorehouse and Angove officially presented the tape to more than seventy audiences, securing major funding from the Spokane Valley Rotary Club, Hewlett-Packard, and the outdoor-equipment retailer REI, which hosted brush-clearing events for community volunteers and employees. Constructed with community development funds donated by the Logan neighborhood, much of the trail from Riverfront Park to Gonzaga University was already in place.

In 1988, the Miracle Mile Program was established, enabling individuals and nonprofit organizations to "buy" one foot of a mile-long stretch of the trail. Each donor received a certificate, and a cast-bronze medallion with an inscription of their choice was installed along the trail. The Miracle Mile begins in downtown Spokane at the northwest corner of the Opera House (now the INB Performing Arts Center) in Riverfront Park and runs east to the southeast corner of the Gonzaga University campus. Don Kardong, the founder of the Bloomsday footrace in Spokane, called the Miracle Mile a "chance to plant your name in history." Another initiative, the Adopt-a-Mile program, encourages community groups to sponsor a mile-long segment of the trail over a three-year period to remove litter and purchase amenities such as benches and information signs.

In August 1989, before construction began on the trail, a Washington State University (WSU) archaeological team, headed by Randall Schalk, made an environmental assessment of the proposed Centennial Trail route. Of the thirty-four cultural sites found, ten prehistoric and five historic sites were recommended for further investigation. Discoveries included prehistoric and historic root-gathering and fishing sites, fire-related sites with cracked rock circles, and burned bone fragments. There was evidence of farmsteads dating to before 1900 and glass and china fragments from the early 1900s. A Canadian penny dated 1916 was discovered.

Sacred and mythological sites were also found. At Minnehaha Rocks, Spokane Indian elders recalled two sacred sites among the rocks "where a young man would go to seek fishing power during his vision quest." These sacred sites contain unusual rock formations, which were explained as the result of a great fight between Coyote, friend of the Indians, and a "giant people-eater" and his "horrible pet grizzly bear."

In the WSU report, Alston Thoms spoke of roads mentioned in the Lewis and Clark journals of 1805. Thoms said these references might describe long trails through the Spokane River Valley and one along the river near the mouth of Hangman (or Latah) Creek. "If this interpretation has merit," he wrote, "then the Lewis and Clark journals contain the first reference to a pre-contact road that certainly crossed and may have paralleled the Centennial Trail somewhere between the mouth of Latah Creek and Myrtle Point." Myrtle Point is on the south side of the river, half a mile downstream from the Trent Avenue Bridge.

September 29, 1989, was another milestone in trail history. House Speaker Tom Foley announced that a House-Senate conference committee had approved a second $3.6 million grant to the Spokane River Centennial Trail for phase 2 of the construction. This funding assured completion of the final segment of the trail from downtown Spokane along the river to historic Spokane House.

The initial goal of the Centennial Trail Steering Committee was to secure land for the trail and to generate funding. In 1991, with these tasks nearly complete, the committee evolved into Friends of the Centennial Trail, a permanent nonprofit group to ensure continued operation and maintenance of the trail, with Robbi Castleberry serving as its first president. In August 1991, its executive director, Barbara Marney, said some 1,900 Miracle Mile medallions had been sold. Construction was proceeding on schedule, and the future of the Centennial Trail appeared solid.

Centennial Trail Steering Committee co-chair Joe Custer said he would like to be remembered as "one of many" local citizens who made the dream a reality. But, he said, "The trail itself will remain a legacy for the community." Dean Moorehouse, a member of the committee, observed: "For me, this project represents a powerful symbol, for it reflects all of the values that we must embrace as we prepare for the future. It will serve as a powerful statement to our youth that we care deeply about our special resources, and that we have the vision and courage to protect them for future generations."

In August 1991, the trail was being paved from the Aubrey L. White Parkway in Riverside State Park east to the T. J. Meenach Bridge behind Spokane Falls Community College. The plan was to route the trail under the Monroe Street Bridge on the north bank of the river through land owned by the Metropolitan Mortgage Corporation. In the meantime, the trail route followed existing bicycle routes on the streets just north of the river and over Bloomsday's so-called Doomsday Hill.

The first Centennial Trail run was held on June 15, 1991. It followed the Centennial Trail from Riverfront Park in Spokane to City Park in Coeur d'Alene, a distance of 40.6 miles. On July 13 and 14, sponsored by REI, the Spokane Bicycle Club held the first Spokane River Centennial Trail Bicycle Tour, donating part of every entry fee to the Friends of the Centennial Trail. That September, another bicycle tour, the Spokane/Coeur d'Alene First Annual Tour des Lacs, partially followed the trail.

By the end of the summer of 1991, the dream of the trail was nearly realized. Already crowds of outdoor enthusiasts were enjoying the smooth path. Aubrey L. White would have been overjoyed to see it. The Centennial Trail was a sleek pathway linking numerous parks for all to enjoy.

Since 1991, efforts have been made to fill in gaps in the trail. In the fall of 2013, to connect downtown and Spokane's West Central neighborhood, the trail was rerouted through Riverfront Park, across the Post Street Bridge, under the Monroe Street Bridge, and through Kendall Yards. This stretch offers one of the most spectacular views of the falls in the city. The trail now winds along the north bank of the Spokane River and past the new Olmsted Brothers Great Gorge Park to the Sandifur Memorial footbridge and Summit Boulevard northwest. On August 15, 2016, the Northwest Extension of the Centennial Trail was dedicated. This section runs nearly two miles between Sontag Park and the Nine Mile Recreation Area in Riverside State Park to end at Lake Spokane.

# Aboveground Tank Farms and Our Aquifer

JOHN ROSKELLEY

THREE BURLINGTON NORTHERN SANTA FE RAILROAD EXECUTIVES entered my Spokane County commissioner's office, led by Chris Carlson of the Gallatin Group, a Spokane-based marketing firm that specializes in rebranding corporate environmental scofflaws as stewards of nature.

"John, we're here today to give you the facts on Burlington Northern's proposed refueling depot," Carlson began. "There's been a lot of misinformation out there, and we want to make sure elected officials like you are up to speed."

I liked Chris. In fact, he and another Gallatin Group partner had voluntarily helped me improve my presentation skills before my second election campaign. But many of Chris's clients, such as Burlington Northern and Plum Creek Timber, needed environmental damage control, and the Gallatin Group were the Picassos who helped paint lipstick on pigs.

I knew what they were selling: promises and prayers couched in a high-performance package of statistics and technology. I also knew what they wanted: for the Spokane County Commission to stay neutral in the permitting process for a proposed diesel-locomotive refueling depot a few miles south of Rathdrum, Idaho, above a portion of the aquifer on which the city depends for its drinking water.

"In fact, John," Chris continued, "the project has been scaled down to two 250,000-gallon tanks with state-of-the-art protections." He handed me a glossy promotional brochure for the project. As I paged through it, the term *tertiary protection* caught my eye.

"Well, that's certainly a smaller project than the two or three one-million-gallon tanks originally proposed," I conceded. "But what is tertiary protection, and how does that protect the aquifer if a tank has a catastrophic collapse?"

I wasn't alone in my concern for the Spokane Valley–Rathdrum Prairie aquifer. Local county commissions, city councils, and public health districts on both sides of the state border had lined up against the refueling depot for good reason: our regional aquifer was the sole source of drinking water for more than half a million people.

The 370-square-mile aquifer, an underground body of water, percolates from east to west up to fifty feet per day through a mix of gravel deposits, ranging from sand to boulder-sized, dating from the Missoula Flood. In some places these deposits lie less than fifty feet below a thin skin of soil. Geologists estimate that as much as ten trillion gallons of water is coursing through the aquifer at any one time.

In a symbiotic relationship, water from the Spokane River, which has its source at Lake Coeur d'Alene, flows into the aquifer when the riverbed is higher than the aquifer. Farther west and downhill, as the river cuts deeper into the valley floor and into the underground water table, it receives water from the aquifer through springs.

If one of the Burlington Northern refueling tanks collapsed or ruptured, a quarter of a million gallons of diesel fuel would permeate this mix of sand and boulders. The fuel would disperse in a fanlike pattern west into the valley, contaminating a number of municipal water supplies, including Spokane's, as well as the Spokane River.

Burlington Northern expected a groundswell of dissent—and got it—because the aquifer is permeable. Its shallow cap of soil is highly susceptible to contamination by hazardous industrial waste, residential septic-tank pollution, contaminated storm water, and accidental fuel spills. In response to such threats, the US Environmental Protection Agency designated it as a sole-source aquifer in 1978. Sole-source designation, identifying the aquifer as the source of at least 50 percent of the region's drinking water, gave health districts and local governments in Washington and Idaho the impetus and federal money to initiate programs to protect the aquifer. These include a comprehensive wastewater management plan, which in turn includes a septic-tank elimination program (1981), an aquifer sensitive overlay zone (1983), and a wellhead protection program (1998), which are still in effect today.

My conversation with the Burlington Northern executives continued. "We weren't satisfied with just monitoring the interstitial space of the double-bottom tank. The tanks will also be built inside a concrete basin overlying two 60-mm-thick plastic liners. This is state-of-the-art protection." The rhetoric sounded great, but then I thought of a statement in the *Spokesman-Review* newspaper a few months previously from Sy Thompson, a foe of the refueling depot. He wrote, "People thought the *Titanic* was state-of-the-art."

After the meeting I thumbed through the brochure and the railroad's "tertiary protection" safety measures for their small tank farm. I realized their proposal was indeed state-of-the-art, at least compared to Spokane County's archaic regulations for aboveground tank farms. (A tank farm is a field area used exclusively for the storage of oil in tanks.) Around the Spokane metropolitan area, I knew, there were sixty to eighty million gallons of fuel stored in aging 1950s-era tanks that had virtually no safety protections in place. As a community, we were ignoring a hazardous-material time bomb in our own backyard.

The Burlington Northern tank-design schematic and safety details were a wakeup call for me. I went to work with the county's planning department to develop an aboveground tank plan and to convince my two fellow commissioners to pass legislation that would bring Spokane County's regulations into the twenty-first century.

My research began at the ExxonMobil Spokane Terminal, a few miles east of downtown Spokane, between Trent and Sprague. There the manager of the facility gave me a tour. On thirty-nine acres, thirteen tanks ranged in volume from 500,000 gallons to a staggering 3.2 million gallons. Across the street on ten acres were six tanks of under 500,000 gallons, owned by ConocoPhillips.

The nearest tank was a cylindrical, whitewashed steel monolith with rusty streaks along the welded seams. "This tank is as old as me," I said. "If it ruptures or has a catastrophic collapse, what protections do you have in place to prevent fuel from reaching the aquifer?"

"These tanks are double-bottomed, and the interstitial space is electronically monitored," the manager said. "We can detect the smallest of leaks. Every tank you see here has a containment berm to hold 110 percent of the volume of the tank."

I stared out over the tank's spill-containment area. "Well, not to state the obvious, but the berm is just gravel," I said. "It won't hold fuel for a second before it disappears into the ground and into the aquifer."

"We continually maintain these tanks and completely overhaul them every ten years," he responded. "They're not going to rupture or collapse."

His confidence mirrored that of Melissa Papworth, environmental engineer for Burlington Northern. At a public meeting concerning the two tanks proposed for the refueling depot, she said, "It's designed to not leak." Papworth made this declaration six years before the state-of-the-art refueling depot opened in September 2004. Three months after the opening, a major fuel spill and ground contamination were detected under the new facility because of faulty construction. The depot was quickly closed for extensive repair work and hazardous material cleanup. Fortunately, the spill never reached the aquifer.

We discussed other safety precautions, but my thoughts kept coming back to the rusty streaks along the welds, and the age of the tanks. These tanks were built a year before the first Air Force B-52 Flying Fortress left the assembly line to protect America during the cold war in the 1950s. "Don't you think it's time to consider tank failure?" I asked.

The manager of the Holley Refining and Marketing Company off Market Street told me the same story. It was like listening to a recording. Holley has thirty aging tanks capable of holding a total of seventeen million gallons on forty-six acres. The tank farm sits between the main aquifer flow through northeast Spokane and a secondary aquifer area below the Little Spokane River valley to the north. Like the tanks I found at ExxonMobil, none of them was in an impermeable concrete holding basin or had a plastic liner, let alone a combination of the two protections.

After visiting all the aging tank farms, I came to one conclusion: the collapse of one of these tanks would be a hydrological Armageddon. And it was impossible to guarantee against that happening: human error can and does occur.

Good government demands a process. That process can be messy, time consuming, and difficult. Nonetheless it is important. I started the lengthy legislative process at a regularly scheduled Tuesday morning meeting of the county commissioners.

"We've all been visited by the same contingent of Burlington Northern executives concerning the refueling depot," I said to commissioners Kate McCaslin and Phil Harris. "I think we should weigh in with a letter to the Kootenai County hearing examiner voicing our concern about the refueling depot and ask the hearing examiner to deny the permit." After a half-hour discussion, we agreed to ask the Idaho commissioners to deny the permit.

"I also think we should examine our own aboveground tank regulations for Spokane County and bring them up to par with the same safety procedures as those being proposed by Burlington Northern for their tanks," I said. "I've done some preliminary investigation of the tank farms around here, and they're operating in the Dark Ages. If we think the Burlington Northern tanks are a threat, they're nothing compared to what we have in Spokane County."

There was more discussion before McCaslin and Harris tentatively agreed, but they insisted we wait to see my team's final recommendations. I got to work.

"Give me everything you've got on aboveground tanks: how many, who owns them, present regulations, everything," I said to my planning director. "Then I want our tank regulations rewritten in draft form to mirror Burlington Northern's tertiary safety precautions proposed for their new tanks in Rathdrum." I handed him the brochure. "Make sure any changes to the regulations are vetted by our civil attorneys."

Our sole-source aquifer, fed by Idaho and Montana snow and rain, begins at the south end of Lake Pend Oreille and flows south and southwest, being recharged underground from several lakes: Coeur d'Alene, Spirit, Hayden, Twin, Hauser, Newman, and Liberty. The Spokane River contributes 49 percent of the aquifer's inflow during its journey from Lake Coeur d'Alene to Lake Spokane but receives almost 59 percent of the aquifer's discharge as the river exits the Spokane area.

Like so many early communities along rivers, Spokane disposed of raw sewage, storm water, and industrial and manufacturing effluent in its river. As the main artery for many of north Idaho's smaller creeks and rivers, the Spokane River was also contaminated with heavy metals from the mining smelters in North Idaho. Colloidal heavy metals and PCBs traveled down the Coeur d'Alene River and accumulated during flood events in Lake Coeur d'Alene, settling in the sands and gravels along the Spokane River.

Today, the state and local communities have passed environmental legislation to protect the quality and quantity of the Spokane River and the related aquifer. But the river is still being used—by industries such as Kaiser Aluminum, Inland Empire Paper, and occasionally by local cities—to flush state-permitted levels of hazardous wastewater and storm water into the river. The aquifer, although not visible like the river, has also seen its share of contamination from tens of thousands of septic tanks, tons of chemicals from farm and residential fertilizer, and oily scum and other hazardous material washed from our roads into storm drains. And despite all the efforts by federal, state, and local authorities to clean and protect the aquifer, perhaps the most serious threat—aboveground tank farms storing hazardous materials—has evaded our environmental radar.

After dozens of staff meetings, months of research, and multiple rewrites, we prepared a draft amendment to the Spokane County Code concerning standards for tanks with a capacity of ten thousand gallons or more. A public hearing was scheduled for November 1, 2000. Staff gave a presentation, and then a few concerned citizens thanked us for considering a change to regulations. The tank-farm managers were not pleased, however, and a representative read a prepared statement voicing the industry's concerns.

Twenty days later, after minimal deliberation, the county commission approved the resolution that amended chapter 3.15 of the Spokane County Code to bring the safety standards for aboveground tanks up to standard of the industry's state-of-the-art designs. It was one of the few times throughout my nine years as a commissioner that our Republican-dominated commission was unanimous in what many perceived as a vote for environmental protection. Not only did the resolution require new tanks to be built according to updated safety standards, but it also required older tanks to be retrofitted and brought up to the same standards over time.

Not long after the commission passed our resolution, we received a short letter from the oil and gas industry explaining that tanks and other necessary fuel infrastructure, such as pipelines, are considered interstate commerce and therefore come under federal law. The letter ended by telling us that since the industry's regulation was not under local jurisdiction, the resolution was nonbinding, and they would not be voluntarily complying.

It's been over fifteen years since the aboveground tank resolution was passed, and it's still on the county books. ExxonMobil, Conoco, and Holly Refining have refused to comply with local regulations. If they had, most, if not all, of the tanks currently perched over the aquifer would now have been retrofitted in conformity with the new safety standards. The risk to the aquifer from a catastrophic tank failure from these old tanks increases with each passing day.

Industries always claim that their technology is safe when first developed—unsinkable, like the *Titanic*. Refusing to upgrade sixty-year-old tanks to a safer modern standard because of lost profits is criminal and immoral. No doubt about it, there is another iceberg floating in the dark, this time capable of sinking the tank-farm industry and tainting or destroying our aquifer.

# An Indian Named Lokout

PAUL LINDHOLDT

THE NAME QUALCHAN—A YAKAMA WARRIOR WHO, LIKE HIS FATHER, died at the hands of Col. George Wright in 1858—is well known in the Spokane area. It has been appropriated to name a golf course, a housing development, and a footrace. Qualchan's hanging is also commemorated in the renaming of Latah Creek (a tributary of the Spokane River) to Hangman Creek on federal maps. Fewer local residents know that Qualchan had a half brother, Lokout, who survived him by fifty-six years. Lokout's life is in some ways more inspiring than Qualchan's. By outliving most of his friends and adversaries as well as his brother, Lokout became an archetype of Indian persistence.

Qualchan and Lokout were sons of the Yakama chief Owhi, who was shot in 1858 while trying to escape white captivity. Born of two chieftain families, Lokout was also a grandson of the Columbia chief Sulktalthscosum. As a boy, he traveled with his band to hunt bison east of the Rockies, where his grandfather died in battle with the Blackfeet, and west to Puget Sound, where he stayed with a paternal aunt and a cousin who later became the Nisqually chief Leschi. As a young man in 1853, Lokout guided Theodore Winthrop through Washington Territory for a portion of the journey described in Winthrop's 1862 book, *The Canoe and the Saddle*. Fighting alongside Qualchan, Lokout waged many of the battles for which his tribe became known. In one 1856 battle, a blow from a soldier's gunstock caused a gouge in his forehead that marked him for the rest of his life.

After capturing both brothers, Wright hanged Qualchan but set Lokout free. Lokout then married one of Qualchan's widows. Lokout claimed to have fought at the Battle of Little Bighorn in 1876. After that, he settled down beside the Spokane River to live out his remaining decades in relative peace. Lokout went by many names (a practice common in his time), including Loolowcan, Quo-to-we-not, Soka-tal-ko, and Rain Falling from a Passing Cloud.

Lokout's family lived in what is now Yakima County, around the present-day towns of Wenas, Selah, and Naches. The family made trips to the Salish Sea (Puget Sound) to visit family and exchange goods. One destination was the Nisqually River, where Lokout's aunt lived, and Fort Nisqually, the first European trading post on the Salish Sea. Few records of those days remain, but Mary Moses, a half sister of Lokout and Qualchan, recalled a trip east of the Rockies her family made in 1847 or 1848, with the family of old Chief Sulktalthscosum. They met some friendly Kalispel Indians who were gathering roots. The groups stuck together, rode to bison hunting grounds, and were heading home when they ran into a camp of Blackfeet Indians. A long battle ensued, and Moses's grandfather died from a Blackfeet bullet. In later years, Lokout's band sojourned for months or years on the Great Plains to hunt and fight.

While Lokout was honing his skills as a warrior, he had a bad experience with Theodore Winthrop that deepened his hostility to "the Bostons" who were already occupying his homeland. In 1853 at Fort Nisqually, Winthrop engaged Lokout, who was then in his late teens and went by the name Loolowcan, as a guide. The destination was Fort Dalles, where Winthrop was to meet some traveling companions. Winthrop, who held his Yankee ethnic group and culture to be infinitely superior to Lokout's, gave his guide a poor report in his memoir, *The Canoe and the Saddle*. Even so, it remains the most detailed record of the young Lokout's appearance, behavior, and dress.

When the two men met at Fort Nisqually, Lokout was gambling among a group of Indians. "Squalid was his hickory shirt," Winthrop noted, "squalid his buckskin leggings, long widowed of their fringe. Yet it was not a mean but a proud uncleanliness, like that of a fakir, or a voluntarily unwashed hermit." The fastidious Winthrop conceded that "there was a certain rascally charm in his rather insolent dignity, and an exciting mystery in his undecipherable phiz." Lokout "had been selected for his knowledge as a linguist and his talents as a guide." When he met a fellow Indian youth on the trail, he displayed his boyish side. The two "laughed sunset out and twilight in, finding entertainment in everything that was or that happened—in their raggedness, in the holes in their moccasins, in their overstuffed proportions after dinner, in the little skirmishes of the horses, when a grasshopper chirped or a cricket sang, when either of them found a sequence of blackberries or pricked himself with a thorn—in every fact of our little world these children of nature found wonderment and fun. They laughed themselves sleepy, and then dropped into slumber in the ferny covert." Later, after the rigorous crossing of Naches Pass, Winthrop wrote of Lokout, "He has memory and observation unerring; not once in all our intricate journeys have I found him at fault in any fact of space or time." The two communicated in the trade patois of the Northwest known as Chinook Jargon.

Like some others of his time, Lokout claimed a totem, or *tamanous*, a spirit power to pilot and protect him. His totem animal was the wolf, Talipus, "a very mighty demon," Winthrop wrote. The wolf is "a link between himself and the rude, dangerous forces of nature. Loolowcan has either chosen his protector according to the law of likeness, or, choosing it by chance, has become assimilated to its characteristics." Wolves as totems generally signify acute instinct, social connections, hunger for freedom, and intelligence. "Wolfish likewise is his appetite; when he asks me for more dinner, and this without stint or decorum he does, he glares as if, grouse failing, pork and hard-tack gone, he could call to Talipus to send in a pack of wolves incarnate, and pounce with them upon me." On their journey, Winthrop often felt intimidated by Lokout, particularly at night.

Their relationship reached its nadir when Winthrop roused Lokout from rest one morning with a kick. This was the "deadliest of insults to an Indian. It is a wonder that Lokout did not knife him then and there," wrote the historian A. J. Splawn. A group of thirty road builders camped beside them probably emboldened Winthrop to deliver his *coup de pied*.

Once Lokout came in contact with his people in the Wenas Valley, he refused to go any farther. He had suffered enough abuse. Because of this desertion, Winthrop reneged on his promised reward of trade blankets. But,

Winthrop recorded, "'I no die for lack of it,' said Loolowcan, with an air of unapproachable insolence." Winthrop reasoned that Lokout had already received compensation in the form of "a journey home and several days of banqueting." Winthrop got off cheap —and alive. "I fear," he wrote, "that the traitor escaped unpunished, perhaps to occupy himself in scalping my countrymen in the late war." He was right. But what the Yankee blueblood failed to acknowledge is the way his personal behavior antagonized his guide.

The so-called Yakima War began two years later, in 1855. According to the Eastern Washington jurist William Compton Brown, "The fact became apparent to the Indians that the occupation of their country by the Americans was at hand." In Brown's account, the first governor of Washington Territory, Isaac Stevens, started the war through "the illegally presumptuous stunt of publishing in the Olympia and Portland newspapers a declaration to the effect that the treaties negotiated at Walla Walla had cleared the way for immediate entry of the whites upon all Indian lands east of the Cascade Mountains, other than those expressly mentioned as held out for Indian reservations." Those treaties needed to be ratified by the US Senate and the president, which did not occur until April 18, 1859. But the flood of miners and settlers had already begun, hastened by the discovery of gold on lands set aside for the Yakama Tribe. As Yakama opposition to the illegal invasion grew, Lokout, now twenty-one years old, was among those who took arms against it.

The warring tribes united under the Yakama chief Kamiakin, although Lokout's brother, Qualchan, led the charge in many fights. Brown dubbed the brothers "the Castor and Pollux of Yakima Indian history," an allusion worth exploring. In Greek mythology, these figures were the twin sons of Leda. Castor was the mortal son of Tyndareus, the king of Sparta, and Pollux the divine son of Zeus. Both were skilled horsemen. When Castor was killed, Pollux asked Zeus to let him share his immortality with his twin to keep them together. Zeus transformed them into the constellation Gemini. Likewise, Qualchan and Lokout hailed from a family that prided itself on horsemanship. Though they had different mothers, they had a common father, Owhi. And by contrast with Qualchan, Lokout proved almost immortal.

They learned the art of open warfare from Plains Indians. "[Yakama] Indians fought individually instead of in concerted groups," Stephen Emerson has written, and "were proficient at shooting from horseback, whereas most of the soldiers had to dismount, fire, and resume pursuit." In the Indians' guerrilla style of fighting, which included night raids and horse rustling, grass fires and sniping, these brothers became partners in "one of the greatest federations of Indian tribes ever recorded in history." Qualchan's early death was due in part to his renown, which marked him as a target of the US military. Lokout, by contrast, went underground.

One well-documented incident in the Yakima War embodies Lokout's spirit as a warrior. In May 1856, on the banks of the Naches River, some four hundred Indians, led by Kamiakin, were preparing to besiege Wright's camp. Lokout's father, Owhi, openly opposed Kamiakin's plan and pleaded for peace. Disgusted, Kamiakin rode away and took half the warriors with him, never to return. Lokout, although he remained with his father, was also disgusted and ashamed. "Mounting his horse," according to Splawn, "he said in a loud voice, 'I am the son of a chief and a tried warrior. After hearing my father talk, I do not want to live. I will swim the river on my horse. I will go to the soldiers' camp and be killed.'"

Wright had promised to shoot any armed Indian who approached his camp. Lokout went anyway, bearing a bow and a quiver, first swimming his horse to an island in the Naches River. After resting briefly, "he then swam on to the other shore which was lined with blue-coated soldiers." According to Splawn, whose account is based on an interview with Lokout in 1906, Lokout delivered the following speech to Wright: "If I am killed, my father and brother will fight on, which is what I want them to do. I have one life to give and am ready to give it now, that war may continue until the whites are driven from our country. If I live, Ow-hi will fight no more. You now know the object of my coming. I am waiting." Carrying a gift of tobacco from Wright, he swam back and then returned the next day with another message from his father: "Ow-hi is glad to quit fighting. His people are tired and poor. It seems when he drinks water or eats food that it tastes of blood. He is sick of war."

The peace Owhi secured did not last, in part because his sons opposed it. Even though his cause was doomed, Lokout persisted in the fight. Splawn claimed that Lokout was active in battles in Toppenish, where Maj. Granville O. Haller was defeated; at Union Gap, "when they fought Major Rains; also at the battle of Walla Walla, when the great chief Pe-peu-mox-mox was killed; [he] also participated in the attack on Governor Stevens, a few miles above the present city of Walla Walla; was in the fight that defeated Colonel Steptoe in the Palouse country; was in the attack on Seattle in 1856, and again at Connell's Prairie."

Lokout's firsthand accounts of these exploits are impossible to verify today, but other histories corroborate some details. According to Splawn, "When Col. Steptoe was defeated in 1858, Lokout was one of the Indian sharpshooters selected by Ka-mi-akin to pick off Captain O. H. P. Taylor and Lieutenant William Gaston, saying, 'These two men must die if we are to win,' after which these officers were special targets of the unerring rifles. Thus fell two gallant men, victims of an ill-advised expedition." Other histories address Lokout's skill with a rifle and his fierce resolve to repel the invaders. Less often acknowledged are his capacity for self-preservation and his will to survive.

On September 19, 1856, Lokout was fighting against Governor Isaac Stevens following a second Walla Walla treaty meeting. Stevens had affronted tribes by coercing them to sign away their lands. The Nez Perce and Yakama were firing at full gallop; the less seasoned white troops had to dismount to take aim. The cover was scrubby and sparse. Qualchan, leading the charge, ordered his people to set the prairie burning and keep on fighting after dark. Although Lokout sustained two shots to his chest, he fought on, killing a trooper in hand-to-hand combat before falling over, prostrated by fatigue and pain. As night came on, the fighting continued. Grass fires set by his tribesmen smoked and flamed.

A passing trooper spotted Lokout on the ground and swung near enough to smash him in the forehead with his gun butt, caving in his skull. Militiamen delivered such strikes to save bullets. Although "his skull had a hole in it that would hold an egg," as Splawn wrote, Lokout survived the injury. Photos from Lokout's adoptive Spokane Tribe confirm the astounding gouge it left.

Lokout was also a player in a pivotal event in the Yakima War. On September 25, 1858, according to David Wilma, Wright, who was "engaged in a punitive military expedition against the Yakama, Palouse, Spokane, and Coeur d'Alene tribes after their defeat of a force under Lieutenant Colonel Edward Steptoe in May," tricked Owhi into camp and took him captive. Wright "sent word to Qualchan that if he did not surrender, Wright would hang his father. The next day Qualchan appeared carrying a white flag. He wore Yakama finery of beaded buckskin and rode his best horse. His wife carried his rifle, and his brother Lokout accompanied them." Qualchan was seized, and fifteen minutes later he was hanged.

Lokout and Qualchan's wife knew their lives were on the line. What happened next remains in dispute. Many say that a Spokane Indian lied for Lokout by identifying him as a member of the Spokane Tribe and thus securing his release. Others say Lokout wrested a noose from his neck to mount Qualchan's warhorse and escape. Some claim Qualchan's wife grabbed a saber and slashed her way to freedom, while others say she plunged a lance defiantly into the ground and left it quivering after Wright released her. Whatever happened, on the shore of what would come to be named Hangman Creek, it was the beginning of the end of the Yakima War. Lokout later married his brother's widow—variously named Mary, Whisto, Swista, Whist-alks, Tat-sa-misa-quest, and Walks in a Dress. They lived together for five decades on the Spokane Indian Reservation near the confluence of the Spokane and Columbia Rivers.

The dent in Lokout's forehead became a sign of his valor and tenacity. If Lokout actually fought in the Battle of Little Bighorn in 1876 (though my colleague and friend Larry Cebula doubts he did), it might have been his last hurrah as a warrior. By then he would have been about forty-two. He reportedly told his wife that he was done fighting. He joined the Spokane Tribe by virtue not only of his wife's bloodline but of his mother's also.

Thirty years later, he participated in long interviews with Splawn, who was doing research for his book *Ka-mi-a-kin: Last Hero of the Yakimas*, and later with Edward S. Curtis, whose documentary record of the tribes includes voluminous written transcripts as well as photos.

We might wonder, with Splawn, how Lokout managed to survive that fearsome blow to the skull. We might also wonder what he did and where he lived before he spoke with Splawn in 1906. My guess is that he went underground to protect himself and his wife. If the trials he endured in guiding Winthrop were not enough to make a warrior of him, having his head bashed in would surely have been enough to dedicate him to the cause of fighting white incursions as long as he could.

In 1910, four years after Splawn met the disfigured Lokout, the Seattle photographer Edward Curtis and his entourage made a visit. Curtis was compiling interviews and photos for the seventh volume of his twenty-volume work *The North American Indian*. That volume was to focus on the Yakama of Washington and the Kootenai of Idaho. Curtis costumed his models and paid them a dollar or two for each sitting. How Curtis heard about Lokout is impossible to say, but Lokout agreed to grant him interviews and to have his photo taken. The resulting image, shown here, portrays the former warrior in profile. His face is lined, his chin raised, the decorative necklace and feathers imposed by Curtis belying his seventy-nine or so years of age.

Remarkably, this photo shows less than it hides. Curtis was essentially a fashion photographer, one who often posed and dressed his indigenous subjects in ways they would not actually have appeared from day to day. Using a comb-over, much like a makeup artist in Hollywood, Curtis had Lokout's hair styled to hide the legendary gouge. Perhaps Curtis considered the wound too unsettling to behold—too graphic a reminder of the brutality of the white invaders—rather than a mark of courage and endurance.

Ethnologists and historians fault Curtis for manipulating his images. He portrays his Indian subjects, some say, in stereotypical ways, as a vanishing race unable to endure a modern onslaught. He makes noble savages of

"Luqaiot [Lokout], Kittitas Indian man." Photo by Edward S. Curtis, March 11, 1910. Reproduced courtesy of the Library of Congress.

them. In one of his images, Curtis erased a clock that blighted a traditional teepee scene. And always Curtis turned his photographic gaze away—from the automobiles that he used to haul his gear to reservation grounds, from the squalor in which some tribes had to live, from the factory-made clothing they got in trade and often preferred to wear. Curtis traveled with his own collection of quaint regalia to ornament the Indians, to fit them out to match popular notions of the times. He might have provided the necklace and feathers that adorn Lokout like so much costume jewelry for actors on a stage. Tribal photos, by contrast, show Lokout dressed, like many of his contemporaries, in hair braids, cowboy hat, and trade blankets.

If no one before this time has connected Lokout with the Curtis photo, it might be because Curtis spelled the name Luqaiot. Field linguists transcribed Indian names phonetically or relied on erratic sources. To confound the history further, Lokout went by other names, as noted above. Some

Indians took different names at different periods in their lives, or gave fake names to whites who might do them harm. Had Wright not known the name of Qualchan, for instance, Qualchan might have survived to live and fight as long as his brother.

Because of the superficial charm of the Curtis photograph, it took on a life of its own. In the 1930s it was altered, colorized, and packaged as a trading card by the Goudey Gum Company of Boston. The chin was given a more pugnacious tilt. The dented forehead, now artificially laid bare, was restored to its original shape. Lokout's profile, altered at first by Curtis for one commercial purpose, was appropriated and altered again for another.

# Two Poems

SHERMAN ALEXIE

## The Powwow at the End of the World

I am told by many of you that I must forgive and so I shall
after an Indian woman puts her shoulder to the Grand Coulee Dam
and topples it. I am told by many of you that I must forgive
and so I shall after the floodwaters burst each successive dam
downriver from the Grand Coulee. I am told by many of you
that I must forgive and so I shall after the floodwaters find
their way to the mouth of the Columbia River as it enters the Pacific
and causes all of it to rise. I am told by many of you that I must forgive
and so I shall after the first drop of floodwater is swallowed by that salmon
waiting in the Pacific. I am told by many of you that I must forgive and so I shall
after that salmon swims upstream, through the mouth of the Columbia
and then past the flooded cities, broken dams and abandoned reactors
of Hanford. I am told by many of you that I must forgive and so I shall
after that salmon swims through the mouth of the Spokane River
as it meets the Columbia, then upstream, until it arrives
in the shallows of a secret bay on the reservation where I wait alone.
I am told by many of you that I must forgive and so I shall after
that salmon leaps into the night air above the water, throws
a lightning bolt at the brush near my feet, and starts the fire

which will lead all of the lost Indians home. I am told
by many of you that I must forgive and so I shall
after we Indians have gathered around the fire with that salmon
who has three stories it must tell before sunrise: one story will teach us
how to pray; another story will make us laugh for hours;
the third story will give us reason to dance. I am told by many
of you that I must forgive and so I shall when I am dancing
with my tribe during the powwow at the end of the world.


## That Place Where Ghosts of Salmon Jump

Coyote was alone and angry because he could not find love.
Coyote was alone and angry because he demanded a wife

from the Spokane, the Coeur d'Alene, the Palouse, all those tribes
camped on the edge of the Spokane River, and received only laughter.

So Coyote rose up with his powerful and senseless magic
and smashed a paw across the water, which broke the river bottom

in two, which created rain that lasted forty days and nights,
which created Spokane Falls, that place where salmon travelled

more suddenly than Coyote imagined, that place where salmon swam
larger than any white man dreamed. Coyote, I know you broke

the river because of love, and pretended it was all done by your design.
Coyote, you're a liar and I don't trust you. I never have

but I do trust all the stories the grandmothers told me.
They said the Falls were built because of your unrequited love

and I can understand that rage, Coyote. We can all understand
but look at the Falls now, and tell me what you see. Look

at the Falls now, if you can see beyond all of the concrete
the white man has built here. Look at all of this

and tell me that concrete ever equals love, Coyote,
these white men sometimes forget to love their own mothers

so how could they love this river which gave birth
to a thousand lifetimes of salmon? How could they love

these Falls, which have fallen farther, which sit dry
and quiet as a graveyard now? These Falls are that place

where ghosts of salmon jump, where ghosts of women mourn
their children who will never find their way back home,

where I stand now and search for any kind of love,
where I sing softly, under my breath, alone and angry.

# Writing on Water

## Sherman Alexie's Poetry on Salmon and Spokane Falls

CHAD WRIGLESWORTH

SHERMAN ALEXIE IS A SPOKANE/COEUR D'ALENE INDIAN, A DESCENDANT of tribes whose biological, economic, and spiritual identities are historically interwoven with the ecology of rivers and the migratory patterns of Pacific Northwest salmon. This way of life was contested in the early twentieth century, after a series of seven dams were constructed on the Spokane River by Washington Water Power (established in 1889) and other organizations to support the industrialization of Spokane, a resource-rich community that local boosters marketed as the center of the "Inland Empire" of the Pacific Northwest. After the construction of Little Falls Dam, forty-five miles downstream from Spokane Falls, in 1910, salmon continued to spawn in a twenty-nine-mile stretch of water below the obstruction. Salmon migrations ceased after the Army Corps of Engineers and Bureau of Reclamation (established in 1902) identified the Columbia River basin as a latent powerhouse with "mighty possibilities" for national progress. Subsequently, Franklin D. Roosevelt's Columbia Basin Project (1933)—part of the New Deal plan for economic renewal—laid the groundwork for the Grand Coulee Dam and for a forty-year plan of watershed reclamation that produced a network of hydroelectric dams and irrigation canals throughout the Columbia Basin, effectively transforming the watershed into what the environmental historian Richard White calls an "organic machine."

The largest of the dams proposed by the Columbia Basin Project, the Grand Coulee, built in 1941, cut off salmon migration to the upper Columbia River basin. This included the entire Spokane River, the center of life for indigenous peoples living on the Spokane Indian Reservation and the place where Sherman Alexie grew up. Alexie, who was born in 1966, explains that before the dams, "our religion, our culture, our dancing, our singing—had everything to do with the salmon. We were devastated by the Grand Coulee Dam. It took away seven thousand miles of salmon spawning beds from the interior Indians in Washington, Idaho, and Montana."

This lament is no exaggeration. According to the historian John Fahey, anthropologists speculate that prior to the damming of the Spokane and Columbia Rivers, the Spokane Tribe of Indians alone harvested at least five hundred pounds of salmon per person each year, accounting for more than 60 percent of their annual consumption of food. Research conducted by Robert H. Ruby and John Arthur Brown indicates that when Spokane Indians, along with tribes such as the Colville, Kootenai, and Coeur d'Alene, fished at nearby Kettle Falls (now inundated by the Grand Coulee), it was not uncommon for the fishery to yield two thousand salmon in a day (see also Allan Scholz's chapter in this volume). Plans to restore salmon above the Grand Coulee today are driven also by a desire to return salmon to Canadian waters.

The interior tribes of the Pacific Northwest felt the deepest economic and cultural repercussions from the salmon loss caused by the Grand Coulee Dam, but indigenous peoples were not the only groups questioning the vision of progress enacted by the Bureau of Reclamation. By the time the Columbia Basin Project was completed in the 1970s, many citizens of the Northwest were already challenging the exploitation of the Columbia and Snake River system. In 1968, the regional publisher and historian Oral Bullard wrote *Crisis on the Columbia*, one of the first regional works to speak out against the Columbia Basin Project for environmental reasons. Meanwhile the city of Spokane, once celebrated as an economic hub of the Northwest interior, had continued so far down the path of industrialization that Spokane Falls, the city's main attraction, was inaccessible and barely visible because of the railways and other infrastructure that lined the waterfront. In the late 1960s, a group of business leaders formed an organization called Spokane Unlimited and used an emerging interest in local watershed reclamation to make a bid to host Expo '74, marketed as the first environmentally themed world's fair. After Spokane—then a city of only 170,000—was selected as a venue for the fair, the Expo Corporation set to work scraping away the industrial buildings and railways that had defined the downtown waterfront for nearly one hundred years. In the spirit of ecological renewal, concrete structures of the past were replaced by a one-hundred-acre green space of sod and trees that set the stage for pavilions, footbridges, and a gondola to usher visitors across river islands, over the roaring Spokane Falls, and through a city park that lined a newly reclaimed Spokane River.

Sherman Alexie, who grew up in the historical wake of the Grand Coulee Dam and the Columbia Basin Project, attended Expo '74 and witnessed local attempts to reclaim Spokane Falls. His poetry, written in response to federal and local efforts at watershed reclamation, addresses the challenges and possibilities posed by the efforts of nonindigenous groups to remake Spokane Falls. Artistically and politically, Alexie enacts and participates in a new era of reclamation by offering a Native perspective on the meaning of Spokane Falls, one that has all too often been silenced or simply unheard throughout the contested history of this place.

## A Reclamation of the Promised Land

During the 1930s, when the Grand Coulee Dam was under construction, Franklin D. Roosevelt and political leaders of the New Deal promoted the Pacific Northwest as an emerging Promised Land. Roosevelt visited the Grand Coulee construction site in 1934 and spoke to more than twenty thousand supporters, encouraging them to embrace the future of hydroelectricity and irrigation by becoming "dam minded." He reminded them that their work would provide "many families back in the older settled parts of the nation . . . the opportunity of still going west." In Roosevelt's view, the Grand Coulee would fulfill a national "prophecy" in which the "unlimited natural resources" of the Pacific Northwest would be harnessed and distributed to benefit the entire nation. Three years later, after the Grand Coulee had transformed the Columbia River basin, Roosevelt returned to predict the future prosperity of the region: "Coming back to Grand Coulee after three years, I am very happy by the wonderful progress that I have seen. And I can't help feeling that everybody who has had anything to do with the building of this dam is going to be made happy all the rest of his life." Roosevelt reminded those in attendance that their labor was cause for great "rejoicing," for they were ushering in a vision of progress that would help families—both regionally and nationally—to "live better than they are living now." Yet the fulfillment of this promise eluded tribes such as the Colville, Spokane, Kootenai, and Coeur d'Alene, whose lives the New Deal altered forever.

Sherman Alexie's response to the Grand Coulee Dam and the larger Columbia Basin Project is articulated in a religiously and historically inflected poem titled "The Powwow at the End of the World" (included in this volume). Alexie's apocalyptic poem imagines an era of indigenous reclamation that restores the salmon runs and eliminates dams. The poem begins by addressing those who urge the speaker to forgive and forget the economic and ecological injustices inflicted on the Spokane River and indigenous peoples. The speaker informs his petitioners that he "shall" forgive all wrongs done to the river and Native peoples only after a specific set of conditions is met:

> I am told by many of you that I must forgive and so I shall
> after an Indian woman puts her shoulder to the Grand Coulee Dam
> and topples it.

The visual and rhythmic force of these lines awakens two opposing images. By letting the first line hang on the archaic and biblically inflected word *shall*, the speaker leads readers to believe that he will extend forgiveness. That hope is revoked in the second line, however, when the speaker invokes the condition for this forgiveness: a mythical-indigenous woman rising up and dismantling the Grand Coulee Dam. With the 548-foot-high dam rhetorically toppled, Lake Roosevelt and eighty thousand acres of the harnessed Columbia River race down the lines of Alexie's verse, triggering a flood that destroys the concrete monuments of the New Deal and the cold war. Drawing on the rhetorical power of repetition and unrestrained lines, the water and verse gain momentum to "burst each successive dam / down-river from the Grand Coulee."

When the floodwaters of the Columbia River reach the Pacific Ocean, a new possibility of restoration enters the mouth of a single salmon. Biological memory then triggers a long-awaited journey from the Pacific Ocean up the Columbia River and back to Spokane Falls. At that point, the rhythm of Alexie's poem shifts to enact the salmon's migration upriver. Ascending the free-flowing Columbia River, the fish turns and fights through a watery graveyard of "flooded cities, broken dams" and the "abandoned reactors / of Hanford." At the confluence of the Columbia and Spokane Rivers, the salmon turns "upstream again," marked by a pair of commas that signify the turn of the fish from the mainline Columbia and up the Spokane River toward the falls.

"The Powwow at the End of the World" ends with a gathering of indigenous peoples to reclaim a Promised Land from its colonizing occupants. The image of crushed hydroelectric dams and inundated cities evokes images of ancient Egyptian irrigators consumed by floodwaters and pride while the oppressed Israelites head toward freedom. This comparison is apt: during the 1930s the Grand Coulee Dam was repeatedly described as "the biggest thing on earth," a monument to American innovation that would rival the engineering wonders constructed by the Egyptians. Richard Neuberger, the author of *Our Promised Land* (1938), wrote articles for *Harper's* and the *New York Times* assuring readers that the Grand Coulee would surpass "the ancient Pyramid of the Pharaohs." Such extravagant rhetoric was not uncommon. More recently, Richard White notes in *The Organic Machine* that "like Superman, [the Grand Coulee Dam] was always greater than its objects of comparison: larger than the Great Pyramid, higher than Niagara, more concrete than a transcontinental highway. Only the new world it would help produce dwarfed Grand Coulee."

At the closing of "The Powwow at the End of the World," the vision of a nationalist Promised Land is undermined, and Spokane Falls is restored to indigenous peoples. In the biblical exodus, the Israelites are led by a pillar of fire toward the Promised Land. Alexie manipulates this imagery when a salmon carrying lightning returns to Spokane Falls and ignites a burning bush that ushers indigenous people into an era of restoration. This new era replaces cheap electricity with fire and lightning. Local rituals of prayer, laughter, and dancing upstage all visions of the New Deal and national progress. Only when the first salmon returns to the Spokane Indians, and the champions of unrestrained progress are consumed by floodwaters of their own making, will the speaker of the poem forgive the injustices inflicted on indigenous peoples, the salmon, and the Spokane River. Alexie's best-known and most frequently anthologized poem of indigenous reclamation gains force through repetition, syntactic finesse, and the image of a mythic salmon that delivers its people from bondage and leads them home.

Fusing historical reality with imagination, the poem envisions how story-telling and poetry can breach dams, prompt political redemption, and revise the flow of the Columbia and Spokane Rivers.

## Speaking against Walls of Concrete and Steel

The force of poems to enact change is evoked in the public, physical presence of a second poem by Alexie that has gained political force not only as an anthologized text but also as an installment of public art at Spokane Falls. To grasp the ecological and cultural importance of Alexie's poem "That Place Where Ghosts of Salmon Jump" requires some knowledge of the role played by indigenous peoples at Expo '74, the environmentally themed world's fair that Alexie attended as a child. The celebration was noteworthy because it was the first to include an exhibit developed and administered by local Native peoples. Members of the Spokane, Colville, and Coeur d'Alene tribes were invited to participate for a range of complex and often superficial reasons.

Throughout the 1970s, environmental organizations such as Keep America Beautiful cast Native peoples—older and wiser figures like Iron Eyes Cody, the televised Crying Indian—as models of ecological stewardship that could teach white followers how to reject pollution and learn to reinhabit the land. In an *Orion Magazine* article, the essayist Ginger Strand describes the emotional power of watching "a black-braided, buckskinned, cigar-store native come to life, complete with single feather and stoic frown." The actor, who navigates a canoe through pristine waters and into a polluted city, is then struck by litter hurled from a car window. The Indian looks over the creation of modern America and weeps because, as Strand states, "the crying Indian wept for our sins, and from his tears sprang forth a new Green Age."

But as many cultural critics now recognize, that moment of indigenous identification was riddled with false assumptions about Native peoples and practices. Richard White explains that during the 1970s, environmental activists might have found the so-called "ecological otherness" of Native peoples alluring, but few activists "acquired more than a superficial acquaintance with Indian practices or beliefs." The Native historian Philip Deloria suggests that a figure like Iron Eyes Cody says more about white consumers than about Native peoples, mostly because "Americans have returned to the Indian" less for authentic cultural and ecological guidance than out of a desire to commodify and appropriate an assumed and largely false set of indigenous practices designed to help disoriented citizens make sense of their own tumultuous times.

Like other environmental efforts of the day, Expo '74 in Spokane used stereotypical and often colonizing images of indigenous figures to urge white tourists to reject modernization by embracing the ecological and spiritual wisdom of Native traditions. For example, when the celebration opened to a gathering of more than eighty-five thousand people, visitors met at Spokane Falls to confess their environmental sins and to make a renewed profession of faith. They listened to promoters read the "Credo of Expo," an oath that began with a confession of ecological negligence and concluded with absolution, as participants committed themselves to the "restoration of the reverence of Nature" in the spirit of the "American Indian" who "roamed in respectful concert with his environment."

Alexie, an heir to this culture of appropriation, remains critical of ongoing attempts to promote ecological wisdom through Indians. He insists that modern environmentalism has now become a "luxury," a set of gentrified practices that were inaccessible to indigenous tribes who lived by subsistence and under "the absence of choice" when seeking food and shelter. Ultimately, Alexie suspects that lines of separation between actual white and

Indian environmental practices are quite thin. For those still seeking models of ecological stewardship based on indigenous practices, Alexie points to the Spokane Indian Reservation, where there are abandoned uranium mines, toxic rivers, and "a whole lot of tin cans on the road."

Visitors at Expo '74 were led to believe that the World's Fair stood for a new era of social harmony between white and indigenous peoples in a common environment, but this display was little more than a masquerade. In 1973, only months before the fair opened, the Expo Corporation sent out a belated invitation to disgruntled Spokane, Colville, and Coeur d'Alene tribal leaders, inviting them to discuss ways that local indigenous peoples might participate in the event. Expo organizers then allotted tribes a total of one acre on the one-hundred-acre site. With this allotment, the tribes established an educational exhibit on Indian customs titled "Native Americans' Earth," one of the fair's most popular attractions. Alex Sherwood, a leader of the Spokane tribe, criticized the entire arrangement. Sherwood reminded developers that "the fair was being held on lands once occupied by the Spokane tribe . . . but the Indians were hardly involved in its planning." Sherwood "felt neglected because the Expo people had not contacted his people for Indian participation at the fair." Sherwood insisted that despite appearances of ecological health, the city of Spokane and organizers of Expo had not improved the environment: the Spokane River was polluted and had been devoid of salmon since the Grand Coulee Dam was constructed.

The Expo Corporation's belated invitation to include neighboring tribal leaders in planning the World's Fair proved ironic considering that Chief Seattle, a revered figure among 1970s environmentalists, held a position of prominence at the US Pavilion. Having crossed Spokane Falls in an airborne gondola, visitors filed toward the ecologically themed structure. It welcomed them with totem poles and a creed attributed to Chief Seattle: "The Earth does not belong to Man, Man belongs to the Earth." Dawn Bowers, author of *Expo '74 World's Fair Spokane*, wrote that visitors who entered the US Pavilion were then channeled through educational exhibits that informed them, without any irony, of the ways that organizations such as Washington Water Power and the Bureau of Reclamation "have taken an active role in protecting the environment with major pieces of legislation in the environmental field dating back 100 years." On the way out of the building, visitors passed "a kiosk which housed a life-like, talking mannequin of Chief Seattle." The simulated Indian chief reiterated the need for everyone—Indians and whites—to take responsibility for the Earth and then closed with a sagacious benediction: "Go now, and do the work that must be done."

Alexie no doubt encountered the figure of Chief Seattle while attending the fair in his youth. He writes about Expo '74, the US Pavilion, and Spokane Falls in *The Lone Ranger and Tonto Fistfight in Heaven*, a 1993 collection of interrelated short stories that he calls "a thinly disguised memoir." It includes a vignette of two brothers, Victor and James, who make a trip from the reservation into the city to visit the World's Fair. Victor, the narrator, is impressed by international exhibits hosted by Mexico and Japan, but he finds stories presented in the US pavilion to be utterly foreign to his experiences as a Spokane Indian. After he hears about state and federal commitments to environmental protection, Victor sees the mannequin of Chief Seattle and listens to the message its white organizers have programmed into it. The old sage tells the boy: "We have to take care of the earth because it is our mother." Victor, who fails even to recognize the identity of the tribal leader, then points it out to James as "a statue of an Indian who's supposed to be some chief or another." James, the younger brother, wise beyond his years, assesses the concrete and steel embedded in the Spokane River and tells the gathered crowd that the earth is, in fact, not our mother but actually "our grandmother" and that "technology has become our mother and they both hate each other." As evidence, the boy directs the crowd to the Spokane River, "only a few yards" away from where they stand, telling everyone that those falls out there are "all we ever need to believe in."

In 1990, Alexie was presented with an opportunity to write "That Place Where Ghosts of Salmon Jump," a poem about Spokane Falls that documents its ecological reclamation. The invitation arrived shortly after citizens of Spokane approved a $28.8 million bond measure for the construction of a new library in downtown Spokane. In an attempt to integrate local history and the aesthetic appeal of the falls into the structure of the new building, the library board of trustees worked with local and state organizations—including the Washington State Arts Commission, the City of Spokane Parks and Recreation Department, and the Spokane Arts Commission—on a plan to present Alexie's poem as part of the Sculpture Walk, a collection of public art installations in Spokane's Riverfront Park and along the Centennial Trail. Funding for the project was made available through Spokane's Percent for Art ordinance, legislation passed in 1981, which mandates that 1 percent of certain capital construction costs be used to "purchase artwork for enhancing public buildings and spaces."

The library reclaimed a former parking lot across the street from the library and developed it into Overlook Park, the site that houses the installation of Alexie's poem. In 2008, while reflecting on the poem and its place at the falls, Alexie told Stefanie Pettit, a writer for the *Spokesman-Review*, that the decision to have his work installed at the site was "a risky move, risky to put the work of a relatively unknown artist in such a permanent location, risky to put the work of a Spokane Indian there." At the time of the invitation, Alexie remembered how "the river was the center of our lives, the center of our religion, so that location, there overlooking the river, is just where I wanted the poem to be."

In an essay titled "The Poetics of Water," previously published in *The Bioregional Imagination* (2012), I discuss how "That Place Where Ghosts of Salmon Jump" contributes to the reclamation of Spokane Falls by reinterpreting a Salish Indian story about their creation of the place. The indigenous story tells of a meeting with Coyote, the mythical trickster. Coyote was known to assist or impede the migration of salmon to upriver Indians depending on the tribes' willingness to accommodate his voracious appetite for beautiful women. According to Salish legend, a dispute over a young woman led to the creation of the falls. Coyote was traveling up the Spokane River, to the place where Spokane Falls now exists, when he decided to take a Salish woman as a wife. The trickster asked the tribal leaders to provide him with a young woman, but they refused and mocked him. An enraged and lonely Coyote punished those gathered at the salmon fishery by smashing his paw across the river. In so doing he remade the river into a massive set of falls so that salmon could no longer pass upstream.

Alexie speaks directly to this creation story. Setting the scene for upheaval and mythic transformation, the poem opens:

Coyote was alone and angry because he could not find love.
Coyote was alone and angry because he demanded a wife

from the Spokane, the Coeur d'Alene, the Palouse, all of those tribes
camped on the edge of the Spokane River, and received only laughter.

Rejected and mocked by tribal leaders and those who have gathered to fish, Coyote crushes the river, splitting open the bottom so that salmon cannot travel beyond the falls.

The speaker then confronts Coyote, arguing that the loss of salmon at Spokane Falls has nothing to do with mythical powers but was caused by companies such as Washington Water Power (now Avista Utilities), part of an industry that poured a "graveyard" of "concrete" over the water. Calling Coyote a liar, the speaker points out that it was rather the work of white engineers and laborers who have installed a network of dams, penstocks, and turbines—creating a place of extinction where only the "ghosts of salmon jump" and the "ghosts of women" come to mourn. As evidence, the speaker challenges the old trickster—as well as readers at the public installation of the poem—to look over the falls and try to "see beyond all of the concrete / the white man has built here."

As published in his book *The Summer of Black Widows*, Alexie's poem reads as a sequence of couplets, but at the public installation at Spokane Public Library's Overlook Park, the verse is set out as a single line like a current, a string of spiraling words etched on granite and concrete. Readers of the poem step into a textual version of the Spokane River. Migrating, like the metaphorical salmon, toward the poem's center, they spin and turn with a series of currents. When they reach the center to read the last phrase of the poem, they are left with the words "alone and angry" at a dead end of concrete.

Ten years after its installation, "That Place Where Ghosts of Salmon Jump" as public art has contributed to revising the flow of water on the Spokane River. A major controversy over the dams operated by Avista has been the diversion of water by Upper Falls Dam, constructed in 1922. In summer, the company was diverting all of the river's water through a series of storage penstocks, leaving Lower Spokane Falls dry. The speaker in Alexie's poem informs Coyote that in recent years the falls have "fallen further" and now "sit dry and quiet as a graveyard."

In 2009, the Upper Falls Dam operational license was up for a fifty-year renewal. Through the efforts of the Seattle-based Center for Environmental Law and Policy, the Sierra Club, and the Environmental Law Clinic at the University of Washington, a court settlement was reached with Avista to guarantee a steady flow of water year-round so that neither the Upper nor the Lower Spokane Falls go dry during the summer. As part of a local campaign for this change, activists wrote letters to the Washington State Department of Ecology, posted letters and alerts on websites, and spoke on behalf of the falls at public hearings with the Federal Energy Regulatory Commission. John Osborn, webmaster and board member for the Center for Environmental Law and Policy, explains that throughout the campaign, Alexie's poem was cited as a cultural and historical testament to environmental injustices on the Spokane River. Overall, he estimates that excerpts from "That Place Where Ghosts of Salmon Jump" went out to at least two thousand local activists during their campaign to restore year-round flow at Spokane Falls.

The Spokane River, part of the Columbia River watershed, is caught up in a process of watershed reclamation that reflects our cultural values and environmental priorities. Words shape actions and lead to policy changes, whether in the form of Roosevelt's persuasive speech about the Columbia Basin Project or localized reclamation efforts at Expo '74. Rhetoric, art, and literature have power to reshape the way we inhabit places. At their best, Robert L. Thayer Jr. suggests in *Lifeplace* (2003), "a distinctly regional art, aesthetics, literature, poetics, and music can evolve from and support" a culture sensitive to ecological and human health. Sherman Alexie's poetry on salmon and Spokane Falls powerfully reminds us where we have been and points us toward a horizon that we are still trying to reach.

# Beneath
# the Surface

# Spokane River Archaeology

SARA L. WALKER, STAN GOUGH, AND JERRY R. GALM

> Deciphering meaning from objects in context is the business of
> archaeology.
>
> —DAVID HURST THOMAS, 1998

ARCHAEOLOGY PROVIDES A GLIMPSE OF ANCIENT LIFEWAYS THROUGH
the study of the material remains of people's lives and activities. Such relics
reveal the plants and animals the people ate, their shelters, tools, and raw
materials. Many of the objects of daily life were perishable. Only objects made
of durable materials—stone, bone, and shell—typically survive for study and
interpretation. Spokane River archaeology, like all archaeology, is fragile. It is
limited by the vagaries of site preservation, and it is nonrenewable.

The Spokane River archaeological record is incomplete for several
reasons. Geological processes erode and destroy sites, as do modern
human land-use practices; perishable materials decay. In addition, fewer
investigations have been conducted along the Spokane River than along
the Columbia and Snake Rivers, where the federal legislation driving the
construction of hydroelectric dams included provisions for archaeological
investigations. There, surveys located sites; tests evaluated the scientific
potential of individual site contents; and large-scale excavations recovered
some artifacts and information before it was submerged and lost to time.
Such research, new in the United States, was driven by a national movement
to obtain a better record of Native prehistories and interpretations of stasis
and change in Native lifeways.

But development on the Spokane River, including the construction of dams, occurred mostly before relevant legislation to empower recovery of a more comprehensive archaeological record. Despite what laypeople might see as an impersonal and often inadequate record of Native life, the ability to acquire baseline information forms the starting point in what is most commonly a long and difficult path to understanding Native land-use practices. For the Spokane River valley, the very limited information available for study represents a challenge. That challenge can be met through comparisons to other regional data sets; through renewed study of available data; and through vigilance to preserve, protect, and (as needed) investigate remaining archaeological resources.

Motivated by the research potential of two fur-trade posts (Spokane House and Fort Spokane, the first permanent Euro-American settlement in Washington State) and the adjacent Spokane Indian village, the National Park Service and Washington State Parks funded the Spokane region's first professional archaeological excavations. Limited funding resulted in far more attention to the fur-trade site than to the Indian village, but a few recent comprehensive surveys and excavations in the Spokane River valley help to fill the information void. Before construction of the Centennial Trail in the late 1980s, archaeologists surveyed a near-continuous path along the Spokane River between the Washington-Idaho state line and the mouth of the Little Spokane River. That project expanded the number of recorded prehistoric and historic-period sites almost sixfold. Additionally, reservoir-inundated land was briefly exposed and surveyed as part of the process for relicensing the Spokane River hydroelectric dams. Piece by piece, each investigated site provided evidence of the intimate and sustaining relationship between Native peoples and the river.

Large-scale excavations funded by the City of Spokane, at the aptly named Spokane Site, provide the bulk of Spokane River archaeological information. Those excavations occurred near the confluence of Hangman Creek and the Spokane River. Eastern Washington University archaeologists did the excavating, with the assistance of the Spokane Tribe culture staff and under the interested watch of Spokane elders. The results provided a unique window onto human occupation of the Spokane River valley. The Spokane Site reflects the broad sweep of Columbia Plateau archaeology and the intimate relationship of Native people to the Spokane River. Excavations sampled periods of site use beginning 8,000 years ago and deposits dating throughout the last 3,500 years of prehistory. Was the site abandoned between those documented time periods? Probably not. More likely, the archaeological record for the intervening 4,500 years was not preserved in the relatively small site area investigated. Archaeological evidence of site use between 8,000 and 3,500 years ago likely exists in unexcavated site areas. The site holds much regional prehistory information, including the record for the longest continuous occupation of any Washington city.

## Subsistence and Sustainability

Spokane River basin archaeology reveals subsistence and residential patterns similar to the archaeological records in the better-documented Columbia and Snake River basins. Those similarities include an economy based on hunting, gathering, and fishing of seasonally available plant and animal resources; on residential life centered on major rivers and streams; and on ritual celebration of root crops and salmon. While a sustainable hunting-gathering-fishing economy is represented throughout Spokane prehistory, the archaeological record also documents significant technological and adaptive changes.

The earliest people in eastern Washington likely traveled in small groups or bands. They moved systematically across the land, foraging for a broad spectrum of animals and plants and using a deceptively simple but highly flexible (and necessarily portable) set of tools. For all of prehistory, dogs were the only beasts of burden until the arrival of the horse in the early 1700s, and thus the capacity to carry heavy loads overland was limited. Beginning around eight thousand years ago, subsistence activities appear to shift toward more locally available resources. People had settled in and begun exploring and exploiting plants and animals in specific environmental niches, such as river environments that contained a variety of aquatic species. Approximately five thousand years ago, Columbia Plateau Native people developed semisedentary habitation patterns, often overwintering as settlement clusters in pithouses along major rivers. A pithouse is dug partly underground and covered by a roof to provide shelter from extreme weather.

Prehistoric houses have yet to be excavated along the Spokane River, again not because they are absent but because site samples are sparse. The seemingly simple shift to winter sedentism required enormous changes to the people's lives. Not only did food have to be gathered in sufficient quantities in the spring, summer, and autumn to feed the community through the winter, but those foods also had to be processed for long-term storage. Evidence suggests that stores of dried salmon, meat, and starchy edible roots such as camas, lomatium (or biscuitroot), and bitterroot served as staples. As villages expanded in size and complexity, preservation and storage methods intensified and grew more efficient, eventually resulting in a surplus of storable foods. In time, stored foods became an important commodity in local and regional trade spheres.

## Oldest Evidence

Native peoples inhabited eastern Washington at least twelve thousand years ago. While sites of similar antiquity might yet be found in the Spokane River basin, nothing yet has been documented. Evidence of human occupation along the Spokane River extends back eight thousand years, which equates to more than 260 human generations. Spokane Site dates are the earliest archaeological radiocarbon ages yet obtained in the entire Spokane River drainage basin. At that time, the climate of the western United States was hotter and drier than at any other period since the last ice age. The earliest layers of the Spokane Site contain small, informal hearths that imply construction and use by small groups during brief site occupations. Butchered animal bones, debris from chipped stone-tool manufacturing, and the occasional tool were found around the hearths. In an area lacking abundant high-quality stone sources for tools, quartzite cobbles were favored. Such rocks, residues of Pleistocene Lake Missoula Floods, were abundant in streamside gravel bars.

Most stone and bone tools from the site are consistent with portable tool-kits and thus imply relatively mobile lifeways. They include Cascade-type dart points to kill game; knives to butcher and prepare carcasses; stone chisels, drills, and scrapers; and bone awls and needles. Chinook salmon and large mammals such as deer and wapiti were the favored foods. Recovered bones also indicate a broad array of other food species: marmot, rabbit, beaver, porcupine, muskrat, otter, bear, bird, turtle, and canids ranging from coyote to wolf size. Large-mammal long bones were broken to extract the fat-rich, nutritious marrow. Abundant salmon bones littered the ancient ground surface, but specialized fishing tools—likely wood spears, traps and weirs, and twine lines or nets—have not survived.

At the Spokane Site, these first people repeatedly camped on a riverside sand bar. Each season's campsite debris was covered by a protective layer of sand deposited by the next spring freshet. For archaeologists, that is a fortunate circumstance: the spring floodwater velocity was such that the sands buried the campsite and perfectly preserved that season's artifacts. Evidence of four campsite occupations was buried in that manner. Such deposits create a layer cake, a textbook example of a stratigraphic sequence of spring flood sands. One layer lacking artifacts is capped by a layer of campsite artifacts, which in turn were buried by another layer of culturally sterile flood sands. Radiocarbon ages of campfire charcoal from the layers are statistically the same, indicating occupation over a few seasons eight thousand years ago, not centuries. Over subsequent millennia, the accumulation of sediment slowed. By 2,500 years ago the river channel had cut deeply into the ancient floodplain, and floodwaters no longer inundated the site.

## Middle and Late Prehistoric Times

Subsequent Spokane Site periods of occupation documented through excavation fall into the late Middle and Late archaeological time periods. The second and major period of investigated Spokane Site occupation began some 3,500 years ago. After the preceding hot and dry climatic period had ended, modern climatic conditions prevailed. Although modern vegetation communities may not have been established for another thousand years, forests fostered by a cooler and moister climate would have replaced sagebrush steppe in the Middle Spokane River valley. In contrast to the small individual hearths of the earliest occupations, the Middle and Late layers of campsite debris are marked by expansive scatters of fire-cracked rock and charcoal-stained sediments, indicating the presence of larger aggregations of people and more intensive plant and animal processing.

Despite evidence of greater artifact diversity and debris, indicating more-intensive site use, such occupations appear to represent not villages but rather warm-season fishing and hunting camps. Individual hearths discernible in the broad and unpatterned scatters of fire-cracked rock were small and informal. Surrounding tools and animal bones indicate a variety of daily activities. The people fished, hunted, manufactured, and maintained tools. Their foods included mammals, fish, turtle, and river mussels, and the remains of these foods provide more clues about habitation patterns.

Around this time, the people began to cook larger quantities of mussels in pits. River mussels contain the highest concentrations of calcium and iron of any local plant or animal foods. Those two minerals, necessary elements in human diets, are especially important to pregnant and lactating women. Western painted turtle remnants suggest warm-season occupation; such turtles hibernate from October to March and are unavailable for late fall and winter harvest.

Again, gravel bar quartzite cobbles were used to manufacture pounding and chopping tools, fishing-net weights, and flake tools for cutting and scraping. Specialized tools such as knives, drills, perforators, scrapers, gravers, and abraders suggest a range of activities. A ground adze blade made of nephrite (jade) documents sophisticated woodworking. As is the case throughout the site record, hunting and fishing were important economic activities. Deer and wapiti were hunted with atlatl darts until about two thousand years ago, after which the bow and arrow became the primary weapon.

Traps and snares likely would have been used to capture smaller animals—such as marmot, rabbit, beaver, muskrat, otter, bird, and turtle—although no archaeological evidence of these techniques has survived.

Fish bones include both chinook salmon and resident suckers, a pairing that could reflect changing seasonal availability. Suckers congregate for spawning in late spring, and major runs of chinook arrive in July or August. The increasing emphasis on salmon acquisition is clear from the archaeological record. Occupation surfaces are littered with notched fish net weights that indicate mass-harvest salmon netting. Although it is an efficient method for catching large numbers of salmon in deeper water, net fishing is undoubtedly overrepresented as a fishing method in the archaeological record because of the durability of stone net weights. In other words, implements of wood, bone, antler, and plant fibers—such as clubs, spears, hooks and lines, gorges, harpoons, dip nets, traps, and weirs—quickly deteriorate and therefore are rare or completely absent in open archaeological sites, despite being well referenced in Columbia Plateau ethnographies.

Net fishing suggests formalized efficiency and increasing social complexity among the people, because it is necessarily communal: it requires many hands to construct, set, work, and repair the nets. And when large numbers of salmon are caught in a short period in seasonal runs, still other hands must quickly gut and fillet the fish and hang the processed slabs on racks to dry before they spoil.

A variety of ethnographically documented ritual ceremonies and honorary positions, such as the Salmon Chief, accompanied formalized efficiency in this time period and survive in oral tradition. Fragments of what appears to be a stone club recovered from the middle Spokane Site occupation period might have had a ceremonial or ritual function. This ground and incised stone object, while incomplete, resembles paddle-shaped ceremonial clubs found in Columbia River sites and other Columbia Plateau locales. Such objects are sometimes referred to as salmon clubs, but the ornamentation and very evident effort of construction, as well as the prohibitively heavy weight of the clubs, point to a ritual rather than strictly utilitarian function. During the ethnographic period, clubs used by Spokan bands to stun or kill trapped fish were instead made of wood, very often pieces of driftwood expediently gathered onsite.

There is limited evidence of plant processing at the Spokane Site, but perishable vegetal materials would have been a crucial part of camp life, both for food and for tool construction. Cordage and string would have been used for fishing nets and lines, tule mats, lashing of structural supports, twining bags, and other residential, storage, and transport needs. (Tule, a bulrush growing in abundance in local sloughs, springs, and ponds, was used to make mats to cover winter log houses and summer tepees.) Various edge-ground stone flakes evince fiber preparation, the edges deliberately blunted to remove pulp and to soften but not cut the desired fibers. Pestles and hopper mortar bases, while limited in number, indicate the processing of roots and berries as foods. More remarkable, perhaps, is the presence of distinctly nonportable artifacts in a seasonal camp. Those items suggest that this site was repeatedly if not continuously occupied. Items constructed of valuable materials and requiring considerable labor investment might have been cached at this favored place for use during future visits.

## Recreation

Recreational activities played a large role in the most recent site occupation. Among the fishing camp debris were a number of decoratively incised bone gaming pieces, including one matched pair. Those specimens are strikingly similar to ethnographic examples of gaming pieces used in a dice game popular throughout the Columbia Plateau and Northwest Coast culture areas. The bone dice were typically blank on one side and marked on the other (the face), creating two opposing matched pairs. Common designs included dots paired with transverse lines or dots with a double zigzag pattern. Pigments were often rubbed into the incised decoration. In some accounts, one of the four dice was specially marked (wrapped around the middle by sinew or thread) and designated the "man," while the other three dice were the "women." The four dice were thrown onto a blanket or the ground, and the various permutations (such as specific designs face up or face down, the "man" face up or down) were assigned different scores.

The dice game and other "sitting" games were commonly played by small groups during long winter evenings and were popular at fish camps where bands from different locations came together and formed rival teams (by one ethnographer's account) for "every possible form of competition." During the ethnographic period, dice games were typically, and in some groups strictly, women's games, in contrast to male-associated guessing games such as *lahal*, the so-called hand game or stick game. Archaeologists must be cautious not to blithely project the rules of a game or gender roles 1,500 years into the past, but these small pieces of fire-hardened and decorated bone offer intriguing glimpses of social life into settlements that date well into prehistory.

## Trade

Obsidian and nephrite artifacts demonstrate that local populations could obtain resources from distant areas through networks of trade. Geochemical fingerprinting of obsidian artifacts and source materials allows researchers to correlate and identify artifact origins. Almost all the high-quality obsidian found in eastern Washington sites comes from sources in eastern Oregon, but some examples come from southern Idaho and even from Yellowstone National Park's Obsidian Cliff. The obsidian trade from sources so remote from eastern Washington is evident from the earliest prehistoric time at the Spokane Site. One obsidian graver, found in eight-thousand-year-old deposits, originated at Indian Creek Buttes, three hundred miles south of Spokane. (A graver or burin is an incising tool made by chipping or pressure flaking stone on two edges in order to leave a sharp point.) Spokane-area obsidians dating from Middle and Late prehistoric times come from northeastern Oregon, southern Idaho, and Obsidian Cliff in Wyoming.

Obsidian trade and use occurs throughout prehistory, but late prehistoric use in Spokane Basin sites ranges from two to eighteen times the average of other samples documented at Columbia and Snake River region sites. The Spokane Site nephrite adze blade indicates trade links to the Fraser River valley in British Columbia, a nephrite source more than two hundred miles northwest of Spokane. Local resources furnished daily food and shelter requirements, while extensive trade networks provided access to exotic materials.

## A Perpetual Resource

Scientifically excavated archaeological collections retain importance long after being analyzed and reported. Collections provide materials for public education, museum exhibition, and research. People visit museums to see informative exhibits and to become excited by what they learn. Students and professionals access collections for scholarly research. Archaeological analyses are never exhaustive: new ideas, approaches, and technologies make additional study possible and are vital to creating new knowledge.

Archaeological collections are particularly useful because the materials have been very carefully recovered. Artifact and feature contexts are documented and their ages confirmed. Archaeological animal bone collections provide information about ancient distributions of animals in an ever-changing local and regional landscape. Research on archaeological site collections demonstrates the presence of species in places and under climatic conditions that often vary greatly from today's. For example, biologists for many years debated whether wapiti were present in the dry environs of prehistoric eastern Washington. Confirmation of their presence through archaeological finds aids elk-management efforts today.

Likewise, in 2015 a Washington State University doctoral student in biology sequenced DNA from Spokane Site salmon bone, using research techniques that did not exist when the site was excavated in 2005. That student's research objectives included not only methods of determining salmon species but also salmon DNA lineage characterization. The research provided an understanding of Spokane River salmon variations in the larger context of salmon stocks of the Columbia River basin. The DNA sequenced from forty-five salmon bones, ranging from 2,500 to 8,000 years in age, proves to be chinook and derives from six different genetic lineages. By identifying the existing salmon lineages that most closely resemble the now-extinct Spokane River chinook lineages, biologists can identify the best candidates for salmon restoration to the river. Such a goal will require cooperation not only between archaeologists and fish biologists but also between tribal representatives and the general public.

## A Sense of Place

Before dams were built along its course, the Spokane River possessed the highest gradient of any major tributary of the Columbia River. This singular fact unquestionably affected the ways in which different generations of Native peoples used and settled the environment. The gradient of the untamed river must also have generated dramatic noise at the many falls and rapids along its course. The roar of the river in prehistory cannot be replicated through archaeological research, but it was certainly significant to those who fished it and settled along its shores. Indeed, the river's current remains one of the most common and consistent details of recollections by Native elders.

*Place* in an archaeological context has a special meaning. It demands a thorough examination and knowledge of landscapes and landscape interactions, especially those that involve the people whose adaptations influenced and altered the landscapes. For this reason, the future of archaeological research in the Spokane River valley holds tremendous potential, not only for archaeology but also for the establishment of an enduring partnership between all constituencies—tribes, the archaeological community, and the lay public. All those communities might share the common goal of someday hearing the river roar again.

# First Post

*Spokane House, 1810–1825*

JACK NISBET

## Jaco's House

EARLY OCTOBER 1809 FOUND THE NORTH WEST COMPANY FUR AGENT
and surveyor David Thompson exploring the Pend Oreille River and visiting a small Kalispel village near present-day Cusick. On October 5, he
noted in his journal: "At 11 a.m. 4 men arrived; they made me a present of
a Horse & a few [musk] rats—they smoked a few Inches of Tobacco, all I
had left; they seem to be of the Spokane tribe." This encounter obviously
made a lasting impression on Thompson, for six months later he dispatched
his clerk, Jaco Finlay, to build a new trade house in the homeland of the
Spokane people.

Jacques Raphael Finlay, born in eastern Canada of Scottish and Cree
parentage, had honed his skills as a guide and interpreter in the Canadian
prairies. He scouted the trail for Thompson's 1807 thrust across the Rockies
and established new trade relationships with tribes west of the mountains.
Having received his orders in the spring of 1810, he made his way to a Spokane village at the junction of the Spokane and Little Spokane Rivers.

## The Gathering Place

The confluence of the two rivers is a rich place, cut by streams and full
of birdsong. The ice age floods left behind gravels graded into a perfect
size for salmon and steelhead redds, and here the Middle Spokane people

established fisheries that became an important meeting place for neighboring Salish, Sahaptin, and Kootenai bands. The Spokane elder Alex Sherwood explained that the lure of the place stemmed from abundant fish runs: steelhead on the Little Spokane and salmon on the main river.

The tribal name for the Little Spokane River is nxweme'a'tkxy, meaning "river where the steelhead trout run." Early white visitors often called steelhead "salmon trout" because they exhibit traits of both species, and the Middle Spokane people who lived on this part of the river were known as "the salmon trout people."

The fur traders who arrived at the site described a landscape of large, orange-barked, widely spaced ponderosa pine. It was a habitat managed by set fires: mentions of smoke along the river are common in early written accounts of the area. The vigorous, clear understory that emerged after these low-running blazes bristled with edible berries and several species of nutritious bunchgrass, an excellent source of fodder for horses. A horse and rider could canter easily through such an open forest, with good views all around. Finlay would have been less interested in the site's view than in its fisheries, its timber supply, and its proximity to the Spokane village and trade center. The trading post that he and his crew dubbed Spokane House probably mirrored the post-on-sill structures typical of the North West Company. Good relations with the local tribes rendered a stockade unnecessary.

The Spokane elder Louie Wildshoe recalled that his mother-in-law was a little girl when Finlay and his French-Canadian crew arrived. She said these first white people were called *seme*, the Spokane term for "wonder." They cut round wheels out of big logs and built wagons; they dug a garden and planted potatoes. Other novelties included trade goods such as axes, calico cloth, guns, and flints and steels for starting fires.

## Three Companies

Spokane House entered written history on June 14, 1811, when David Thompson arrived with a fresh supply of trade goods, noting: "Thank Heaven for our good safe journey; here we found Jaco &c with ab[ou]t 40

Spokane families." Thompson spent three days at the post, during which he found time to calculate its latitude and longitude. He then rode north to Kettle Falls, where he built a canoe to speed him on an exploratory tour down the Columbia to the Pacific. When he returned in August, he brought news that the North West Company's monopoly on the fur trade west of the Continental Divide was coming to an end: five months earlier, members of the Pacific Fur Company, founded by the New York City entrepreneur John Jacob Astor, had arrived at the mouth of the Columbia and erected a post they called Fort Astoria.

Thompson also brought a Hawaiian Islander called Coxe, whom the Astorians had hired during a stopover at Honolulu. While visiting with the Pacific Fur Company partners on the lower Columbia, Thompson had arranged to exchange one of his aging voyageurs for the "powerful well made Sandwich Islander," whom he regarded as "a prodigy of wit and humor." In Canada, a voyageur was an expert woodsman, boatman, and guide to remote regions who was employed by fur companies to transport supplies. When Thompson departed for his post on the Flathead River in western Montana, he left his new crew member under the tutelage of Jaco Finlay for the winter. Here Coxe experienced his first snowfall, and his Polynesian tongue joined the English, French-Canadian, Scottish Gaelic, Iroquois, Salish, Kootenai, Sahaptin, and other languages spoken at Spokane House.

In spring 1812, David Thompson made his last stop at Spokane House before crossing the Rockies on his way to eastern Canada. He used his astronomical observational skills to render the first accurate map of the Columbia drainage. A series of dotted lines radiate from Spokane House, representing the network of tribal trails that led from the Spokane confluence north and west to the Columbia, south to the Snake River, and east to the ancient Road to the Buffalo, across the Rockies to the Montana plains.

A few months after Thompson's departure, a contingent of the Astorians whom he had met at the mouth of the Columbia arrived at Spokane House, intent on building a post to compete with the Nor'westers. Their agent, John Clarke, was accompanied by four clerks, twenty-one voyageurs, and four Hawaiians. Among them was the Irish clerk Ross Cox, then nineteen years old, who wrote in his memoir *Adventures on the Columbia River*: "The spot selected for forming our establishment was a handsome point of land . . . thinly covered with pine and other trees, and close to a trading post of the North-West Company." The compound that Clarke constructed within sight of Jaco Finlay's post included a dormitory for the clerks, a trading store and warehouse for furs, and a "gentlemen's house" for the chief trader, with four rooms and a kitchen. Although the Nor'westers had never felt any threat from the Spokanes, Clarke erected a pole stockade around his "Spokane Fort."

Cox noted that the "N[orth] W[est] Com. has had an establishment for trade here for some years, & did not much like the idea of our opposing them." Another clerk referred to "the sly and underhanded dealings of the competing parties," but on one issue the rivals agreed: "to abstain from giving the Indians any spiritous liquors, to which both parties strictly adhered." By fall 1812, Clarke's traders had gathered half a ton of furs, a promising beginning. But around Thanksgiving word arrived that war had broken out between the United States and Great Britain. A cloud of uncertainty descended over the Astorian enterprise, for it was clear that a single Royal Navy frigate could easily capture the company's small fort at the mouth of the Columbia. After several rounds of negotiations, the North West Company purchased the entire inventory of Pacific Fur in October 1813.

For the next decade, Spokane House served as the headquarters for outposts in western Montana, northern Idaho, and southern British Columbia. Fort George (formerly Fort Astoria, established 1811), Fort Okanagan (established 1811), and Fort Nez Perce (also known as Fort Walla Walla, established 1818) completed the company's Columbia District.

One of the articles of the agreement in the purchase of the Pacific Fur Company specified that the North West Company would hire any Astorians who wished to remain. Ross Cox took advantage of this offer, and his memoir provides most of what we know about Spokane House between 1813 and 1822. He recorded the arrival of the first chickens, hogs, and goats at the post, backgammon games between the clerks, and the bear cub that one of the voyageurs taught to dance. He accompanied the annual treks to Fort George to deliver fur packs and pick up trade goods shipped from England.

During his time at the post, he made the acquaintance of Illeum-Spokanee, the headman of the Middle Spokane band. He watched the pervasive gaming among the Native peoples, observed the horse trading between the Spokanes and the Nez Perces, and enthusiastically joined in tribal horse races. He recorded the food supplied by the Spokane people around the post and venison brought in by Coeur d'Alene hunters. He remarked that the Spokanes would never eat horses but willingly traded them to the fur traders, who used them not only for transport but also for food when fish and game ran short.

In summer 1821, the North West Company merged with its longtime rival, the Hudson's Bay Company (HBC). At first, Spokane House saw few changes beyond a new flag and a new chief trader. The post journal for the outfit of 1822–23, kept by the veteran agent Finan McDonald and a young clerk named James Birnie, provides a detailed look at the routines of daily life at the trade house. Tribal parties came in to trade horses and furs from across the region. Relationships with the tribes remained amicable, and the gates to the stockade were shut on only a single night during the entire year. The Native wives of the traders tended potatoes, turnips, and melons in a large garden, while the Spokane people disappeared in the spring to gather edible roots in the plains. Workers remodeled the post, building a new trade store, enlarging the stockade, and adding a gallery and bastion.

Chief Factor Alexander Kennedy's 1823 annual report described the geography, extent of tribal territories, game, weather, and future possibilities for Spokane House. His account included many valuable details of tribal life, including a description of the weirs or fish traps that the tribes constructed and tended during the most important fish runs: trout and steelhead, chinook and silver salmon. Combined with the counts of captured fish from the journal, his account provides a snapshot of one of the key aspects of tribal life before the Little Falls Dam blocked the salmon runs in 1910.

### Demise

In October 1824, the Hudson's Bay Company governor, George Simpson, stopped at Spokane House during a tour of his new domain. He was impressed with its setting and its prospects for self-sufficiency, but he was critical of the amount of provisions being imported from England. Known for his keen eye for the bottom line, Simpson declared that the denizens of the Interior "had better Hoard the European provisions and Luxuries they have got now in Store, as their future supplies will be very scanty."

By the following spring, Simpson had decided to move the HBC operations from Spokane House to a new post at Kettle Falls, to be called Fort Colvile. The move would eliminate the costly horse brigades to the mouth of the Spokane by placing this key post directly on the Columbia, and company trade houses in the Kootenai and Flathead regions could be just as easily supplied. The only difficulty that Simpson saw in abandoning Spokane House was that "it may give offence to the Spokan Indians who have always been staunch to the Whites."

During a conference with a group of chiefs who had come to meet him, Simpson promised to look into the possibility of sending Christian missionaries to the area. He baptized two young boys, "the Sons of the principal Spokan and Coutanais [Kootenai] War Chiefs, men of great Weight and consequence in this part of the Country; they are named Coutonais Pelly and Spokane Garry." Pelly and Garry, named for two governors of the Hudson's Bay Company, accompanied Simpson's brigade east to attend the missionary school at the Red River Colony in Manitoba.

Agent John Work spent the next year overseeing the construction of the new Fort Colvile. In March 1826, he reported on the move from the old Spokane post: "The blacksmith & cook, the only two men we have now here, employed collecting all the iron about the place, stripping hinges off door &c. The Indians much regret our going off." When the naturalist David Douglas visited the abandoned post two months later, he found Jaco Finlay and his family still in residence. Soon after moving to the area in 1810, Jaco had married Teshwintichina, a Spokane woman. Their daughter Josephte arrived in 1812, followed by several other children. Between 1826 and 1828, the Finlay family greeted and fed numerous visitors to the outpost.

Jaco Finlay passed away in 1828, at the age of sixty. John Work heard the news while gumming a canoe on the way down the Columbia River.

According to lore passed down among the fur traders, Finlay was buried beneath one of the bastions, in accordance with his wishes. The American businessman Nathaniel Wyeth passed the site in 1835 and recorded in his journal that he found "the remains of old Spokan House one Bastion of which only is now standing which is left by the Indians from respect to the dead one clerk of the Co. being buried in it."

Over a century later, in the fall of 1951, the archaeologist Louis Caywood was directing excavations on the grounds of the old Spokane House when he noticed one of his assistants "dancing an archaeological jig." According to the newspaper account of the find, the young man had just uncovered a grave site that held a skeleton, a comb, a drinking cup, a hunting knife, the nose piece of a pair of spectacles, and five tobacco pipes. When examination of one clay pipe revealed the faint initials "JF" scratched into the bowl, Caywood concluded that the grave was that of Jaco Finlay, resting beneath a corner of the trading post he had founded. The rich confluence of two rivers that lured people for thousands of years still swirls around that bastion.

# Aboriginal and Historic Sport Fisheries

ALLAN T. SCHOLZ

THE SPOKANE RIVER DISPLAYS THE QUIRKY TEMPERAMENT TYPICAL of Western rivers. It dithers across gravel riffles in places, appearing to levitate above its banks and defy gravity by flowing uphill, resembling a woodcut by M. C. Escher. Unlike most rivers of the region, however, the Spokane River is recharged not by surface runoff but by the underground water source to which it is inextricably linked.

The population of salmonid fishes in the Spokane River was likely related to the abundance of food organisms the river produced. In 1894, in the first fish survey of the Spokane River prepared for the US Bureau of Fisheries, Charles H. Gilbert and Barton W. Evermann observed that it was "clear, cold and pure, . . . An abundance of fish food such as insects and their larvae, small mollusks, and crayfish was noticed in this river." The large numbers of both salmon and the organisms the fish fed on depended on connections to the aquifer.

At certain points along the river, called gaining reaches, the water table is higher than the riverbed. Here cold aquifer water seeps into the river. It furnished sufficient discharge and the cool temperatures necessary to maintain both the salmon and their food organisms during low summer flows. During the winter, aquifer water keeps the river from freezing because it is warmer than surface water, thus extending the growing seasons for insects and fish.

At other points, called losing reaches, the water table is below the riverbed. River water seeps down into the aquifer. Such disparities stabilize flows during periods of high discharge because water sinks into the ground rather than causing flooding. This protection from devastating floods prevented the disruption of key habitats for both salmon and their prey. Thus, the Spokane River seldom suffered from stochastic events—that is, unpredictable events due to random variables—that affected many other salmon-producing streams in the Columbia River basin.

## Aboriginal Fisheries

Among the Plateau Indians, the Spokane was a famous salmon river. In sign language, Robert H. Ruby and John Arthur Brown reported, one could identify Spokane Indians by their imitation of a salmon in the act of spawning and then being consumed. The North West Company fur trader Alexander Henry noted in 1809, "The Spokan dwell along the Spokan River . . . noted for its salmon fisheries. [They] seldom leave their own country, [live] upon the produce of their own lands and upon vast quantities of fat, well flavored salmon, which they take in their river . . . where salmon enough could be procured for any number of people." The Spokane River produced some of the largest chinook salmon (*Oncorhynchus tshawytscha*) in the Columbia Basin, many exceeding forty pounds. Both the large numbers and large size of chinook might explain why Indians from several nations annually came to the Spokane River as part of their subsistence round.

Spokane could mean either "children of the sun" or "great fish place." (See also the chapter by Barry Moses in this volume.) The historian William T. Youngs reconciled these views by pointing out in 1996 that the tribe's name might be better interpreted as "children of the rainbow (refracted light)," a name that would better reflect their relationship to the river. "For untold generations the Spokane Indians were beguiled by the falls. . . . The central feature in the Spokane region was the falls and the Indians' paramount experience was standing at the base of the falls amid the water and the salmon. In the river . . . the Spokanes were touched by the refracted light of the sun radiating through the spray of their falls."

It is a romantic as well as historically accurate notion to imagine that the Spokane River, with its numerous falls and turbulent rapids, was a river of rainbows, illuminated by light refracted through perpetual mist cast up by its falls or through spray from wind gusting through its innumerable rapids. Today the river is dammed, its flow regulated, and a portion of its discharge used for irrigation. We have traded the rainbows produced by its agitated waters for rainbows produced by center-pivot irrigation systems that draw water from the reservoirs and pump it up onto agricultural lands on the benches above the river. There they appear in outrageous contradiction to the dust devils that swirl through farm fields.

The five major fisheries along the Spokane River, where various bands of Indians fished communally to procure their annual supply of salmon, included Detillion, Little Falls, Tum Tum, Little Spokane, and Spokane Falls. Indians also harvested anadromous fish at twenty-two other sites in the Spokane drainage. The Spokane therefore provided the principal subsistence for a large number of the region's Indians. At each of the five major fishing stations, Spokane salmon chiefs directed the construction of apparatus used for communal fishing. According to the anthropologist John Ross, they also directed the escapement of fish, the daily harvest, and the daily distribution of fish to each family present at the fishery. The historical notes below provide details about each station. RM means river mile: for the Spokane River, this is measured upstream from the confluence with the Columbia River.

DETILLION (RM 7.2)

The naturalist David Douglas first described this fishery on August 20, 1826. He recorded a Lower Spokane village a short distance above the mouth of the Spokane River, where Indians were busy harvesting salmon from their weir on that date. In 1870 the Indian agent William Winans observed a large salmon weir at Detillion and noted that it was the most important of all the Indian fisheries on the Spokane. He also reported that in addition to the many Spokane and Sanpoil Indians, Columbia/Yakama and Palouse Indians also frequented the site. All these peoples fished there for salmon that would last them through the winter.

The US Army constructed Fort Spokane at the confluence of the Spokane and Columbia Rivers in 1880 because of its strategic proximity to the largest salmon fishery on the Spokane River. There, Lieut. Col. H. C. Merriam noted, "hundreds of Indians annually congregate from all directions. All the great Indian trails center on this point."

## LITTLE FALLS (RM 28.5)

The Lower and Upper Spokane, Sanpoil/Colville, Columbia, Yakama/Palouse, and Kalispel Indians sometimes came together at the Little Falls fishery under the control of a Middle Spokane salmon chief. On July 25, 1825, the Hudson's Bay Company fur trader John Work reported that the Indians at Little Falls were "catching 700 or 800 salmon daily."

Cushing Eells and Elkanah Walker, Presbyterian missionaries, lived among the Spokane from 1839 to 1848 at Tshimikain Mission, ten miles north of Little Falls. Their diaries recorded the numbers of salmon caught and methods of catching them, the most efficient ways to capture them, and the duration of the run at Little Falls. The two missionaries kept meticulous records because they traveled to Little Falls each weekend to teach and minister: the Indians were too busy harvesting their winter's supply of salmon to go to the mission. While men and boys fished south of Tshimikain Creek (Chamokane today), women and girls harvested camas and baked the roots in earth ovens about ten miles north of the mission, "and daily horses passed between the two places, loaded both ways, so that all could share both kinds of food." Each weekend one of the ministers traveled south to the fishing grounds, and the other north to the camas grounds. Salmon runs began in mid-June and ended in mid-August. Some one thousand Indians gathered there annually. The daily harvest consisted of four hundred to eight hundred fish, occasionally as many as one thousand. Many salmon escaped through this fishery to continue their upstream migration. Eells remarked that the Spokane Indians so much preferred fish and native roots to farming that they would not soon be induced give up their nomadic subsistence round and take up an agrarian lifestyle. Indeed, Eells lived to see his prediction borne out in 1875: "Their mode of living was much as it had been 35 years previous, for they lived upon fish, roots, and berries, with some wheat and garden produce, and consequently were continually migrating as of old." His partner, Walker, described Indians fishing at Little Falls: "It is not uncommon for many [salmon] to pass the [weirs] and these [were] taken [after] they laid their eggs."

Others corroborated the descriptions by Walker and Eells. Lieut. Robert Johnson, a member of the United States Exploring Expedition, traveled along the Lower Spokane River in June 1841 and wrote, "The river is pretty, its waters transparent. . . . To judge from the number of sheds [the Indians employed] for drying salmon it must abound with that fish." In 1869, the cadastral surveyor L. P. Beach recorded in his field notebook that the Spokane Indians "put up at least 250 tons of dried salmon during the fishing season" at Little Falls.

## TUM TUM (RM 44.7)

The British naturalist David Douglas visited the Tum Tum fishery on August 4, 1826. That morning he left Spokane House, at RM 56.3, and rode downriver for one hour to the vicinity of Tum Tum, where he passed a village of Spokane Indians engaged in salmon fishing. He observed that the Indians took 1,700 salmon and steelhead (that is, anadromous Columbia River redband trout, *Oncorhynchus mykiss* var. *gairdnerii*) by 2 p.m. one day out of a weir they had constructed in the Spokane River and noted, "1500 and sometimes 2000 [salmon] were taken in the course of a day [at this site]."

## LITTLE SPOKANE (RM 56.3)

The Middle and Upper Spokane peoples and various bands of Coeur d'Alene Indians made extensive use of this fishery at the confluence of the Spokane and Little Spokane Rivers. As many as 350 Indian tents were counted in the vicinity at one time. The Kalispel, Colville, and Columbia Indians occasionally camped and caught salmon here. The Nez Perce were frequent visitors, coming to trade horses for salmon and other goods supplied by the Spokane Indians. The Little Spokane was known for steelhead and the Spokane for chinook salmon.

George Heron, deputy sheriff of Stevens County, was a frequent visitor in most years between 1844 and 1892. He stated:

Wild Columbia River redband trout (*Oncorhynchus mykiss* var. *gairdnerii*) caught in 1997 in the Spokane River Arm of Franklin D. Roosevelt Lake, the reservoir behind the Grand Coulee Dam. Photo courtesy of Allan T. Scholz.

> The flat between the two rivers was a great meeting place for the Indians. . . . During the summer there were from a hundred to a thousand Indians camped [there] catching and drying salmon. . . . Weirs were comprised of two fences across the river. The upper one was tight but the lower one had frequent small gates made by lashing sticks to the upper horizontal pole and leaving them loose on the bottom, so the fish could push into the enclosure going upstream but the current could close the gate after them. The fish came into the traps in countless thousands and were speared by the Indians.

Capt. Charles Wilson, who surveyed the boundary between Washington and British Columbia from 1858 to 1862, recounted: "At the junction of the Great and Little Spokane Rivers, an elaborate contrivance [was] made for catching salmon." He described V-shaped runs of stones that funneled salmon downstream and onto a landing platform where they were "speedily dispatched by attendant Indians."

The United States Fish Commission biologist L. Stone reported that forty to fifty thousand salmon and steelhead were seen in 1882 on drying racks at the Indian encampment on the Little Spokane, but in 1883 the Indian catch was only about two thousand fish. He attributed this decline to the commercial fishery for salmon downstream from Celilo Falls.

## SPOKANE FALLS

Upper and Middle Spokane and Coeur d'Alene Indians exploited the Spokane Falls fishery intensively. Lieutenant Grover of the US Army described Spokane Falls in late February 1854: "Just below the falls, where a bar divided the channel, the Indians had constructed wing walls of loose rocks across one arm, leaving a race between their extremities, in which, by means of nets, they caught [steelhead trout]. . . . A long trestle work was also built on the bank upon which their captives were laid to dry."

Chinook and coho (*Oncorhynchus kisutch*) salmon were harvested here in summer and autumn. Indians harpooned or dip-netted salmon from rocks or scaffold platforms or caught them in J-shaped basket traps at the base of the falls. In 1857, A. J. Miner noted, "I saw 300 Indians drying fish in the sun in the woods where [Spokane] city hall now stands. This was a great fishing place for the Indians in those days. [They] took fish in dip nets and after the women cleaned them, they would dry them in the sun." Spokane Falls was a migration barrier for salmon and steelhead: it forced them to turn back downstream. The Indians built elaborate traps near the mouth of Hangman Creek to corral thousands of those diverted fish. James Glover, the founder of Spokane, wrote in his memoirs: "The first fall I was here, in 1873, and for several years after that, Spokane was the great rendezvous for all the Indians in this part of the country. . . . At that time the salmon used to come up in great numbers. I have seen them so thick in the river that the rocks on the bottom would not be visible. . . . The Indians took the fish out of a [weir set in] shoal [water near] the mouth of Hangman Creek. . . . They [built] high scaffolds of willow limbs for drying fish."

A second weir was placed across the mouth of Hangman Creek to trap fish attempting to migrate up it. We know for certain that chinook salmon ascended Hangman Creek to near its headwaters in Idaho because US Army Capt. Charles Bendire, a naturalist trained at the United States National Museum (Smithsonian Institution), collected one there in 1882. He sent it to the museum, where it still resides in the collection.

The cadastral surveyor Claire Hunt surveyed Hangman Creek in 1876 and described the weir at the mouth:

> The trap consisted of two barriers across the stream about 100 yards apart. Each barrier was made in panels, at ends of which were supported by large tripods set in the water and resting on the river bed. The panels were made of two parallel and horizontal poles about 30 inches apart. Woven willow mats attached to the poles on the downstream side made a continuous fence across the river. The mats extended down to the bed of the river. They were woven in an open pattern to permit the flow of water and yet closely enough to prevent the salmon passing through. The lower barrier had a large opening in the center to allow the salmon to enter. The upper barrier had no opening. . . . When the fish were to be taken out, the opening in the lower barrier was closed . . . with a mat . . . to prevent the escape of salmon. Men went into the cold water naked except for loin coverings. With their hands they caught the fish and threw them out rapidly on the grassy bank.

## Aboriginal Consumption of Salmon and Total Run Size

Estimates vary, but all commentators agree that the consumption of salmon along the river was very high. G. A. Paige, the Indian agent at Fort Colville, Washington Territory, wrote on September 19, 1866: "The Spokane draw at least 5/8ths of their subsistence from the salmon fisheries of the Columbia and Spokane Rivers and their tributaries." In 1870, Paige's successor, C. W.

King, reported that while many Indians in his district "had taken up farming yet $4/5$ths of their support is derived from their salmon fisheries." Because these Indian agents did not account for the importance of camas and other root crops, they might have overestimated the importance of salmon in the subsistence diet. But I believe that some 50 percent of the calories in the Native diet came from salmon. In 1947, the anthropologist Gordon Hewes computed a base consumption per capita of 365 pounds per year for Plateau Indians, then used ethnographic information about the relative importance of salmon to each tribe as a weighting factor to adjust this number up or down from the average value. By this method, Hewes estimated the Spokane and Sanpoil consumption to be five hundred pounds of salmon annually and the Coeur d'Alene consumption three hundred pounds annually.

In 1985 Randall Schalk noted that Hewes had failed to account for two factors in making his calculations: the portions of fish not eaten and the fact that salmon don't eat after entering the river and therefore must burn a portion of the energy stored in their muscles and fat for locomotion as they migrate upstream. The further the distance upriver, the more calories lost. Thus Indians living further upriver would have to eat more pounds of fish than Indians living downriver to gain equivalent caloric intake. By the time a fish reached the Spokane River, its flesh would contain only about 660 calories per pound. Estimates of minimum numbers of salmon harvested were 1,139,468 pounds of chinook (61,593 individual chinook), 687,610 pounds of steelhead (94,193 individual steelhead), and 137,522 pounds of coho (15,452 individual coho).

Assuming that Indians harvested 85 percent of each species, the total run size would be 72,680 chinook, 111,148 steelhead, and 18,233 coho, with 11,087 chinook, 16,955 steelhead, and 2,781 coho escaping the Indian fisheries to spawn in the river and tributaries. Further assuming that half the fish escaping to spawn were females that contained three thousand eggs each, and that only 1 percent of the offspring survived until adulthood, this number of spawning fish could potentially produce 166,305 chinook, 254,326 steelhead, and 43,065 coho in the next generation, more than enough to replace the total run size of each species.

These estimates are conservative for several reasons. First, they are based on a maintenance diet of two thousand calories, whereas nomadic Indians almost certainly burned more calories per day in their subsistence quest. Second, these estimates don't account for the quantity of fish consumed by other tribes who came to the Spokane River to fish, which I am unable to estimate. Third, these estimates account only for salmon actually consumed and not for the number taken for barter or trade.

Adding up the daily catches tallied by historical observers at just three of the five major fisheries suggests that on a good day, at least 3,093 to 3,292 fish could be harvested from the Spokane River, whereas dividing the total number of fish harvested as calculated above yields an average of 2,854 fish per day for the sixty-day peak of the fishing season. The number of salmon harvested daily from the Spokane River therefore probably exceeded the number harvested at more celebrated fisheries like Celilo Falls and Kettle Falls, where we estimate a respective 2,000–3,000 and 1,000–2,000 salmon were harvested daily.

## Destination Sport Fishery

In 1884, weirs at the junction of the Little Spokane and Spokane Rivers were torn out by the Colville Indian Agency in an effort to force the Spokane Indians, who still resided there, to move onto the Spokane Indian Reservation, which was created by executive order in 1881. After this relocation, the Spokane River became a destination sport fishery for anadromous salmon, steelhead, and resident trout. James Glover stated in his reminiscences in the *Spokane Daily Chronicle:* "In those days [1873, we] caught all the fish [we] wanted in [the Spokane River] and for many years we almost lived on the trout we caught." In August 1877, Gen. W. T. Sherman toured the Pacific Northwest. While encamped on Lake Coeur d'Alene, he sent Lieut. W. R. Abercrombie ahead to reconnoiter Spokane Falls. Abercrombie proceeded to the falls and purchased tackle from Glover's store. Then he and a friend fished in downtown Spokane in 1927, where, he recalled, "We caught 400 or 500 fish, salmon trout Mr. Glover called them. In fact as fast as we dropped in a hook baited with a grasshopper we would catch a big trout .... The greatest part of the work was catching the grasshopper. We dropped [the trout] into gunny sacks and when the men came we distributed them around the camp." Gilbert and Evermann likewise reported in 1894 to the US Bureau of Fisheries, "Steelhead is an abundant fish . . . especially about Spokane. Several fine examples . . . were taken by B. A. Bean in September 1892, near Spokane [using] a spoon."

In an article published in the *Spokesman-Review* in 1903, A. C. Ware stated that the Spokane River drew sport anglers throughout the United States and Europe in the early 1900s. He noted, "Salmon can be got in the Spokane River below town. Specimens caught within an hour's walk have weighed 50 pounds." The potent mixture of occasional large chinook, along with abundant steelhead and large resident trout, apparently attracted anglers in droves to Spokane from about 1880 to 1910. One distinctive feature of Spokane's hotels was some of the best fishing the West had to offer within a few blocks.

Newspaper articles published in Spokane newspapers document the extent of local sport-fishing opportunities. The *Spokesman-Review* of February 17, 1894, wrote that steelhead were coming up the [river] in good numbers . . . fishing in the Little Spokane is said to be excellent." The *Spokane Chronicle* of August 4, 1895, reported of fishing in the Bowl and Pitcher area, "F. E. Buchanon yesterday established a record for fish catching that will be hard to break. In the company of another young man he landed seven [chinook] salmon," all weighing between twenty-five and forty-five pounds. According to the paper, "He found it necessary to hire a rancher to bring their harvest of over 200 pounds to the city in a wagon."

## Factors in the Collapse of Indian Subsistence and Sport Fisheries

The factors that contributed most to the collapse of both Indian subsistence and sport fisheries in the Spokane River included the commercial fishery that developed in the lower Columbia River, the destruction of habitat by agricultural development along Hangman Creek, construction of dams along the Spokane River, and the construction of the Grand Coulee Dam, beginning in 1939, that blocked anadromous fish above Columbia RM 596.6.

Large numbers of chinook salmon were observed below Spokane Falls until 1882. That decline coincided with a ramped-up commercial fishing industry beginning in 1866, when the first cannery opened. Commercial fishermen caught salmon in gill nets, beach seines, traps, and fish wheels. Collectively, these formed an intimidating gauntlet salmon had to run. Gill nets caught more than any other method. The large mesh of these nets (8.0–8.5 inches) initially targeted chinook salmon and allowed smaller fish to pass through. By 1904, 2,569 boats festooned the lower Columbia River and set approximately 875 miles of gill nets each year. Beach seines (between 600 and 2,400 feet long by 35 to 40 feet deep) deployed from skiffs encircled schools of salmon. Some fifty-seven of them operated in 1934. Teams of horses and crews of between twelve and twenty-four men pulled the seines to shore. During the fishing season, according to reporters, seining was "carried on with little interruption, hauls being made in quick succession all through the day."

Other devices were also used to capture salmon. A series of funnels anchored on the shore led to traps. In 1885, 1886, and 1934, the number of traps was 105, 154, and 228, respectively. Fish wheels were constructed like Ferris wheels, fitted with steel mesh buckets to scoop fish out of the river. Positioned in chutes in the river where the current was strong enough to drive the wheels, they collected salmon by lifting and shunting them into a hopper. The first fish wheel operated in 1879. By 1899, seventy-six were operating. Commercial catches peaked at forty-three million pounds in 1883 and 1895. For the first twenty-three years of the fishery (1866–88), chinook was the only species harvested. Only after chinook stocks began to fail did commercial fishermen pursue smaller, less desirable species.

Gilbert and Evermann noted that by 1893, the numbers of chinook salmon harvested by Indians in the Spokane River had already declined dramatically. They placed the blame squarely on overharvest by commercial fishermen: "It is … certain that the decrease in … number of salmon [is] due to ill regulated fishing in the lower Columbia." They further pointed out that steelhead, a species not initially targeted by commercial fishermen, was still relatively abundant in the Spokane River. This observation indicated that the chinook decline was related to commercial fishing and not some other factor such as altered habitat, which presumably would affect chinook and steelhead equally.

Commercial fishing drove many upriver stocks to the brink of extinction, typically harvesting more than 85 percent and sometimes as much as 98 percent of each stock. With only 2 to 15 percent of the fish escaping, it was likely that weak stocks would be overharvested, since they were mixed in with strong stocks, and fishermen had no way to distinguish between them. (A *stock* is a population of salmon that spawns in a particular tributary of the Columbia River. If the salmon enter a particular tributary in small numbers, the population of that tributary is called a weak stock. If the salmon enter a particular tributary in large numbers, the population is called a strong stock.) Overfishing occurred because commercial fishermen intercepted salmon in the lower Columbia River rather than harvesting them as individual stocks ascending tributaries.

The indigenous fishery was more sustainable. Indians fished salmon in known-stock terminal fisheries in each main Columbia River tributary: that is, they harvested fish after the salmon had returned to the tributaries where they spawned. When the Indians noticed that the numbers of fish returning to one tributary were low, they simply moved to a different location, allowing the weak stock to recover. Salmon chiefs shut down the fisheries at certain times to assure that sufficient numbers of salmon escaped the fisheries and continued their upstream migration to reproduce and sustain the fish population.

Equal distribution of the catch was also very important to the salmon chiefs. Christine Quintasket (Mourning Dove) of the Colville Confederated Tribes provided an explanation in her autobiography: "Everyone got an equal share so that the fish would not think humans were being stingy or selfish and refuse to return." The Canadian artist Paul Kane, who visited Kettle Falls in 1847, reported that the salmon chief frequently shut down the fishing to allow fish to escape upstream. He wrote, "Infinitely greater numbers of salmon could be readily taken here, if it were desired; but as the chief considerately remarked to me, if he were to take all that came up, there would be none left for the Indians on the upper part of the river; so they content themselves with supplying their own wants."

The states of Oregon and Washington did little to curb exploitation of salmon in the early years of commercial fishing. State legislatures moved at a glacial pace to regulate gill nets, traps, seines, and fish wheels. Although both states enacted a weekly closure, they didn't provide appropriations to hire sufficient wardens and enforce their laws. The *Oregonian* reported in January 1882, "The purpose of the laws restricting fishing was to give part of the run each year a chance to reach the spawning grounds up the river and deposit their eggs. . . . These laws if enforced to the letter would amply protect the fish but . . . all along the river this law was openly violated during the season just closed." Even as late as 1938, regulations were ineffectual in stemming harvests of declining stocks. In 1942 Willis Rich, director of research for the Oregon Fish Commission, lamented: "Such regulations and restrictions as have been imposed upon the Columbia River salmon fisheries apparently [had] very little effect insofar as they act[ed] to reduce the intensity of fishing and provide a greater escapement. . . . On the whole it would appear the Chinook salmon runs . . . [were] subjected to an exceedingly intense fishery without any effective protection whatsoever." The states of Oregon and Washington bear partial responsibility for fish decimation.

Habitat destruction in Hangman Creek between 1860 and 1892 was a second factor causing declines of anadromous fishes in the Spokane Basin. The first historical records, made by cartographers with the Pacific Railroad Survey (1853–55) and US Army personnel (1856–59), described Latah Creek (as it was then called) and its tributaries as flowing clear and cool through "well timbered" canyons and rolling upland prairies carpeted by a "luxuriant" growth of native grasses and wildflowers. Settlers who moved into the watershed by 1860, attracted by the rich Palouse soils, damaged salmon habitat in many ways. They broke sod, replaced biologically diverse prairies with cropland monoculture, and caused extensive erosion of fine sediments into the creek. Sediments clogged the interstices between gravels in salmon redds (egg-laying areas), preventing the flow of oxygenated water and thus suffocating developing eggs and embryos.

The settlers also cut timber to burn for fuel and to construct homes, barns, and corrals. Most of the timber grew in the riparian corridor along the creek's edge and provided both shade that cooled the water and large woody debris that increased the complexity of the habitat for juvenile salmonids. They channelized watercourses, widening river channels, reducing their depth, and eliminating pools in which juvenile salmon were reared and adults rested.

Channelizing also resulted in reduced discharge because of the loss of connectivity between the creek and its floodplain. Cold groundwater in the floodplain had formerly discharged into the creek through springs and seeps. Settlers also diverted irrigation water out of the stream into croplands, further reducing the discharge of Latah Creek. Reduced discharge exacerbated the shift in water temperature. The water eventually became too warm and the discharge too low to attract salmon into the creek.

By the time the first fish survey was conducted in 1892–93, Latah Creek had already been seriously degraded. Gilbert and Evermann in 1894 described its waters as "roily" and unsuitable for salmon production. A sugar-beet processing factory near Waverly, Washington, constructed a dam across Latah Creek in 1898 to provide water for washing the beets before processing them into sugar. Old photographs of this dam suggest that the plunge pool was too shallow to provide the takeoff velocity that salmon needed to leap the dam.

Construction of hydroelectric dams on the Spokane River was the third factor contributing to the decline of anadromous salmonids. When Little Falls Dam was constructed in 1910, it blocked the salmon runs above it. Although Little Falls had a fish ladder, it was essentially a wooden flume that lacked baffles to provide resting areas for fish, so it acted as a velocity barrier. Tests performed by the Washington Department of Fisheries showed conclusively that it passed no fish, and it was eventually removed. In 1916, Long Lake Dam was constructed a few miles upstream without a fish ladder, in lieu of which the fisheries department negotiated a settlement with the Washington Water Power Company to construct a fish hatchery at Natatorium Park in Spokane. By 1939, only remnant runs were left in the Spokane River, although members of the Spokane Tribe still fished for salmon below Little Falls Dam.

Construction of the Grand Coulee Dam, without a fish ladder, finally eliminated anadromous fishes in the Spokane River. Grand Coulee blocked runs between the dam site and the headwaters, including the Sanpoil, Spokane, Colville, Kettle, Pend Oreille, and Kootenay/Kootenai Rivers. All told, Grand Coulee Dam blocked salmon and steelhead from 1,140 linear miles of river habitat. In 1955, Chief Joseph Dam at Columbia RM 545 blocked anadromous fishes from an additional fifty-two miles of habitat. All of the Indian tribes that occupy the Columbia Basin in the United States, as well as Canadian First Nations, have now petitioned both countries to restore salmon to the Upper Columbia Basin above Chief Joseph and Grand Coulee Dams as part of their renegotiation of the US/Canada Columbia River Treaty. Natural-resource agencies for affected tribes are currently assessing the feasibility of salmon restoration throughout the blocked area, including the Spokane River.

# Mining, Climate, and the Giant Salmonfly

CAMILLE MCNEELY AND CARMEN A. NEZAT

INSECT GEEKS AND FLY FISHERS ALIKE MIGHT CONSIDER THE GIANT salmonfly (*Pteronarcys californica*) one of the more charismatic animals of the Spokane River. Hatches of the two-inch-long adults attract fly-fishing enthusiasts throughout the western United States. The Spokane River, a relatively large, cold, fast-flowing, cobble-bottomed river, provides the ideal physical habitat for this species. The success of salmonflies in the Spokane River is likely due in part to the inputs of cold groundwater from the Spokane Valley–Rathdrum Prairie Aquifer. These inputs are also critical to the survival of native fish, as Al Scholz and others explain in this book.

Giant salmonfly larvae live in river water for three years. Then, like many aquatic insects, they complete their lives on land and in the air. The larvae are dark brown, with tufts of hairy gills under their legs. In their third spring, they mature and crawl out of the water, their exoskeleton splits down the back, and the winged adult form crawls out of the old shell. This is their metamorphosis. Unlike the butterflies whose life cycles we observed in elementary school, they do not form a still and bundled pupa: instead they pupate like grasshoppers. The transformation of their breathing and their way of moving to fit their new environment takes place within the old skin while the animal is still maintaining its active underwater life.

After a few hours drying their new exoskeleton and wings, the newly hatched adults seek mates. Males court females by drumming a distinctive rhythm with the abdomen on a tree trunk or another surface. Females use the drumming to identify the males' species and find them. The males' initial mating call is six beats about one-quarter of a second apart. Interested females respond with six thumps also, softer and slightly slower. The courting male uses the female's thumps to find her by a process of triangulation while she waits for him. The females mate only once. Mating pairs rest on rocks, bushes, and tree trunks, facing away from each other but attached at the ends of their abdomens.

After mating, females drop egg clusters while hovering over the water; these clumsy fliers often plunge into the stream while laying their eggs. Each female lays more than one hundred eggs, possibly many more. Neither males nor females feed or live more than a few days as adults. They form locally dense patches with others of the same kind. One of these areas is the Spokane River between the Maple Street Bridge and the confluence with Latah Creek in the city of Spokane. People's Park is a great place to observe a hatch, including the sight of the mature larvae crawling out of the water and new adults expanding and drying their wings, drumming, and mating, usually in mid- to late May. Of the many eggs that each female salmonfly deposits, only a few survive to emerge from the river as adults. Most perish during the three-year larval stage, washed downstream or eaten by other river animals.

Juveniles shelter beneath the boulders that line the river bottom, in clumps of dead leaves, and on sticks and logs. The leaves and sticks likely double as both food and shelter. Juvenile salmonflies often feed on dead plants and other decomposing material on the river bottom. In some rivers they feed mostly on algae. From the Spokane River, we have collected some whose guts contained mostly algae and others that contained mostly dead leaf material. Feeding on terrestrial plant detritus may help to protect these bugs from the toxic trace metal (or heavy metal) pollution that deeply affects all aquatic life in the Spokane River.

Much of the metal contamination in the river today is a legacy of earlier generations. Hard-rock mining and milling of ores for silver, lead, and zinc began in Silver Valley, Idaho, in the late 1800s. The tailings were carried from the mills into the streams. Today, hundreds of miles of riverbank in Idaho and Washington are dotted with signs that advise the general public to limit contact with the sediments to prevent ingestion of the toxic metals.

## How Mining Contaminates

Some areas of the world have an abundance of natural resources, the result of millions or billions of years of geological processes. In the Coeur d'Alene mining district (Silver Valley), rich veins of metals such as silver, lead, and zinc run through 1.4-billion-year-old rocks. Those veins are exposed at the land's surface in small amounts and also extend deep below the surface. Miners dig deep into the earth, carry these rocks to the surface, and crush and smelt them to extract the metal. An ore is a rock that is worth mining because it has a relatively high concentration of a metal, but ores may contain less than 1 percent of the desired metal. The process therefore generates a lot of crushed (or milled) waste rock, known as tailings.

Before the consequences of these actions were fully understood and environmental regulations implemented, tailings were dumped into nearby waterways, in this case the South Fork of the Coeur d'Alene River and its tributaries. Although these tailings were typically not commercially valuable, early processes for extracting metals were inefficient, and the tailings still contained metals such as lead, zinc, cadmium, and arsenic in concentrations high enough to have harmful effects on life. Zinc is a necessary nutrient in low concentrations, but in high concentrations it is toxic, especially to algae and to fish, which absorb the metal through their gills. In fact, some tailings from early Silver Valley production were rich enough in zinc and lead that in the 1940s the Hecla Mining Company extracted metals from them again.

## Mine Tailings

Underground, rocks have limited contact with water and oxygen. Once solid rock has been mined and crushed, water seeps through it, carrying dissolved oxygen from the atmosphere. The resulting chemical reactions break down the rock, releasing sulfuric acid and toxic metals.

The starter reaction for this process is often caused by the interaction of water and oxygen with pyrite, better known as fool's gold. Pyrite contains one atom of iron for every two atoms of sulfur. When it is exposed to oxygen and water, the iron and sulfur are forced apart and may combine with oxygen atoms or a hydroxide ion, part of a broken water molecule. One result of this process is rust. Except in very acidic conditions, oxidized iron forms a solid, a reddish mineral that discolors water and coats rocks. Its blood-red color can be seen in areas affected by acid mine drainage. When atmospheric oxygen combines with the sulfur from pyrite, it produces sulfuric acid, which permeates surrounding water. This acidic water increases the disintegration rate of the tailings, releasing lead, zinc, mercury, arsenic, copper, and other metals into the water.

Fortunately, in the Coeur d'Alene mining district, carbonate minerals are also present in the same rock as the ore, and they work to buffer the acid—much as Tums neutralizes stomach acid—so that the acidity of stream water is circumneutral, similar to streams unaffected by mining. Despite this buffering, natural processes (including biological processes) release metals from the tailings in the Spokane and Coeur d'Alene Rivers. While the water in the Coeur d'Alene River may appear clear and harmless, its concentrations of lead, zinc, and cadmium are higher than the US Environmental Protection Agency's criterion for continuous concentration, the limit above which these metals harm aquatic life.

Since mining in this district began in the late 1800s, more than fifty million metric tons of tailings have been dumped into the South Fork of the Coeur d'Alene River and its tributaries. The tailings are still moving downstream, especially during spring snowmelt and floods. They are carried into the Coeur d'Alene River, into Lake Coeur d'Alene, and into the Spokane River, which drains from the lake. Tailings persist in the sediments that line the stream channels and banks. They accumulate where the water slows down, in broad, flat floodplain areas like the lateral or chain lakes along the lower Coeur d'Alene River in Idaho and even in spots along the Spokane River. Tailings generated during the early decades of mining can contain up to one thousand times more lead than is naturally found in the local river sediments. Finer sediments in the Spokane River can contain up to one hundred times more lead and zinc than occurs naturally. In fact, warning signs along the upstream portion of the river caution beachgoers to avoid accidentally ingesting sediment and to wash hands and toys thoroughly after visiting. One of these telltale signs, at Sullivan Road on the Centennial Trail, reads, "Attention: lead and arsenic in shoreline soils." At key shoreline recreational locations and also over trout spawning grounds above the Upriver Dam, the Washington State Department of Ecology has removed contaminated sediments or placed protective sediment caps over metals-contaminated soils.

## Heavy Metals in Water

Although cadmium, lead, and zinc concentrations in the Spokane River have slowly decreased over recent decades, these metals persist, and their concentration increases in the river each spring when water levels rise and flush them downstream. The harm they pose to aquatic fish and animals depends on the individual species and on the interactions between the river and the Spokane Valley–Rathdrum Prairie Aquifer.

Lead and zinc in Spokane River water may come from locally contaminated sediments or from sediments upstream in the Coeur d'Alene River and Lake Coeur d'Alene. While most of the lead attaches itself to sediment particles, zinc is likely to stay dissolved in the water. Zinc concentrations in the Spokane River often exceed safe limits for fish and other aquatic life.

Between Lake Coeur d'Alene and Sullivan Park in Spokane Valley, the river is fed primarily by Lake Coeur d'Alene. Along this reach, some river water seeps into the ground below, feeding the aquifer. Once the river reaches the area near Sullivan Park, the water level of the prolific aquifer is higher than the river bottom, and groundwater seeps back into the river. During periods of low flow, the emerging groundwater is visible in the form of springs in places like Sullivan and Mirabeau Parks.

The aquifer, the sole source of drinking water for half a million people, protects the river's biota in unexpected ways. First, cooler water contains more dissolved oxygen, which even underwater creatures depend on. Salmonflies absorb oxygen through the hairy gills under their legs and, like all insects, have a complex network of tubes to distribute oxygen through their bodies. Second, the groundwater has higher levels of dissolved calcium and magnesium (the elements that create hard water and stain our bathroom tubs and sinks). These minerals reduce the absorption of zinc and other toxic metals by fish, thus diminishing the harmful effects. During the summer months, when stream flow is low, the proportion of groundwater in this reach of the river is higher, and conditions are better for fish. Upstream of aquifer inputs, however, calcium and magnesium concentrations are insufficient to counteract the effects of the toxic metals, and summer water temperatures are higher than downstream.

## Effects of Toxic Metals on Salmonflies and Other Insects

Aquatic animals, including fish and insects, are exposed to toxic metals through three routes: dissolved in the water, in sediments on the river bottom, and in their food. In the late 1990s, the United States Geological Survey estimated that without chronic pollution, primarily toxic metals, two or three times as many insect species might be living in the river. In addition, dissolved levels of zinc in the river are high enough to reduce growth of algae as far downstream as Long Lake (or Lake Spokane). Since algae are the most important source of food and energy at the bottom of the food web, less algal growth likely means fewer insects and, in turn, fewer fish. The insects that are common in the Spokane River—midge larvae, blue-winged olive mayflies, and caddisflies (i.e., spotted sedge larvae), which build underwater nets to trap food particles carried by currents—are comparatively tolerant of metals.

Flathead mayflies are conspicuously absent from the Spokane River. The extremely flat shape of these insects allows them to cling to rocks without being washed away. They are common in many local streams and should thrive among the loose cobbles in riffles and at the edge of the Spokane River. Unfortunately, they are relatively sensitive to toxic metals and therefore absent from the river.

The giant salmonfly is an interesting denizen of the Spokane River in part because its tolerance and intolerance to different types of pollution neatly reflect the water quality in the free-flowing portions of the Spokane River, including the stretch through downtown Spokane. Salmonflies, like other stoneflies, are quite intolerant of extensive silt and gravel, warm water, low oxygen levels, too many nutrients and algae, pesticide runoff, and high levels of most toxic pollutants. Generally, if salmonflies are thriving in a stream, it must be pretty clean. Yet, unlike most aquatic insects, they are relatively tolerant of harmful metals. Our beautiful Spokane River now has excellent water and habitat quality by many measures. Toxic metal contamination is the largely invisible flaw.

Large, two- or three-year-old salmonflies can tolerate levels of dissolved cadmium, lead, and zinc much higher than those in the Spokane River, and much higher than the level set by the US Environmental Protection Agency or the Washington Department of Ecology to protect aquatic life. However, salmonflies in their first year of life may be more vulnerable. In a study of a closely related species, all very young individuals were killed by a cocktail of dissolved cadmium, copper, and zinc that did not appear to kill any older, larger individuals: the concentrations of dissolved zinc that killed the young salmonflies were similar to those in the Spokane River, although levels of cadmium and copper in the cocktail were higher. Smaller, younger larvae may be more vulnerable because they face greater exposure to the metals through all three routes—food, sediment, and water. They feed on smaller particles more likely to contain contaminated algae or particles of the toxic metals. Also, they have a higher ratio of skin to internal body tissue, which increases their exposure through contact with sediment and water.

No one knows for sure what mechanisms allow salmonflies to tolerate levels of metals that are toxic to more sensitive insects such as flathead mayflies, but there are several possible explanations. Some protective mechanisms could be fairly simple, the result of the giant salmonfly's way of life in the river. The salmonfly mostly lives among large cobbles with water flowing around them. These areas retain relatively little fine sediment, likely limiting the insect's contact with metals. The Spokane River upstream of the Hangman Creek confluence also has a low load of fine sediment today, in contrast to the years when tailings were flushing through.

Feeding on dead plants could also help reduce the salmonfly's exposure to toxic metals because the plant material comes mostly from outside the river channel, from trees on the riverbank or from river tributaries. These food items likely contain much less metal than algae do. Animals that feed on dead leaves in streams are called shredders, and many studies have found shredders to be more tolerant of toxic-metal pollution than insects that eat algae or other insects. Finally, abundant giant salmonflies in some tributaries of the Spokane River, such as Marshall Creek, travel downstream to repopulate the Spokane River after periods of stress, such as floods.

Other protective mechanisms may result from the ways that the salmonfly's body processes metals. Their resistance has been shown through controlled exposures to metals in laboratory studies, where habitat and diet are the same for all insects in the experiment. Insects have several ways of limiting the accumulation of metals within their cells. We don't understand all of these mechanisms, but we do know that the toxicity of metals seems to be determined by how much metal an organism accumulates in sensitive parts of its cells. These sensitive parts are responsible for making proteins, moving things around, and converting food to energy. Some of the salmonflies' tolerance to toxic metals undoubtedly comes from subtle differences in how their bodies work, compared to those of other aquatic bugs.

All animals that live in freshwater face the challenge of managing the salt balance in their bodies, which is higher than that of their environment. Salts are necessary for a range of cellular functions, but they are lost to the environment through parts of the skin that are permeable to water and oxygen. Fish and aquatic insects alike have special cells in their skin that help them absorb salts from the water into their bodies. In insects, these cells take up toxic metals as well as necessary salts. The more of these salt-absorbing cells the insect has, and the larger its skin area relative to its body size, the more metals it absorbs, increasing its exposure. The giant salmonfly has salt-absorbing cells on the hairy gills underneath its legs, but it perhaps has fewer than other species that are more sensitive to metals.

Once a bug such as a salmonfly absorbs toxic metals, the damage they cause may be limited by special proteins that bind the metals chemically, preventing them from disrupting bodily processes. Some of these proteins are found in almost all animals, including mollusks, mammals, and insects. Others are unique to insects. Giant salmonflies seem to produce more of these proteins than do closely related bugs that are more sensitive to toxic metals.

Finally, the giant salmonfly appears to be pretty good at removing some metals from its body, particularly cadmium. Insects remove waste and toxic materials using tiny tubes that float in their body fluids and select unwanted chemicals, passing them into the lower gut to be expelled with food waste. Just as in human kidneys, large metal particles are difficult for the membranes of these tubes to process. Unlike salmonflies, flathead mayflies are essentially unable to excrete cadmium. This may be part of the reason they are absent from the Spokane River.

## The Future of Heavy Metals in the Spokane River

Cadmium, lead, and zinc concentrations in the Spokane River have declined since the 1970s, when federal laws were enacted to prohibit mining companies from discharging tailings into surface waters. Cleanups also began in the Silver Valley about this time. Concentrations will likely remain elevated for many decades, however, because of the millions of tons of old tailings still moving through the river and lake systems upstream of the Spokane River.

Certain processes could increase the release of these metals from sediments into the water. For example, lead and arsenic released from mine tailings are recaptured by oxidized iron compounds and accumulate in the bottom sediments of Lake Coeur d'Alene. Currently, zinc concentrations and low nutrient levels in Lake Coeur d'Alene limit the growth of floating algae. But if zinc concentrations continue to decrease and nutrients such as phosphates from human and agricultural activity increase in the water, algal blooms may occur and deplete the oxygen near the bottom of the lake. If this happens, the iron oxide particles will dissolve and release the toxic metals that were chemically bound to them. Maintaining the quality of the water in Lake Coeur d'Alene to protect aquatic wildlife in the lake and the Spokane River will be a duty for generations to come.

## Other Future Changes

The Spokane River will undoubtedly be affected by altered temperature, rainfall, and snowfall in our region caused by climate change. These effects will be strongest in areas where the aquifer does not recharge the river with cooler water. Throughout the western United States, we expect increased rain, a reduced snowpack, and earlier spring floods. Longer periods of low water and warmer air temperatures in the summers will warm waters, threatening animals like the giant salmonfly and trout that depend on cool water.

In the short term, salmonflies are somewhat tolerant of warm temperatures and the resulting low oxygen levels. They typically live in waters between 40°F and 60°F, but they can survive temperatures in the seventies for brief periods. In warmer, oxygen-poor water, salmonflies do "pushups," bouncing up and down to move more water over their gills to collect more oxygen. Every year, students in Eastern Washington University's introductory biology laboratory observe this behavior. We expose the animals to a range of water temperatures, from 40°F to 77°F, and count the number of pushups per minute. In the coolest water, the salmonflies usually remain still; in the warmest water, they do a pushup about every 1.5 seconds. (Handling these large, prehistoric-looking insects never fails to produce a good thrill in some students and revulsion in others. Either way, the energy level in the room rises, and students remember the lesson.)

Salmonflies do not, however, thrive in consistently warm water. At temperatures above 60°F, their survival and growth rates decline, and they are rarely found in such waters. Already, temperatures in some reaches of the Spokane River that lack local inputs of water from the aquifer are too hot for salmonflies in the summer. As our climate warms, will the entire Spokane River become too hot for these ecologically significant creatures? It is hard to predict how much warmer our city and river will become. The temperature in the river will depend partly on the future pace of global climate change and partly on how much water is taken from the aquifer during the summer. As flows in the river decline, water warms. If we can limit global warming, and aquifer flows into the river remain strong, salmonflies should continue to delight fish, fly fishers, and students of the Spokane River for many years to come.

# More Than a Bathtub Full of Rocks

STAN MILLER

SPOKANE BOASTS THE MOTTO "NEAR NATURE, NEAR PERFECT." THE Spokane River constitutes a key component of the "nature" we are near. Reexposing the downtown section of the river was a driving force behind Expo '74, the Spokane World's Fair dedicated to "celebrating a fresh new environment." When I joined the staff at the Spokane County Engineers Office to work on the newly organized protection program for the Spokane Valley–Rathdrum Prairie Aquifer in 1977, Riverfront Park had just been established. Creation of the park, which allowed Spokane citizens a fresh new outlook on the river, closely followed the deindustrialization of the downtown reach of the river for the Expo. The increased access to and awareness of the river through the park and associated events spawned a number of organizations dedicated to improving access to and recreational use of the Spokane River. Most of the river uses—canoeing, kayaking, rafting, fly fishing, and enjoying the sight of the falls—rely on abundant water in the river.

## 2015 Temperature Blip

The summer of 2015 was a bellwether period for the river and aquifer system. For the first time since records have been kept, water temperatures near the Spokane River at the Spokane gaging station, just downstream of the Monroe Street Bridge, exceeded those critical for the survival of native fish. Prior to that, the river temperature over most of the river's free-flowing reaches remained suitable for native cold-water fish: redband trout, whitefish, and extirpated salmon species. During that noteworthy summer, the unusually warm water from the river's source at Lake Coeur d'Alene and abnormally low levels of cold groundwater recharge led Spokane River temperatures below Monroe Street to exceed 60°F, the established stress level for cold-water species.

While the weather patterns that led to this condition were unusual, current climate models predict that the weather in the near future will be more like that of the 2014–15 water year than like that of past decades. The summer of 2015 may be the new normal. Grasping this situation and its implications requires an understanding of the overall flow regime of the river and aquifer system.

## River-Aquifer Interchange

Two major impoundments dominate the lower half of the Spokane River. River mile (RM) 0 to RM 23 constitutes the Spokane River Arm of Lake Roosevelt, the reservoir created by the Grand Coulee Dam on the Columbia River. Lake Spokane, the reservoir behind Long Lake Dam, occupies another twenty-four miles (RM 33–RM 57). Little of the lower half of the river is the free-flowing habitat preferred by trout.

The upper half of the river begins at Nine Mile Dam at about RM 58. The dam sits at one of many waterfalls on the natural river, constructed between two granite outcrops. It represents the westernmost point of the gravel-filled valley that contains the Spokane Valley–Rathdrum Prairie Aquifer. From RM 58 to RM 111 at Coeur d'Alene, the river flows above the aquifer. While there are several dams along this reach, each with a small impoundment, only Post Falls Dam at about RM 103 in Idaho creates a sizable reservoir. For several months of the year, Post Falls Dam impounds water that is part of Lake Coeur d'Alene and holds the lake at what is referred to as the summer recreation level. This eight-mile-long reach is an important source of recharge to the aquifer.

Between Nine Mile Dam and Lake Coeur d'Alene, the river's bed is formed by the sand and gravel deposits left by the outburst floods from glacial Lake Missoula at the end of the Pleistocene. This porous medium allows water to leak through to recharge the aquifer whenever the river surface is higher than the groundwater level. During the late winter, spring, and early summer, the river is often a "losing stream" over the entire reach from RM 58 to RM 111. Because the gradient of the aquifer beneath the river differs from that of the river itself, the river changes from losing to gaining several times when the river surface is at summer low-flow levels.

The major gaining reaches, where aquifer water enters the river and helps to maintain the summer flow through Spokane, are between RM 78 and RM 80, below Upriver Dam, and RM 84 and RM 89, roughly between Plante's Ferry Park in Spokane Valley and the Sullivan Road Bridge. While Lake Coeur d'Alene is the source of most of the river's flow, these two reaches may constitute more than half of the river's flow during some summers.

The aquifer occupies an L-shaped valley that extends north to south between Hoodoo Mountain and Coeur d'Alene in Idaho (the Rathdrum Prairie) and then east to west from Coeur d'Alene to Nine Mile, Washington. The Spokane River flows along the entire length of this east-west arm. The aquifer lies beneath an area of about 320 square miles. Only some 125 square miles of that area lie in Washington. Outwash from the glacial Lake Missoula Floods filled this prehistoric valley with silt, sand, and gravel. The fill varies from an overall thickness of several hundred feet at the thinnest portion, near the East Spokane city limits, to nearly one thousand feet in Northern Idaho and north of the city of Spokane. The surface of the water-bearing layer itself lies anywhere from a few feet below the surface along the bank of the river to several hundred feet underground in northern Idaho. The water-bearing stratum is several hundred feet thick and has been estimated to contain over ten trillion gallons of water.

## Sources of Water in the System

Two units of measure are used to quantify water flow: cubic feet per second (cfs) and million gallons per day (mgd). Scientists studying river flow usually use cfs, while those interested in water supply use mgd. One thousand cfs is approximately equal to 650 mgd.

Lake Coeur d'Alene, the source of the river, derives its water from a large drainage area in the Rocky Mountains. Most of the water entering the lake comes from the Coeur d'Alene and St. Joe Rivers. Flow in these rivers varies widely through the year. The peak flow comes in late spring, when mountain snow is melting, and it drops to a trickle in July and August. The average flow in the river is about 6,000 cfs. Over a typical year, this flow can range from a low of around 500 cfs to a high of over 20,000 cfs. Several times in the recorded history of the river, peak flows of nearly 50,000 cfs have been observed.

Since 2008 the minimum flow at Post Falls Dam has been regulated by Avista Corporation's operating license, issued by the Federal Energy Regulatory Commission. The license requires that a minimum of 600 cfs be released from the dam except when the level of Coeur d'Alene lake drops three inches below the summer recreation level, in which case the flow can be lowered to 500 cfs. Typically, the river flow mirrors the inflow to the lake. However, at extremely low and high flows, other factors come into play. Post Falls Dam regulates low flows. A geologic feature at the lake outlet limits river flow out of the lake. Even when inflow exceeds 100,000 cfs, the outflow to the river does not exceed 50,000 cfs.

The source and amount of water recharging the aquifer has been an important area of study for several decades, beginning in the early 1950s, when the Bureau of Reclamation investigated the effect of irrigation wells on the aquifer. In that era wells were drilled to supply irrigation water to the Rathdrum Prairie and the Spokane Valley. These wells and the associated pipelines replace an extensive system of open canals fed by water from the river. The most extensive study estimated the annual average flow to be about 650 mgd near the state line.

At that time it was believed that most of the aquifer recharge came from the lakes surrounding the prairie and the valley. The largest source was thought to be Lake Coeur d'Alene, which provided about 200 mgd. The other lake basins and drainages adjacent to the aquifer were estimated to contribute another 300 mgd. Leakage from the river accounted for another 150 mgd. For all the basins except the Pend Oreille, the estimates were based on normal precipitation, drainage basin size, and other basin characteristics. The recharge out of the Pend Oreille basin was estimated by difference; what didn't come from the other basins was assumed to come from the Pend

Oreille end of the aquifer. In the 1950s this amount was about 90 mgd. Following years of additional research and the development of flow-modeling technology, the current approach to flow estimates is radically different, as are the flow values assigned to the various recharge sources. Current estimates have increased the river's contribution to over 400 mgd. Lake Coeur d'Alene's contribution is down to 89 mgd and Pend Oreille's down to only 43 cfs. In the current estimates, return flow from irrigation and onsite waste disposal over the aquifer play a significant role in aquifer recharge.

## Spokane River-Aquifer Interaction

To help explain the 2015 temperature crisis, an overview of the dynamics of the Spokane River is in order. Paddlers on the river have long noted the decrease in river flow in the losing reach of the river between Post Falls Dam and the Sullivan Road Bridge during the summer. Yet if we compare the measured flow rates at the Post Falls and Monroe Street gaging stations during the same period, the Monroe Street flow is usually higher than the Post Falls flow. Area water-resource professionals, such as hydrologists from Avista, the United States Geological Survey, and various fisheries agencies, have also noticed this disparity. They focused on the observation that the river flow showed a net increase of 300 to 400 cfs between Post Falls and Monroe Street and the benefit for power generation that the increase created.

In my role as the manager of Spokane County's Aquifer Protection Program, I wanted to gain a greater understanding of the relationship. If water from the river was recharging the aquifer, could contaminants in the river reach our drinking-water supply? Likewise, I wondered about the effect on river quality of large volumes of aquifer water entering the river between Sullivan Road and Spokane Falls downtown. The flow rate and water quality of the river at any given time and location depend on the interaction of the source water (from Lake Coeur d'Alene), the substrate of the riverbed, and the Spokane Valley–Rathdrum Prairie Aquifer. The river and the aquifer are strongly interacting systems.

From its point of origin at the outlet of Lake Coeur d'Alene downstream to near the Sullivan Road Bridge, the river bottom is many feet above the aquifer. River water leaks through the riverbed in this reach to recharge the aquifer year-round. Between Sullivan Bridge and Upriver Dam, the river flow is increased by inflow from the aquifer. A similar set of losing and gaining reaches exists below Upriver Dam. In the final reach where the river flows through the aquifer gravel, Monroe Street to Nine Mile, the river continually gains flow from the aquifer.

Quantitatively and qualitatively, the two downstream reaches are less important than the Sullivan-Upriver reach. The effect of these interactions becomes most noticeable during the summer when river flows are low. During the summer, the gaining reaches upstream of Monroe Street pour between 50 and 100 percent more aquifer water into the river than is lost to the aquifer. If the flow leaving the lake is 600 cfs, then the flow below Monroe Street is typically between 900 and 1200 cfs. In addition to providing an influx of water to the important fisheries below Monroe Street, the cold aquifer water recharging the river offsets the effect of warm water from the lake. Temperature is probably more important than flow to fish in the summer.

## Temperature Effects of Aquifer Recharge

The recharge from the aquifer to the river during the summer is important both because it maintains river flow during the summer and because it provides an influx of cold water to offset the warm water coming out of Lake Coeur d'Alene in the summer. Based on historic norms during a moderate flow year, when surface temperature of the lake is above 70°F and the river flow at Post Falls Dam is regulated at 600 cfs, this aquifer-river relationship is especially critical. Under such conditions the river leaks around half of its flow, or 300 cfs, to the aquifer between Post Falls and Sullivan Road Bridge. Between Sullivan and the Monroe Street gage, about 600 cfs of groundwater from the aquifer leaks back into the river, making for a net flow of around 900 cfs at Monroe Street.

The effect on temperature is significant. Assume the river temperature just above the Sullivan Road Bridge is 75°F. This temperature takes into account the temperature of the water leaving the lake plus added heating in the shallow parts of the river. Based on temperature readings from springs along the river and from monitoring wells, we know that groundwater averages about 50°F.

If we stipulate a flow of 300 cfs and an average temperature of 75°F at Sullivan, and assume that 600 cfs of 50°F groundwater enters the river between Sullivan and Monroe Street, we can estimate the river temperature at Monroe Street. Using a simple dilution calculation, the above conditions produce a temperature of about 58°F, well within the comfort zone for cold-water fish. In a hot year like 2015, where the river temperature was around 85°F at Sullivan, the temperature at Monroe would have approached 62°F. Clearly, warmer temperatures in Lake Coeur d'Alene lead to detrimental effects on fish habitat below the falls at Monroe Street. A warmer lake could result from a low snowpack, prolonged above-average summer temperatures, or both.

## Water-Use Patterns and Development

Opponents of water-conservation pricing on Spokane's water like to point out that the aquifer is like "a bathtub full of rocks" containing over ten trillion gallons of water. They say that even if we do use an average of two hundred gallons per person per day, there's still enough water to last for over six hundred years. There are two flaws in such claims.

First, many more people use this water supply than the 200,000 or so who live in the city of Spokane. About 350,000 people in Washington depend on the Spokane Valley–Rathdrum Prairie Aquifer for their water. And since the ten trillion gallons includes the water under the Rathdrum Prairie in Idaho, we need to account for the use of 150,000 or so Idahoans in the calculations. With half a million users, the life expectancy of the ten-trillion-gallon aquifer drops to only about 250 years. None of these estimates includes water used for irrigating crops.

But this figure is even more misleading because of a second flaw in the assumptions. The aquifer is not a static system. It would be better described as a bathtub full of rocks with the tap turned on, the tub full and overflowing, and half a million people sucking water out of the tub through straws (who are thirstier in summer, so they drink more then). In this metaphor, the tap represents leakage from the river and all the lakes and stream basins that surround the aquifer. The overflow drain is aquifer recharge to the Spokane River. The straws represent the water wells we use to supply our domestic and landscape irrigation needs. Since suburbanization of the Spokane Valley and Rathdrum Prairie began in the 1960s, agricultural irrigation in Washington has been mostly eliminated, and the remaining agricultural irrigation in Idaho uses only a fraction of the total water consumption in the region.

Under natural conditions, spring runoff recharges the aquifer and raises its surface between ten and fifteen feet, until it approaches the level of water in the river. After the spring spate subsides, the river level drops rapidly. Along the gaining reaches, the river surface drops below the aquifer surface, and aquifer water begins to drain back into the river. This drainage maintains river flow during the summer.

When we factor in the extraction through the straws, the water level in the aquifer drops faster than it would naturally. The stress of usage is highest during the summer, when recharge is at its lowest. The maximum daily summer usage has increased so gradually over time that most observers of the river never noticed the change. But over the long term, that summer water use has resulted in a slightly lower average water table, which leads in turn to a gradual lowering of recharge to the river and thus to lower summertime river flows.

Rather than thinking of the whole ten trillion gallons in the aquifer as our supply, we need to look at how our use affects the top ten feet or so of water in the aquifer, which controls both the rate and the amount of overflow to the river in the summer. That top ten feet of the aquifer represents less than 170 billion gallons of water. If the aquifer were just a bathtub full of rocks, the city of Spokane alone, pumping water at a typical summertime rate of two hundred million gallons a day, would lower the water level in the tub by ten feet in less than two and a half years. Half a million people using water from the aquifer would cause the same impact in less than year. In other words, during a three-month summer season, human water use in the region would draw the aquifer down three feet.

As long as water flows out of Lake Coeur d'Alene into the river, the tap filling the bathtub is running. At the regulated flow of 600 cfs, or 400 mgd, about 150 million gallons of water per day enters the aquifer during the summer. Another 50 million gallons per day is added from other sources. That is essentially the same amount of water withdrawn in a day by the city of Spokane.

Even with these drawdowns, the flow and temperature have so far remained suitable for cold-water fish species in the river. Two detailed studies of river flow were conducted between 2000 and 2010 at various locations along the river between Post Falls and Long Lake Dams. They concluded that a 600 cfs minimum summer flow from the dam would provide acceptable conditions for trout between Post Falls and Monroe Street. When the Department of Ecology set 850 cfs as the minimum flow at the Monroe gage, they used the 2000–2007 study data that showed that 850 cfs at Monroe would protect cold-water fish habitat and that 600 cfs at the dam historically yielded a flow above 850 cfs at Monroe.

### The Perfect Storm of 2015

During the summer of 2015, historic norms in the Spokane River basin fell victim to a number of factors. First, the mountain snowpack at the end of March was only about 20 percent of normal in the upper drainages of the Spokane–Coeur d'Alene Basin. Second, in May and June the surface temperatures in Lake Coeur d'Alene reached record highs, above 85°F. Third, the extreme warm temperatures in June caused the region's water use to skyrocket. The city of Spokane averaged nearly 220 mgd for the month of June, a level not typically reached until mid-July.

The hot June negatively affected flows in the river in other ways as well. Consumption of water by evapotranspiration in the forests of northern Idaho—often overlooked as a factor—was far above normal. Such sponging exacerbated the problem of low snowpack that reduced the normal flow into Lake Coeur d'Alene. Low summer inflows into and higher-than-normal temperatures from Lake Coeur d'Alene started a cascade of effects on the Spokane River that multiplied through the summer. First, the combined effect of the warm lake temperature and the warming of the river as it flowed downstream of the Post Falls Dam led to river temperatures in the upper eighties in the reach above the Sullivan Road Bridge. Second, for the first time in the more than one hundred years of recorded flow measurements, the river flow at the USGS Monroe Street Gage dropped below 800 cfs when the flow at Post Falls Dam was at or above 600 cfs. These levels imply that the aquifer recharge to the river fell significantly below the historic norm of 600 cfs. Actual measurements suggest the recharge was more on the order of 400 cfs. Third, the low inflow to the lake caused the lake to fall below the trigger that allows Avista to lower the outflow from Post Falls to 500 cfs.

In the summer of 2015, 500 cfs of water at nearly 85°F entered the river from the lake. That water warmed several degrees as it flowed between Post Falls and Sullivan Road. About half of that warm water was lost to ground-water in the losing reaches. The lost water was replaced by recharge from 50°F groundwater. Based on the observed flow at Monroe Street, only about 400 cfs of cool groundwater was added to the 250 cfs of lake water in the river at Sullivan Road Bridge. Using the simple model presented earlier, we can calculate a flow of about 650 cfs of water, averaging about 65°F, below Monroe Street. Had Avista maintained the 600 cfs flow and drawn the lake down further, conditions would have been even worse.

## Conclusions

The summer of 2015 illustrated several new considerations for regional water-use planning. First, as the climate warms, the 2015 extremes will likely become the new normal. Second, pumping of the aquifer for summer water use reduces the cooling of the river by means of aquifer recharge. Raising overall river temperatures will jeopardize trout survival in the river. Here are some specific lessons for water-use planning:

1. The aquifer is not a static system and should not be viewed as a giant storage tank.
2. Only the top ten feet or so of the aquifer count as a storage unit. If we lower the average summer water level of the aquifer by ten feet or more, we will create a system in which little, if any, water from the aquifer will recharge the river during the summer, and the river will run nearly dry along some reaches.
3. The summer of 2015—when water use almost resulted in the collapse of the river and its flows—could serve as a benchmark for future water-use planning.
4. Because of temperature considerations, taking less water out of Lake Coeur d'Alene, the Spokane River's source, might be preferable under some conditions. Given the limited cooling effect of the aquifer water to offset the warmth of the lake water at the river's source, the amount of warm water entering the river dictates the river temperature downstream. In the summer of 2015, Avista was allowed to limit the discharge from Post Falls Dam to 500 cfs. That low flow likely resulted in the water temperature below the falls at Monroe Street being several degrees cooler than if the discharge had been maintained at 600 cfs. Limiting the amount of water withdrawn from the aquifer by water purveyors could increase the amount of cooling groundwater available, but that would require conservation measures that the public seems reluctant to support.

The Spokane Valley–Rathdrum Prairie Aquifer is not just a bathtub full of rocks. Such a storage-tank attitude overlooks the fact that the aquifer's cold water makes the river habitable for native fish species. Its link to the river through its recharge reaches makes the aquifer an integral part of the river system. As climate warms and our lakes become more like heated swimming pools in the summer, we need to analyze future management of the river carefully, not just on the basis of flow but by considering temperature effects as well.

# Pigments, PCBs, and the Spokane River

DON FELS

I BECAME A VISUAL ARTIST BECAUSE I'VE NEVER BEEN ABLE TO resist the pull of color. I was a kid in the fifties. My family got a TV when I was in fifth grade. *Life* magazine came to the house weekly, the *Los Angeles Times* daily. All appeared in black and white, as if there were no other way of portraying reality. Yet outside and all around, the world was brightly colored. I have always found those colors immensely appealing.

Today, pretty much everything arrives everywhere in glowing color. But centuries before color came to electronic devices, to publications and everyday objects, one of the world's largest trades was the production of color. To control color in past centuries meant mounting a fleet of sailing ships and sending them around the world to places, usually tropical, where sources of natural dye pigments (animal, mineral and vegetable) could be found. That massive undertaking often resulted in large-scale death and destruction. Most of the world's largest chemical companies began as dye manufacturers. Color continues to come at a price, from places usually hidden far from view.

But artists work to make the invisible visible, and I became fascinated by the notion of making art about the world of global trade, finding ways to uncover the layers, trajectories, and overlaps of such networks. That has meant immersing myself in commodity chains—the global linkages that deliver resources from far afield into our personal lives. The production of

A prior version of this chapter was published in *Crosscut*, the online news magazine. It is reprinted here courtesy of the editors.

colors, I came to realize, has created a complex set of troubles for people living and working in Spokane and eastern Washington. Those troubles have tied otherwise well-meaning business, state, federal, and tribal leaders in knots.

When I stumbled on the connection between colors and pollution in the Spokane River, I was knee-deep in research for an art installation in Mumbai. India is one of the most brightly colored places in the world. The streets are covered with all manner and scale of signage ablaze with color, buildings are painted in vivid colors, and even the tiniest object is packaged in the brightest colors obtainable. Indians love colorful clothing. Color offers people in India and everywhere else, regardless of their economic status, a way to shine, a way to project their sense of power and well-being out into the world.

Perhaps not surprisingly, India has led the world in producing the most popular and widely used pigment—blue. For several centuries, India was the primary source of indigo, which in fact is named for the country. The color blue, occurring very rarely in nature, has always been in high demand, not least for uniforms, military and civilian—blue jeans among them. The British, having colonized India, extracted huge profits from the subcontinent by shipping dried indigo cakes, processed with great labor from the indigo plant, to Europe for fabric dyeing and printing.

In the middle of the nineteenth century, at the zenith of the British Empire, the Germans began imagining replacements for what they couldn't get in northern Europe. In the 1880s, after a decade of expensive experimentation, the German chemical company BASF patented synthetic indigo, using nascent organic chemistry (and processes based on coal tar) to produce a color that was chemically identical to natural indigo dye, at a fraction of the cost. Eventually the Germans put the British-Indian indigo trade out of business.

A century after the crash in the trade of natural indigo, color is no longer bound to specific places. Ironically, though, it is still geographically bound by other factors. Phthalo (pronounced *thay-low*) blue, also known as copper phthalocyanine or CuPc, the world's most-used color, is produced almost entirely in India, from petroleum-based chemicals. The azos, another set of synthetic colors—reds, oranges and yellows—come predominantly from China. Thus we might say that India and China now control the primary colors.

One of the many factors that has led to most of the world's color being produced in Asia is weaker environmental regulations there. The processes for making colors often result in nasty chemical wastes and by-products, which are released into the air and water—and not necessarily at their point of origin. Colors are not and have never been manufactured along the Spokane River, yet they befoul the river in dangerous ways.

The falls of the Spokane River, the site of the founding of the city of Spokane, was once the site of an enormously rich fishery, where Native Americans easily caught all the salmon they needed to sustain themselves. By the 1950s, however, the river had become an open sewer. (See William Stimson's chapter in this volume.) It drained the city's toilets, waste from large mines upstream in Idaho, and effluent from closer industrial plants, like the Inland Empire Paper Company and Kaiser Aluminum.

Then Spokane was chosen as the site of the 1974 World's Fair, thanks in large part to the efforts of Sen. Henry "Scoop" Jackson, who helped create the Environmental Protection Agency. Expo '74 billed itself as "Celebrating Tomorrow's Fresh New Environment." The World's Fair was held in the smallest city ever to have hosted the fair, seemingly because Spokane was the first to take on the theme of environmentalism.

The fair didn't result in a cleaner Spokane River, but it did create momentum to rid the area around the falls of an unsightly tangle of railroad tracks and warehouses and to create a large park that would make the river and the falls once again the jewel of downtown. Perhaps most importantly, the Expo inspired the creation of the Spokane River Drainage Basin Depollution Policy Committee, a working partnership of civic, municipal and private entities that met regularly to work out ways to clean up the river.

Four decades after the fair, however, the fish in the Spokane River are laced with polychlorinated biphenyls (PCBs). These chemicals have long been known as potent carcinogens. They accumulate in ecosystems and in the bodies of animals, including fish and humans. Children are particularly at risk because they are exposed to higher concentrations relative to their body weight, and they metabolize the chemicals more quickly. PCB accumulation in kids has been shown to cause serious physical disease as well as cognitive dysfunctions.

Commercial production of PCBs was banned in the United States decades ago, shortly after the fair closed, and pollution in the river is of course not due to any single substance or source. But one of the contributing causes is an unexpected one. In 1991, at a cost of tens of millions of dollars, the Inland Empire Paper Company (IEP), located on the banks of the Spokane River, completely modernized, thus becoming the sixth mill in the country that produced recycled paper. In the late 1980s, California, one of the company's primary markets, had begun legislating that paper would need to contain a high percentage of recycled content. Company owners were doing what they saw as the right thing for the health of both the environment and the company.

Not long before the mill began producing recycled paper, its effluent had been thoroughly tested and found to be PCB-free. Some years later, when PCBs turned up in the tissues of the river's fish, the mill's waste stream was tested again, as was the outflow from all the city's treatment plants and other legacy industrial sites on the river. IEP was shocked to find that its brand-new green facility was discharging PCBs into the Spokane River, even though it did not use or produce PCBs. The dangerous chemicals were in the recycled material IEP used to make paper—specifically in the inks and dyes.

Phthalo blue, discovered in Scotland in the mid-1930s, was hailed almost immediately as an ideal blue. Bright and clear, with unbeatable color strength, it is terrifically colorfast, heat and chemical resistant, and nontoxic to users. It functions very well as a dye for all substrates and cloth, as a well as serving as a pigment for ink. The cyan cartridges we use in inkjet printers are made with phthalo blue. It is also used as a colorant in paints and plastics, including those ubiquitous blue nylon tarps. But phthalo-based blue inks can contain PCBs, as can the azo yellows, oranges, and reds. Most ironically, sales of phthalo-based green inks continue to increase each year because a great deal of consumer packaging now proclaims, in green, that the enclosed product is environmentally friendly. Phthalo green inks can contain even more PCBs than the blue.

As an artist and a researcher, I've interviewed a number of stakeholders in the state about PCB contamination, including federal and regional regulators striving to clean up the Spokane River. I've also talked with manufacturers of phthalo blue in India. I've learned, among other things, that phthalo pigments are found in paper, textiles, cosmetics, leather products, foods, and a multitude of other consumer goods. But the PCBs in phthalo-based inks are not responsible for the dazzling hues or for their intensity: they are a by-product of the manufacturing process. Because phthalo does not dissolve in water, other chemicals must be used to produce liquid colors. The easiest and cheapest manufacturing processes use chlorine-based solvents such as trichlorobenzene. When these react with the other chemicals used in manufacturing process, they produce PCBs.

The same is true of the PCB-containing azo colors. For many years, state highway departments have specified that the yellow paint used to mark stripes on roads must be of a particular azo yellow, because that compound sticks very well to asphalt and stays bright yellow for years. But as chips of the striping are broken off by vehicular traffic and are washed off the roadway with rain, the PCBs in the paint make their way into rivers.

The IEP plant in Spokane recycles publications printed with inks containing phthalo blues and greens and azo yellows, oranges, and reds. As part of the recycling process, those inks are washed out of the paper pulp. Treated wastewater is flushed into the river, taking the PCBs with it. And the practice is perfectly legal. Even though the EPA banned PCBs that "could have unintended consequences in humans" (e.g., cancer), the agency allows imported products that contain PCBs as *unintended consequences* of their manufacture.

Since the discovery of PCBs issuing from the mill, the mill owners—who themselves publish a printed newspaper, the *Spokesman-Review*—have installed the best available waste-treatment equipment in an effort to remove the PCBs from the flow. But it's simply not enough. The PCBs resist the treatment, enter the river and make their way into the metabolisms of fish and other organisms in the food web, including humans.

As the Portland-based science writer Elizabeth Grossman succinctly puts it, "PCBs do not occur naturally, and once they are in the environment, they can last for decades." The persistence of PCBs once made them highly useful in industry. They added chemical stability to products, protecting them from breaking down. In essence, what made PCBs seem very good makes them ultimately very bad: they are persistent in the environment and very difficult to remove. Recycled paper is not the only source of the PCBs showing up in the Spokane River fish.

The world of color has always been associated with danger and some-times with death. In the Middle Ages, those who made colors for textile dye-ing were considered alchemists, practitioners of black magic. During Hitler's regime, several German chemical companies (the largest in the world), under the cover of producing dyes, made mustard gas and the Zyklon B gas (hydro-gen cyanide) used to kill millions in concentration camps. Today we assume that those dark days are over, but colored threads attach themselves to our lives in a multitude of unseen and sometimes dangerous ways.

There is hope, however. Solvents have long been available that produce phthalo blue with no traces of PCBs, though they were, for a long time, more expensive. Scientists have identified several promising avenues for azo pigment formulations that are PCB-free. And on the Spokane River, the collaboration that began after '74 Expo is still remarkably alive. That spirit of collaboration promises the best and perhaps the only way to keep PCBs out of the water—and it has made the river and the resolution of its difficulties a matter of national and even international interest.

There is, it turns out, a connection in this case between India, the Spo-kane River, and the first peoples of the Northwest. The Spokane Indian Reservation of 160,000 acres, created in 1881, is a fraction of the 3 million acres the natives inhabited before the reservation was created, but it is still fed by the Spokane River. Salmon represented a very large percentage of the diet of the Spokanes, but in 1995 the Spokane Tribe demonstrated that the Spokane River salmon contained dangerous concentrations of PCBs. A

2014 letter to the EPA from the Confederated Tribes of the Umatilla Reservation, cosigned by the Spokanes, states: "Water and salmon are among our tribal First Foods. They are first in serving order during our longhouse ceremonies. Our people eat up to nine times as much fish as the 'average' non-Indian. Fish consumption is part of our religion, culture and way of life. The risks to tribal peoples, other fish consumers, and the environment from PCBs far outweigh any possible 'economic considerations.'"

The centrality of salmon to the life and livelihood of the Spokane Tribe moved the Washington Department of Ecology to adopt the country's strictest legal limits for PCBs in the Spokane River. The standards, measured in parts per quadrillion, are so strict that it is technically impossible to measure for such a minute level of contamination, let alone attain it. One of my interviewees likened detecting the presence of chemicals at that level to finding one leaf in the entire landmass of the United States. But the state's water-quality standard has been overruled by, of all things, the US Environmental Protection Agency.

I've asked the EPA directly: if PCBs are leaching into the Spokane River from pigments that contain PCBs, why aren't they banned? PCBs are, after all, one of the most widely studied contaminants in the world. The agency's reply to me included the statement that "an exception is made for inadvertently generated PCBs that are unintentional impurities of many common commercial chemical or manufacturing processes. EPA has concluded that allowing such inadvertent generation has important economic benefits and does not pose an unreasonable risk to human health or the environment."

In July 2016, Judge Barbara Rothstein ordered the EPA and the Washington State Department of Ecology to set limits on the discharge of PCBs into the Spokane River. In its required response to the judge, the agency said that the PCBs are not being added to the pigments but are present as an unintended consequence of the manufacturing process (apparently suggesting that this somehow makes them less to be feared than those intentionally added), and that besides, banning their use in pigments would create problems in the marketplace. What paint would we put down for yellow stripes on highways? What would replace the cyan ink in our home printers? What the EPA actually seems to be telling us all is that a great deal of political pressure has been put on the agency by the chemical industry to allow PCBs in pigments, because banning them would cost companies money.

In a 2010 letter to the EPA, the Color Pigments Manufacturing Association stated that taking phthalo pigments off the market would jeopardize color printing, most blue and green paint, and many plastic formulations. According to industry spokespeople, we'd be left with a discolored or even uncolored world: we would all be transported back to the black-and-white days of my childhood. They say that it is infeasible to alter manufacturing processes to exclude PCBs from the phthalo colors.

It isn't. I have spoken with representatives of major pigment manufacturers based in Mumbai that no longer use chlorine-based solvent to produce phthalo blue. Their spec sheets confirm that they produce and export PCB-free CuPc blue. Just a few years ago, the cost of replacing the trichlorobenzene solvent with alkylbenzene (which produces no PCBs) increased the production cost of the pigment by 5 percent. But enough companies are now using the alkyl-based solvent that the price has dropped precipitously. Producing CuPc without PCBs is no longer prohibitively expensive.

In 1989 a similar pollution drama played out on the shores of the Spokane River. The residents of the tiny Liberty Lake Sewer and Water District, which drains into the Spokane River, were chagrined by floating mats of blue-green algae in the river. Research established that a major culprit was phosphates in laundry detergents that were being discharged into the river from residential sewers and encouraging algal growth. People in the community began boycotting such detergents. In 2005, a new battle heated up around Liberty Lake. The Sewer and Water Commission was considering banning phosphates in automatic dishwasher detergent (just as it would in laundry detergent in 2009 in Spokane County). Well aware of what had happened with washing-machine detergents, mighty Procter and Gamble sent representatives from Cincinnati to Liberty Lake to testify before the commission. The company claimed that without phosphates, dishes wouldn't come clean and would be covered with water spots. Liberty Lake banned phosphate-containing dishwasher detergents anyway. The State of

Washington followed and, again, so did most of the rest of the country. In early 2014, P&G announced that it would no longer use phosphates in any of its laundry detergents, wherever they were sold. Procter and Gamble cited its progress in developing phosphate substitutes as a reason for the change.

Could something similar happen with PCBs in pigments? Judge Rothstein's ruling said that the EPA and Washington Department of Ecology erred in allowing the Spokane River Regional Toxics Task Force to be set up to address the issue of reducing PCBs in the Spokane River instead of simply mandating a clear timetable for their removal. The ruling is another irony in the story of the colors that pollute the river. A lasting legacy of Expo '74 has been the public-private collaboration established to clean up the river. Forty years on, the task force is the latest promising iteration of a cooperative effort to save the river.

Neither the EPA nor the Department of Ecology can clean up the PCBs contaminating fish in the Spokane River, because there is no technology yet available to accomplish such a task. Governor Jay Inslee said as much in his 2016 speech on the matter. What must be done instead is to find ways to keep the PCBs from getting into the river in the first place. That effort will apparently require a groundswell, not unlike Liberty Lake's, to swamp the vested interests that guide public policy in our region and in our country.

Patterns of consumption will have to change. We are going to have to live without the cheapest colors. We are going to have to demand that they be banned from commerce. The chemical industry is going to have to modify pigment formulas. Experience in the Pacific Northwest has shown that collaborative, cooperative efforts can make these changes happen. Such efforts will help to move the EPA to do the right thing in the long term (despite the short-term intransigence of President Donald Trump's EPA chief, Scott Pruitt).

If the EPA enforces its water-quality standards, The Inland Empire Paper Company's recycling plant will not be able to continue in operation. Producing paper with 60 percent recycled fiber is the green thing to do. But it is not, nor has it ever been, enough. We consumers need to rethink our responsibility for maintaining clean ecosystems and clean water: it goes beyond tossing our used paper in the recycle bin.

Color is by nature, by design, and by use distracting. Dressing up merchandise or walls and embellishing printed matter can make designs and products look and feel like class acts even when they really aren't. The application of color is the easiest and usually the cheapest way to induce us to buy. But cheap consumer goods come at a cost: pollution and disease are expensive.

Blue is the color of water and sky, a sign of purity. Those are reasons the color has long been a favorite of artists and (according to polls) everyone else as well. But because blue never occurs in nature in a ready-to-use form (even the indigo plant requires extensive and messy processing to render the color usable), it has always been costly one way or the other. Its cost meant that for centuries its use was limited to purposes such as the depiction of the Virgin Mary's cloak in medieval paintings. At that time, colorfast blue was obtainable only from Afghanistan, in the form of lapis lazuli, a rare mineral that yields an ultramarine blue pigment. Today, in our global marketplace, it's easy to forget that the most widely used blue comes to us from equally far away in India.

As the sick Spokane River illustrates, it is still ultimately expensive stuff. To my mind, the problem of PCBs moving from pigments into fish is not an unintended consequence at all, but rather an un-*tended* consequence. For this polluting practice to stop, people with responsibility would have to tend directly to the problem, and that would be us.

# Spokane River Instream Flows

RACHAEL PASCHAL OSBORN

HOW MUCH WATER DOES A RIVER NEED? WE OFTEN TAKE FOR GRANTED the volume and speed of water we observe flowing in a river. Innately we understand that the quantity of flow—whether a surging spring freshet or a lazy summer eddy—is a function of the hydrologic cycle. Less obvious is the fact that human activities, especially dams and water diversions, manipulate the flow we see.

In the Spokane River, as in all rivers, the volume and timing of water flow are important for ecological reasons. The river's environmental features have developed and evolved through thousands of years of annual water cycles. Human alteration to flow is new in the grand scheme of geologic time, but its effect has proved disproportionate.

The Spokane River is hydrologically complex. Its flows begin as snow and rainfall in the Idaho Rockies, form the Coeur d'Alene and St. Joe Rivers, and feed Lake Coeur d'Alene. Mountain precipitation also percolates downward into groundwater, emerging as ground-to-surface discharges from the Spokane Valley–Rathdrum Prairie Aquifer into the river system, especially below Spokane Falls.

From Post Falls to the Mirabeau Park area, the Spokane River is a "losing" river. That is, water leaks from the river bottom into the aquifer. From Mirabeau Park to the city of Spokane, the river both gains from and loses water to the aquifer. Downstream of Spokane Falls, the river is fully gaining, as water seeps out of the aquifer into springs that feed the river and two tributaries—Hangman Creek and the Little Spokane River.

The Spokane is often referred to as a "flashy" river, with great variation in flow between spring and summer. During winter, snow falls in the upper watersheds. In spring, as the snows melt, river flows increase dramatically, peaking at around 43,000 cubic feet per second (cfs). Views of water thundering over Spokane Falls draw crowds of onlookers. This peak in the annual water cycle drops off as early as February and no later than mid-June, when hydropower company management of the level of Lake Coeur d'Alene begins. Spokane River flows begin to bottom out in July. That drop, from 43,000 cfs or more to 1,000 cfs or less in the matter of a few months, makes the Spokane River interesting, complex, and—during low flows—troubled.

Summer flows are directly affected by operations at Post Falls Dam and by water diversions. The gates at Post Falls Dam are closed in mid- to late June to maintain the surface of Lake Coeur d'Alene at 2,128 feet above sea level. Avista Utilities, the power company that manages the lake, is required to maintain the flow at 600 cfs at the dam unless the lake level drops a few inches, at which point releases are decreased to 500 cfs. These releases combine with aquifer inflows to determine Spokane River flow from July to mid-September, when the spill gates at Post Falls reopen to allow natural outflows from the lake to the river.

The flow releases at Post Falls Dam are controversial. Maintaining higher water levels for Lake Coeur d'Alene pleases Idaho recreationalists and lakefront property owners, but it deprives the Spokane River of water. Determinations of lake levels and dam releases, regulated by Idaho law, directly affect Washington's interests. Conflict between the two states regarding water has yet to precipitate an interstate water allocation fight. But it's coming.

Flows define and affect aquatic habitat. Before 1908, when dam building on the river began in earnest, Spokane Falls was a terminal point for major salmon runs, as were the Little Spokane River and Hangman Creek. (See Allan Scholz's chapter in this volume.) Extirpation of the salmon left a void now filled by such native fish as redband trout and mountain whitefish. Spawning fish and hatchlings require both ample water flow and the cool temperatures that accompany higher flows. To restore salmon to the watershed, protecting flows will be paramount.

Higher flows serve many functions, including recreation. Whitewater rafting and kayaking at Sullivan Hole and Devil's Toenail are extremely popular during the spring runoff. Once flows fall below 3,000 cfs, white-water enthusiasts begin to leave the river. At flows below 1,300 cfs, boats begin to scrape bottom. Flows also produce electrical energy. Along the river's one-hundred-mile length, seven dams bisect it: six are owned by Avista, one (Upriver Dam) by the City of Spokane. Inside these dams, turbines spin and generate power in proportion to the amount of water flowing through.

In addition, flows dilute pollution. Five sewage and two industrial treatment plants process the waste produced by some half a million humans, and these plants discharge their treated effluent to the river. Pollution concentrations in sewage effluent are regulated by law, and they are in part a function of the amount of river flow available to dilute the discharge.

The amount and timing of flow in the Spokane River is a product, then, both of large-scale watershed processes and of human manipulation. That flow also has intimate significance for the people and wildlife that depend on the river. How much water the river "needs," and how much it gets, are largely determined by the priorities we set and the choices we make. Several recent stories illustrate the challenges the river faces and the work being done on its behalf.

## Does the River Have a "Right" to Its Water?

Water rights are permits that authorize private parties or municipalities to pump groundwater or divert water directly out of a river. Pumping from the aquifer in both Idaho and Washington removes water that would otherwise enhance flow in the Spokane River. Both surface and groundwater extraction directly affect the quantity of water flow in the river.

Since the late 1800s, Idaho and Washington have approved or registered thousands of water rights in the Spokane watershed. Most of these rights authorize pumping from the aquifer. Not until 1978, when our aquifer was designated a sole-source aquifer, did scientists formally recognize the connection between the aquifer and the river. This designation by the US Environmental Protection Agency signifies that an aquifer is the sole or primary source of drinking water for a region and therefore requires special protections. In the mid-1990s, the State of Washington imposed an informal moratorium on new water rights. But Idaho continues to issue groundwater rights, deliberately ignoring the effects on the river.

Washington is not guilt-free, however, having issued extensive and inchoate water rights to several municipalities, most notably the City of Spokane. (Inchoate water rights are "paper" water rights, meaning that they are authorized but not actually used.) As the city grows, it will increase water usage pursuant to these rights, with a commensurate increase in effects on the Spokane River. Water purveyors will also access their rights, increase groundwater pumping, and continue to deplete flows in the river. One planning estimate prepared by Spokane County indicates that full use of these inchoate rights will reduce summer flows by up to 250 cfs from already low flows of 1,000 cfs. The exercise of water rights will exacerbate the harm to aquatic habitat and nonconsumptive human use of the river established over the past century.

Both Idaho and Washington have adopted "instream flows" for the Spokane River—a relatively new concept in Western water management. Effectively these are water rights for the river, but they are theoretical numbers that signify what each state thinks the river "needs." In Idaho, during summer, that number is 950 cfs. For the same period in Washington, it is 500 cfs near Mirabeau Park and 850 cfs at the Monroe Street Dam. The recently adopted Washington flow is now the subject of litigation. In practice, neither state is responsible for ensuring that these numbers are met. Indeed, riverine water rights are assigned a lower priority than the thousands of water rights already issued. Neither state has yet recognized that the river came first and deserves first priority in water allocation.

Over the years, Idaho and Washington have tacitly engaged in a race to the bottom of the aquifer. Idaho water managers have expressed a wish to keep all the water in Idaho, as if that were physically feasible, while Washington water managers wring their hands in the quest for what they perceive as a fair share. Each state has allocated very large quantities of water to serve municipal and particularly residential growth. The resulting culture of green lawns elevates nonessential human needs over ecologic, aesthetic, and other nonconsumptive uses of the river.

## The Power Plant Cases: Pump the Aquifer, Rob the River

In the winter of 2000–2001, the ill-fated Texas energy giant Enron manipulated energy markets in California, leading to rolling blackouts and electricity shortages. At the time, it was not widely understood that the energy crisis was a consequence of human machination; instead it was attributed to a shortage of electrical generation capacity. The energy sector responded with a frenzy of proposals to build new power plants around the Western United States. The technology of choice was combined-cycle cogeneration, or *cogen*, which uses natural gas and water as fuel for energy turbines.

On June 25, 2001, Spokane residents woke up to the headline "Demands on Water May Drain Supply: Officials Fear Aquifer Can't Sustain Projects." Two new power plants were proposed for Rathdrum, Idaho, just across the Washington-Idaho state line. Rathdrum, as it turned out, possessed three key infrastructure elements that make it a cogen Shangri-La: two high-pressure natural gas pipelines, originating in Canada and Utah, which would fuel the plants; industrial-scale transmission lines to carry electricity to consumers; and abundant water from the aquifer.

Cheap water in large quantities was essential to the projects. The two plants proposed to pump and evaporate twenty million gallons of water per day to cool the power turbines. The targeted water source was the seemingly prolific aquifer, which lay just a few hundred feet beneath the construction sites. To access this water, developers of the power plant applied for new groundwater rights. In Washington these rights could not be granted. But in Idaho, then as now, new water users were welcome.

The proposed water consumption of the power plants raised red flags. The aquifer is a shared resource, flowing from Idaho to Washington. How much water was in the aquifer? Analysis indicated that the amount of water *already* allocated by the two states exceeded the average annual recharge.

Would these large new uses affect existing water users? Flows in the Spokane River certainly would be depleted. Was evaporating the finite quantity of water in the aquifer to produce power for California consumers the best use of local groundwater?

While state and local policymakers lamented, a consortium of stakeholders organized to appeal the water-right applications. Local 93 of the International Brotherhood of Electrical Workers and Rebound, a union-support project, partnered with Friends of the Aquifer, the Kootenai Environmental Alliance, and the Sierra Club Upper Columbia River Group to challenge the proposed water use. Teresa Hampton of Boise, Karen Lindholdt of Spokane, Gonzaga University School of Law professor Mark Wilson, law student Joel Ban of Gonzaga University Environmental Law Clinic, and I represented the group appealing the water-right applications: that is, the appellants.

The two corporations backing the proposals were Cogentrix Energy, a North Carolina–based energy conglomerate engaged in all phases of power development and sales, and Newport Generation, owned by the venture-capital giant Warburg Pincus, which had money to burn. In response to the appellant group challenges, back-to-back hearings were held in April 2002 before the Idaho Department of Water Resources hearing examiner Glen Saxton.

The appellant group brought numerous legal theories, evidence, and expertise to the proceedings. The hydrogeologists Gary Andres, John Riley, and Stan Miller testified about the intimate connections between the aquifer and the Spokane River. They demonstrated that groundwater pumped and consumed by the power plants would mean less water in the Spokane River and lead to adverse effects on fisheries, water quality, and recreation. The effects would be felt downstream in Washington, not in Idaho.

That fact raised a key legal question. Legally, water rights in Idaho must not harm the "local public interest." But were effects felt in Washington state "local" to Idaho, particularly given the shared nature of the water resource? Idaho and Washington fisheries managers Ned Horner and John Whalen testified that decreased flows would harm fish on both sides of the state line, including Washington trout that migrate to Idaho. Water-quality evidence showed that less water flowing in the river in Washington could lead to more stringent pollution limits for the three Idaho sewage-treatment plants that discharge into the Spokane River.

The appellants also attacked project efficiencies. Idaho water law does not allow wasteful use. The appellants contended that evaporating twenty million gallons per day constituted a waste. They argued that water is not the only way to cool turbines. Instead, some of the electricity the plants generated could be used to power a cooling system, albeit at a cost to profits.

The appellants were the first to offer climate-change evidence in water-rights proceedings. The Washington State climatologist Philip Mote testified that as mountain snowpack decreased, so would the waters that feed our local aquifer. There was (and is) genuine uncertainty about water availability to satisfy future regional needs.

Community support was substantial. The hearings were packed. Citizens and business leaders from both states testified, as did elected officials, including the Spokane city councilor Cherie Rodgers, the Spokane county commissioner John Roskelley, and the Post Falls mayor, Clay Larkin. All were concerned that human use of the local aquifer had reached its limit and that more pumping would harm the community's future.

In a pair of landmark decisions, the hearing examiner denied the two applications. There were too many effects and too much uncertainty to authorize these large, consumptive uses. Future community needs had to be considered. As it turned out, energy markets were not as robust as the corporations had calculated. The economics of new power plants were marginal. Cogentrix and Newport Generation folded up their plans and went away.

The power-plant cases constituted a teachable moment regarding the value of the aquifer and its connection to the Spokane River. For the first time, the regional community heard the message that pumping the aquifer means robbing the river. Public education and awareness translated into political will. One indirect outcome of the power-plant cases was the creation of a common base of information for water-resource management. Washington and Idaho partnered with the US Geological Survey (and Congress obliged with a $3.5 million appropriation) to create the SVRP

Bi-state Aquifer Study. That study evaluated existing water usage, natural recharge to the aquifer, and aquifer-river connections. Using the resulting model, water managers can predict the effects of pumping from any location in the watershed on groundwater levels and river flows.

The power-plant cases also pointedly illustrated the need for an equitable division of water between the two states that share the aquifer. Such an allocation can be made through litigation or a settlement ratified by Congress to become a formal compact between the states. But because almost all the water in the system originates in Idaho, that state has little incentive to agree to limit its use. In the intervening fifteen years, Idaho has issued water rights in excess of what the power plants proposed to use. Meanwhile, the state of Washington lacks the political gumption either to persuade Idaho to negotiate an agreement or to sue. Nonetheless, the Rathdrum power plant cases were a turning point in the Spokane–Coeur d'Alene region's understanding of the limits of the aquifer and its intimate connection with the Spokane River.

## Rehydrating Spokane Falls

Seven dams, especially the uppermost dam at Post Falls, Idaho, limit and control flow in various reaches of the Spokane River. Early twentieth-century dam builders targeted the Spokane's profuse waterfalls as sites for hydroelectric power generation. In the process they dewatered or destroyed important Indian cultural sites at Post Falls, Spokane, Nine Mile, and Little Falls. To operate all but one of its six dams, Avista must hold a license from the Federal Energy Regulatory Commission, the entity that regulates hydropower production. Because FERC's enabling statute, the Federal Power Act, was not in effect when the Avista dams were built, the Avista dams were first licensed in 1972.

Avista's first license extended for thirty-five years. In the intervening period, Congress enacted several laws, including the Clean Water Act and the Electric Consumers Protection Act, which impose important environmental-protection regulations on dams. Citizen litigation used Section 401 of the Clean Water Act to require Avista to return water to the Spokane Falls.

The Spokane Falls gave rise to the city of Spokane. As the city developed, the falls were surrounded by water mills to harness power and create energy for industrial and municipal use. The basalt bed of the falls was gouged and trenched to channel flows for power generation and facilitate access during low-water periods.

In 1890 and 1922, Washington Water Power (Avista's precursor) built two dams at the falls: Upper Falls and Monroe Street. The Upper Falls Dam splits the river between the natural falls channel and a south channel that conveys water around the waterfalls to the powerhouse at the base of Upper Falls. The pool behind the Monroe Street Dam feeds an underground siphon that bypasses the falls and channels water to a turbine at the base of the Lower Falls.

During spring runoff, the falls flow freely, and water is plentiful enough for both the Spokane River and the powerhouses. But in late summer, when river flows drop, a choice must be made between putting water in the falls or channeling it to the forebay and siphons that feed the powerhouses. Lacking regulatory direction, Avista chose to divert water from the falls. As relicensing approached in the 2000s, Upper Falls typically went dry from July to early September, and sometimes until much later in the year. The Lower Falls were maintained with a flow of 100 cfs during daylight hours but "turned off" at dusk.

Under the Clean Water Act, Washington designates specific uses for each river in the state. For the Spokane River, these uses include protection of fisheries, recreation, and aesthetics. When it applied for renewal of its federal power license, Avista asked the state to certify that these designated uses were met. Dry waterfalls did not satisfy the requirement to protect fisheries and aesthetic use. Accordingly, the state permit included not only mandatory conditions to protect water quality but also, as the US Supreme Court had recently approved, conditions regarding water quantity.

Upper Spokane Falls in 2012, showing restored flow after the 2009 settlement between Avista Utilities, on one side, and the Sierra Club and the Center for Environmental Law and Policy, on the other. These channels had previously been dry during the summer months. Photo courtesy of John Osborn.

In response to stakeholder input, the Washington Department of Ecology did impose conditions to require some water to flow over the falls, but it allowed Avista to continue to turn off the water at night and on weekdays. The Sierra Club and the Center for Environmental Law and Policy (CELP), contending that the law required the Spokane River to be treated like a river rather than a faucet, appealed this decision. In May 2009, the Sierra Club, and the CELP, assisted by the University of Washington Environmental Law Clinic, settled the appeal with Avista. The company was required to maintain flows of 500 cfs in the Upper Falls and 200 cfs in the Lower Falls, dropping to 100 cfs at night. Avista had the option of attempting to restore the natural bed of the falls, previously gouged to accommodate water mills, and if successful, to decrease the daily flows in the Upper Falls. Following a pilot study, in 2011 Avista installed concrete weirs to redirect flow in the Upper Falls, substantially improving the aesthetics of the water flow over the north channel. In October 2011, Avista, the Sierra Club, and the CELP agreed on a daily flow of 320 cfs for the Upper Falls.

The 2009 rehydration of Spokane Falls in downtown Spokane marked a turning point in which Avista, the major dam owner on the river, accepted its duty to avoid depleting the Spokane River. The community regained a cultural and aesthetic asset that has, in turn, encouraged further restoration of and access to the waterfall and river environs.

## Climate Change and the Future of the Spokane River

The last twenty years have seen substantial efforts to ameliorate the negative effects of flow depletion in the Spokane River. Through the work of citizen groups, improvements have been seen in managing the issuance of water rights from the river and from its tributary aquifer, mitigating the effects of dams, and establishing ecologically viable instream flows. Citizen advocacy is almost always required to persuade political and commercial powers to do the right thing, but the concept of river restoration is beginning to speak to the entire Spokane community.

Climate change portends great uncertainty regarding future river health. (See Stan Miller's chapter in this volume.) Global climate models indicate that the warming climate is already causing reduced snowpack in the mountains of the western Pacific region, including the western slopes of the Bitterroot mountain range that drain to the Spokane River. Snowpack is a natural storage system: melting snows maintain late summer river flows and recharge groundwater. With warmer winters, precipitation will fall as rain, not snow, and immediately run off into the river systems that drain the mountainous West. As a result, the snowpack-dependent Spokane River will experience lower summer flows. This hydrologic trend change is already evident in Spokane River hydrographs. The hot and arid summer of 2015, in which flows approached the lowest ever recorded, was a preview of future Spokane River flows. Another expected effect of climate change is increased human migration into the Spokane region, as citizens of the southwestern states flee heat and water scarcity. This influx will increase human water consumption, with consequent decreases in Spokane River flows. Ironically, Spokane is perceived as a place of water abundance because of the local aquifer.

Decreasing flows in the Spokane River will shrink native fish habitat, reduce recreational and aesthetic enjoyment, and decrease the river's capacity to assimilate pollution. Climate change and unending human demand for water will exacerbate these problems.

Euro-American attitudes toward the Spokane River have been relentlessly utilitarian for most of the past 140 years. Now it is in the human interest to expand our view of the river's value to include its ecological health and nonconsumptive benefits. To date, however, virtually every effort to prevent or reverse overallocation has required litigation against government and corporate entities. But litigation is not a sustainable model of management. Can the Spokane community recognize and reverse its adverse relationship to the Spokane River?

# The Spokane Riverkeepers

RICK EICHSTAEDT, BART MIHAILOVICH,
AND JERRY WHITE

THE IDEA OF "KEEPING" THE SPOKANE RIVER ORIGINATED WITH THE
Spokane, Coeur d'Alene, and other Salish peoples. Only in their spirit, and
on their backs, has the keeping or maintaining of the river proved possible.
The Spokane Riverkeeper program exists today in part as a tribute to that
past. Officially the idea of a keeper of this river began in 2008, when community leaders in Spokane decided to join the Waterkeeper Alliance. Here we
recount that local history and its origins in an alliance on the Hudson River.
We examine the challenges that face the river and the challenges of working
across state lines. We explain why the mud in Hangman Creek contains
not only normal geological runoff but also pollution from upstream sport,
agricultural, and residential sources. We also recall that four billion global
citizens face water insecurity today.

The worldwide Waterkeeper Alliance began in 1966 with the formation
of the Hudson River Fishermen's Association. Degraded water quality in
that river had begun to erode the finances of commercial fishermen as well
as affecting recreational fishing. The fishermen recognized that outspoken
and citizen-led advocacy to enforce existing water laws would be the best
way to protect their river, livelihoods, and families. Monitoring the Hudson
River and responding to pollution events became an increasingly demand-
ing job. In the early 1970s the association hired Tom Whyatt as the part-
time riverkeeper to monitor the Hudson for pollution. In 1983, the group
launched a patrol boat and hired John Cronin as the first full-time keeper

of the Hudson River. The Fishermen's Association changed its name to Riverkeeper in 1986.

Borrowing that organizational structure and inspired by shared visions and goals, grassroots organizations for protecting waterways emerged across the eastern United States and then in the West, on waterways such as San Francisco Bay and the Salish Sea (Puget Sound). While these waterways faced a variety of problems, and the cultures and approaches taken proved as diverse as the problems, one common feature tied these grassroots efforts together: people were standing up, with the support of their communities, to say they had had enough and were going to take clean-water advocacy into their own hands.

By 1999, some thirty-five independent grassroots efforts across North America had joined together to create the worldwide Waterkeeper Alliance. What began as a loose training initiative for water-quality advocates (called the National Alliance of River, Sound, and Baykeepers) was formalized and launched at a conference on New York's Peconic Bay. There the water advocates gathered under the leadership and ingenuity of Robert F. Kennedy Jr. and trademarked the term *waterkeeper*.

The alliance, which now includes more than three hundred waterkeepers, provides not only opportunities for networking and sharing skills but also a means of collaborating on regional, national, and international efforts. The tiny Spokane Riverkeeper organization might not be invited to participate in worldwide climate negotiations in Paris, but the Waterkeeper Alliance was there, representing the issues and concerns of Spokane Riverkeeper on that global stage.

## Our Local Origins

Imagine getting a phone call from your sister who asks you, "Are you sitting down? If not, you'd better." Your sister informs you that your aunt has died and left you an unexpected and significant inheritance. Such a phone call came Jim Sheehan's way nearly two decades ago, prompting him to quit his job and turn to community service. The former public defender, now a Spokane philanthropist and innovative urban developer, is leading the efforts for urban renewal at West Main Avenue in downtown Spokane. In 1998 he first created the Center for Justice (CFJ), a nonprofit law firm dedicated to protecting human rights, preserving the Earth, and holding the government accountable to the principles of democracy.

The CFJ fulfilled Sheehan's long-held desire to give something back to his hometown and its most vulnerable citizens. As he saw it, the legal system too often favored those with money and political influence, while citizen groups and poorer citizens often could not find or afford representation. His vision of a better community meant fixing all the pieces, addressing social as well as environmental justice. Since Sheehan established the CFJ in 1999, it has served numerous clients and organizations at low or no cost.

Sheehan's windfall also led to an increase in the effectiveness of citizen advocacy for the Spokane River. Finally, nonprofit organizations had lawyers available to help them defend the river. As the CFJ sees it, promoting justice includes protecting the right to a healthy local environment. One CFJ attorney, Bonne Beavers, representing the Upper Columbia River Group of the Sierra Club, worked to ensure that the process of renewing the federal license for Avista Utilities' dams on the Spokane River addressed water quality, water flows, aesthetics, and effects on fisheries. Bonne also began the CFJ's long-term work on implementing the processes mandated by the Clean Water Act to improve the health of the river.

Beavers's initial work was far-reaching, but her part-time efforts were not enough. The CFJ, with Sheehan's support, sought to hire a full-time attorney, with Beavers's continued assistance. In 2004, Rick Eichstaedt, now the CFJ executive director, took up the position.

Eichstaedt and Beavers teamed up to represent the Sierra Club and other environmental organizations until the arrival of Mike Chappell. Mike Petersen, executive director of the Lands Council, set up a meeting regarding the new county sewage-treatment plant. In the meeting, Chappell asked why the river didn't have a keeper and why the Gonzaga University Law School in Spokane didn't have an environmental clinic. Most law schools had such clinics, and the Riverkeeper program began back in 1986. Spokane deserved and needed both.

Coincidentally in 2009, just a few days after the Waterkeeper Alliance had approved the Spokane Riverkeeper project, Chappell was hired by Gonzaga University Law School to head up a new environmental law clinic. Eichstaedt, serving as temporary riverkeeper, was eventually able to expand the program and hire Bart Mihailovich to take over as riverkeeper. In 2011, Chappell died. Mihailovich continued as riverkeeper until 2014, when he took a job with the national keeper program. In 2014, Jerry White Jr. succeeded Mihailovich and continues as the overseer, or keeper, of the Spokane River today.

As the official Spokane riverkeeper, White spends a great deal of time thinking about pipes: pipes that carry sewage or toxic slurry into the Spokane River and its tributaries; and pipes permitted, under complex rules, to flush human-generated waste into the natural world. Increasingly, he also deals with another form of pollution: cattle that denude stream banks and contaminate creeks. Nowhere in the region are such forms of pollution more in evidence than in Hangman Creek (still known on state maps as Latah Creek), a southern tributary of the Spokane River. Bullied by a world that thinks mainly of bottom lines and engineering efficiencies, the creek has the dingy look of neglect and abuse. White lives near the confluence of Hangman Creek and the Spokane River. He has stood on Hangman's banks when it is running foamy and muddy, fouling the Spokane River with a streak of sediment for miles below the confluence.

Hangman Creek meanders over sixty-five miles, draining the mountains of Idaho to the south and east of Spokane, before flowing into the Spokane. It is a neglected and battered sibling of the Little Spokane River, which joins with the Spokane River a few miles farther down. With its high water temperatures and levels of phosphorus, nitrates, and fecal coliform bacteria, Hangman Creek has some of the dirtiest water in Washington State. Agricultural, sport, and residential activities exploit the creek more as a "conveyance," to use the language of the Clean Water Act, than as a living system with complex needs.

The Little Spokane, managed in part by Washington State Parks at a stunning natural area where it meets the main river, enjoys relatively stable banks and shade from forests of cottonwood, alder, and willow. Its waters tend to be clean and clear as they flow out of its complex and vibrant wetlands. By contrast, Hangman Creek at its lower end is crammed into a narrow channel along Highway 195. In the interstate Palouse region where the creek originates, it flows brown with runoff soil. During parts of the winter and spring, its floodwaters blast down the channel in a turbulent mix of silt and runoff. Such stark differences between the two streams are consequences of divergent management practices since white settlement began.

Long ago Hangman Creek was a vibrant and temperate stream, cloaked by black hawthorn, cottonwood, red osier dogwood, and willow. Stories from the Native Coeur d'Alene people describe harvests of salmon and steelhead, which once migrated at least fifty-five miles up the creek from the main course of the Spokane. In the 1980s Herman Seltice, a relative of Chief Andrew Seltice, stated in an interview that his family "went down to Hangman Creek [in Idaho] and caught salmon by spearing and that was the most important meal in those days. Salmon were not the only fish that came up the creek; we also had whitefish and trout. The reason we don't have those now is because the dams were built that destroyed our fishing grounds." Where the creek joins the Spokane River, there was an Indian settlement for eight thousand years. It was supported by an enormous fishery: the Columbia River was once home to migrations of some sixteen million salmon each year. Like a set of great lungs inhaling, the river absorbed massive chinook and coho salmon migrating upriver by the thousands. Exhaling in the spring, it washed millions of tiny smolts downriver to the Pacific. Some of the salmon caught on the Spokane, the Little Spokane, and Hangman Creek were traded with peoples to the east for bison meat, although most were dried and eaten or traded during the long winters.

In those days Hangman Creek ran clear, its cobbles and gravels sustaining populations of trout and salmon. Insects such as mayfly, salmonfly, and stonefly flourished and fed the hatchlings that were storing their energy for the journey to the Pacific Ocean. In Alaska, ocean nitrogen has been detected in the leaves of the alders growing on river banks. At one time, Hangman would have been no different. When spawned-out salmon died in the creek, their flesh nourished a vast network of riparian plants and animals.

The Euro-Americans who settled in the region disrupted this cycle with the farming methods they brought. Native people were pushed out of the area, persecuted, and deprived of the fish that continued to struggle up the changing rivers. The Native people's traditional root-harvesting grounds were ditched and grazed, and the subsistence systems that underpinned indigenous lifeways unraveled. The farmers brought large herds of cattle, which grazed and trampled the riparian groves that cloaked and protected the stream banks. After the great cattle drives of the 1880s, homesteaders and ranchers worked to cultivate even more land, draining wetlands and trenching creeks to raise hay and grain. By the 1930s, and into the 1960s and 1970s, agricultural extension agencies offered incentives to tear out the streamside willows, cottonwoods, and hawthorns. Tributary streams like the North Fork of Spangle Creek were straightened and the adjacent wetlands drained and channeled to Hangman Creek.

Stripped of its natural vegetation and networks of wetlands, the surrounding soil could no longer hold water. Melting snow and rain poured into the creek and its tributaries, carrying soil from roads and tilled fields. The runoff eroded the banks. Today the creek flows as a kind of high-pressure hose, cutting more exposed banks and washing ever more soil into the water. Fine grains of gravel and soil clog the interstitial spaces between river cobbles that provide homes for insects such as caddis and stoneflies. The water has become a slurry, so thick with Palouse soil that the turbidity (degree of clarity) sometimes measures in excess of thirty times the healthy level for trout. Turbid water impairs their respiration, prevents them from feeding, and disrupts normal territorial behavior. For humans, it would be like trying to breathe and function in a world filled with thick smoke.

Practices such as drain-tilling fields, trenching rural ditches to run into the creek, and felling the trees so that the sun beats down on an exposed surface have destroyed the biological fabric of Hangman Creek. Without the shade of cottonwoods and willows, the creek's summer temperatures can exceed 80°F. Trout become distressed in water warmer than 65°F. In addition, negligent ranchers allow cows and horses to graze in the creek, defecate in it, browse down the streamside vegetation, and compact the soils.

Laws like the Washington Water Pollution Control Act prohibit grazing animals in the creeks. But assessments so far say only that human and agricultural impacts create the "substantial potential to pollute" Washington surface waters. The case law clearly upholds Washington State's authority to enforce such legislation for the public good. Yet officials time and again have bowed to political pressure from a powerful agricultural lobby. As a result, the upper management of the Washington Department of Ecology too often turns a blind eye to the problems and violations, making Hangman Creek the victim of a lack of political will.

Agriculture is not the only problem, though. Golf courses and residential practices that strip the banks to the water's edge and overfertilize lawns also degrade the creek's health by creating oxygen-depleting algal blooms. Sewage overflow systems sometimes dump a toxic soup of street runoff and raw sewage. The Department of Transportation has straightened the creek and imprisoned it between steep walls and the armored banks of highway projects. Few species of insects and fish can live in its waters. Still, natural systems possess a tireless and resilient will to survive. Their abilities to work around our ignorance and the problems we have created are impressive and inspiring.

Not long ago, the Spokane Riverkeeper staff decided to canoe a substantial stretch of Hangman Creek. We were hosting a crew of keepers from western Washington and wanted to show them a little local water. They were eager to visit the little creek on the Palouse and see firsthand the pollution issues we had talked about. We showed them. We saw ditching straight from fields into the creek, stream banks that were totally denuded, old chemical drums, tractor tires in the water, cows standing and grazing on the banks, roads pushed through the creek, and chemical burns from glyphosate herbicides sprayed clear to the water's edge. But we saw promising signs on the land and water as well: coyotes, kingfishers, small corridors where hawthorn and willows still provide shade and shelter, owls, an otter, deer, and swallows darting for insects.

Other local groups are also dedicated to rediscovering and recovering the values of this creek, reintroducing beaver in the hope that their dams will promote wetland and stream recovery, and dedicating money to programs to create stream buffers. The Coeur d'Alene Tribe has purchased sections of the streamsides in Idaho with the intention of restoring them. Along one of those sections, on an old section of rail line where Northern Pacific channelized the creek, the tribe is returning it to its original course. A tribal biologist reported that only hours after water was redirected from the old ditch works, redband trout began to move into the creek. Not long ago, Jerry White worked with Eastern Washington University fisheries researchers to catch and tag redband trout in California Creek, a Hangman Creek tributary that still hosts a population of the dwindling fish species. Several were tagged to see if in fact they might travel down to the main stem of the Spokane River.

Hangman Creek demands that we redefine nature, as Greg Gordon suggests (see Gordon's chapter in this volume). We now understand that a stream or river does not end at the waterline. Every river is complete and healthy only if it has its streamside or riparian forest to buffer it from the sun, from road runoff, and from nutrients that drain out of adjacent farm fields. Just as people use clothing to identify and protect themselves, Hangman Creek needs its willows, hawthorn, and cottonwoods to harbor and protect the many forms of life that depend on it. Hangman demands that we fundamentally reexamine the way we see rivers if we are to enjoy clean water and healthy shorelines.

Hangman Creek also demands that we learn something about ourselves and our relation to the systems we live with. When we do, we might cease to devalue and even deny their existence. When we understand and value the shoreline forest, we might choose not to cultivate crops right to the water's edge to maximize profits. We might play golf against the backdrop of riparian forest rather than impose a monoculture of artificially fertilized bluegrass turf into the riparian zone. Perhaps one day our appreciation of the flow of water in our rivers will force us to acknowledge the problems that flow with it. Downstream users on the Spokane River spend on the order of half a million public dollars per year to clean up dissolved-oxygen problems that result in eutrophication and originate, in part, in the Hangman Creek Basin. As the old saying goes, water finds a way.

Hangman Creek demands an end to outdated and compartmentalized thinking. It demands that we recognize causal connections between human activity and habitat degradation and take responsibility for keeping living systems vibrant and our water clean. If we choose the path of recovery, both upstream users and downstream residents will win. As indigenous people have long understood, a healthy river is one measure of a healthy community. Cutting-edge science is gradually coming to the same understanding.

# Waters of Life

WILLIAM S. SKYLSTAD

THROUGHOUT THE CHRISTIAN SCRIPTURES, WE ENCOUNTER references to flowing water and its power to renew life. John baptized Jesus in the waters of the River Jordan, where Jesus began his own public ministry. In the Gospel of John, Jesus meets the Samaritan woman at a well. He tells her of the life-giving, flowing water he offers. And from the time of the apostles, the waters of baptism connected people in the body of Christ.

The symbolic importance of water in the Christian faith prompts awareness of water in our physical world. Over the last two decades, the principle of caring for God's creation has become recognized as a constitutive element of Catholic social teaching. In the late 1990s, the Catholic bishops of the eight dioceses in the Columbia River watershed, seven in the United States and one in Canada, decided to prepare a pastoral letter reflecting on the Columbia River system, which includes the Spokane River. Our "awakening" to the theological significance of the Columbia watershed was part of a new environmental consciousness in the church. Pope John Paul II's message for the 1990 World Day of Peace, titled *The Ecological Crises: A Common Responsibility*, had already highlighted the importance of the environment for the Catholic community. The US Catholic bishops' pastoral letter of 1991, *Renewing the Earth*, and the Canadian Catholic bishops' statement of 1996, *The Environmental Crises: The Place of the Human Being in the Cosmos*, offered Catholic visions of ecology and identified the potential contribution of the Catholic community to public stewardship of nature.

A prior version of this chapter was published in *America: The Jesuit Review* in 2003. It is reprinted here courtesy of the author.

Spokane River, near its confluence with the Little Spokane River, December 2016. Photo courtesy of Rich Leon.

With the assistance of grants from the US Catholic Conference's environmental justice program and the National Religious Partnership for the Environment, bishops from the eight dioceses began work in 1997 on the Columbia River pastoral letter project. "We write this pastoral letter," we said, "because we have become concerned about regional economic and ecological conditions and conflicts over them in the watershed. We hope that we might work together to develop and implement an integrated spiritual, social, ecological vision for our watershed home, a vision that promotes justice for people and stewardship of creation."

## The Columbia Watershed

Rivers throughout the world demonstrate the connectedness of creation. They flow from mountains, pass through all kinds of terrain, and empty into the world's oceans. One of the world's great rivers is the Columbia, immortalized in Woody Guthrie's song "Roll On, Columbia." It is an international river, flowing through southwestern Canada and the northwestern United States. From the snow-capped peaks of British Columbia, it winds through the desert country on the eastern slopes of the Cascades and finally on to the majestic Pacific. Just as it reflects the interconnectedness of creation, the Columbia reminds us of the interconnectedness of the human family.

That human interconnectedness is nearly as complex as the ecosystems through which the river and its tributaries flow on their journey to the sea. For the Native peoples of the region, the Columbia, fed by rivers like the Spokane, is the vibrant and living entity from which they have drawn their sustenance since before the dawn of history. It is the migration route of salmon traveling to and from the Pacific. The Columbia is also a highway that supports commerce through its voluminous barge traffic. Its many dams are a source of electrical energy, supplying homes and businesses across much of the continent. The river also provides water for a vast system of irrigation that transformed agriculture in central Washington. And, through an international agreement, the upper river, in British Columbia, includes large reservoirs to store water for later release and to serve as holding areas during dangerous flood conditions.

The Columbia's complex uses often pit one faction of the population against another. The Hanford Site, where plutonium was produced during World War II, is a source of contention. Hanford is now one of the most contaminated areas in the United States, from which radioactive material has seeped through the ground and into the industrial and agricultural water table. Other pollutants flow into the river, too, and the damage is not easily or cheaply remedied.

Free-flowing water is necessary for salmon migration to and from the ocean. The completion of the Grand Coulee Dam in the early 1940s stopped the migration of these fish to the upper reaches of the Columbia and severely disrupted the culture of the Native peoples, who depended heavily on salmon for food.

Today, efforts to restore declining fish populations compete with efforts to meet the needs of agriculture. There has been a movement to breach the dams on the lower Snake River, an important tributary to the Columbia, for the sake of fish migration. But wheat farmers throughout the Columbia watershed rely on the barge system that transports grain to ports like Portland, Oregon. If the dams are removed, barge transport on the lower Snake River will be impossible. So, even as the Columbia River unites people across borders and ecosystems, competition for its use has the potential to divide them.

### Consultation

Early on, we bishops decided that the pastoral letter should be positive, informative, reflective, and grounded in the church's tradition. It would offer guiding principles for the dialogue about the Columbia's place in our culture rather than specific solutions for the future.

To ensure that our pastoral letter adequately mirrored the Columbia's rich diversity, a steering committee was appointed, consisting of eighteen representatives from the eight dioceses. We began, in the spirit of the Second Vatican Council, with a series of listening sessions conducted across the region to help us "read the signs of the times" as they related to the Columbia. People of diverse backgrounds and viewpoints were invited to these gatherings, and the Catholic universities of the Northwest were involved as well. In every session, although very different viewpoints were expressed, there was always a sense of mutual respect.

The Canadian farmers from the upper reaches of the Columbia voiced hurt and anger about being displaced when their farms were used as part of the reservoir system to control flooding. Native peoples have long felt the same kind of hurt and anger about the changes forced upon their culture. Some of them were removed from their homes with as little as two days' notice to make room for the Hanford nuclear site.

Tension between farmers and those supporting the breaching of the dams on the lower Snake River was also evident. Because of the very poor salmon runs, the advocates of dam removal put considerable pressure on bishops to support breaching the dams. We chose not to do so. Recently scientists have demonstrated that the conditions in the ocean—for example, water temperature—greatly influence the food supply for salmon and therefore their numbers. So preserving salmon habitat requires a more comprehensive approach than simple dam removal. Despite these tensions, the bishops' hearings connected people and contributed to dialogue. Consistently, participants reported they felt they had been heard.

As we began our process, I thought I knew the Columbia intimately. I grew up on one of the river's tributaries, the Methow River in north-central Washington. The river bordered my family's apple farm. Even as a young boy, I felt the connected to the river. One day I asked my mother for a bottle with a cork in it. I put a note in it, threw it in the river, and fantasized that I might someday hear from someone in Japan or China. Though I never received a response, my appreciation of the Columbia was magnified by the sense that my message had connected me with the world beyond my valley. But as well as I knew the river, our listening sessions led me to a greater awareness of the Columbia's significance.

## The Pastoral Letter

The final version of the pastoral letter was divided into four parts. "The River of Our Moment" analyzed current conditions along the river; "The River through Our Memory" reflected on the social and religious history of the Columbia basin; "The River of Our Vision" tried to imagine an alternative future for the watershed; and the concluding part, "The River of Our Responsibility," laid out an ethic of stewardship for the river, its peoples, and its ecosystems.

The letter's underlying theology was creation centered. "The Columbia and all creation," we wrote, "are entrusted to our care." It is "the common home and habitat of God's creatures, a source for human livelihood, and a setting for human community." In keeping with Catholic teaching on the divine purpose of created things, we stressed, the abundance of the Columbia basin, our common home, must be equitably shared. "The reign of God proclaimed by Jesus," we wrote, is "evident in people's efforts to restore

God's creation and to live in harmony with the earth and all creatures, and in struggles to promote justice in human communities."

In the concluding section, we outlined nine specific considerations for taking care of the river for the common good. These included conservation of the watershed, protection of wild species, respect for indigenous people, and justice for the poor. We also gave considerable thought to integrated, community-based resolution of economic and ecological issues and to promoting social and ecological responsibility in the mining, lumbering, and farming sectors.

## Implementation

Rivers speak to us of many things. In the Catholic tradition, they speak to us of the wonder of God's creation and our responsibility to be faithful children of that loving God. Recognizing this, *The Columbia River Watershed: Caring for Creation and the Common Good* was issued on January 8, 2001, the feast of the Baptism of the Lord. The date reaffirmed the ongoing gift of our own baptism.

We sought to produce a document that could be easily understood and also to make the document and its accompanying materials reflect the beauty of the Columbia. Many pictures of the river enliven the final document, and the accompanying video is a beautiful and captivating testimony to the river's majestic place in our culture. Like many pastoral letters on issues of social significance, the statement was addressed not only to Catholics but to all people of goodwill. We hoped to deepen the sense of solidarity among the people of the watershed region.

Our pastoral letter is a living document whose message has been implemented in many ways throughout our region and across the world. Representatives from the seven US dioceses in the watershed have met to address environmental sustainability issues that need to be considered when parishes renovate or develop new buildings. Efforts are under way to implement an annual gathering of the Catholic bishops of the region with the tribal leaders from the watershed. Catholic Conference staff members have met with state legislators to discuss the implications of the issues raised in the pastoral letter on state water policies. Presentations have been given in three dioceses at in-service days for teachers in Catholic schools, and an integrated curriculum for eighth-graders has been developed, inspired in large part by the pastoral letter.

We bishops were clear that we are not experts in matters relating to the Columbia River watershed. We know, though, that God's marvelous creation is far too often taken for granted. We hope that this collaborative effort will continue to help support the common good, increase mutual respect among all participants in the discussion, and deepen appreciation for the wondrous complexity of God's creation.

Since the publication of the pastoral letter, noted scientists have expressed appreciation for the document's call to preserve the natural environment. In November 2000 the World Wide Fund for Nature and the Alliance of Religions and Conservation honored the Columbia River pastoral letter project with an international award presented at ceremonies in Bhaktapur, Nepal.

At the conclusion of the pastoral letter, we offered these words of encouragement: "People live in the world of nature, not apart from it. . . . We can live in greater harmony with our surroundings if we strive to become more aware of our connection to, our responsibility for, the creation that surrounds us."

How wonderful is God's kingdom of creation, of which we are blessed to be a part. And how great is our responsibility as God's people to care for that creation!

# The Once and Future River

GREG GORDON

YOU'D BE HARD PRESSED TO CALL THE SPOKANE RIVER "WILD." SEVEN dams constrict the flow, pulling a succession of concrete nooses around the river and forcing it into penstocks, turbines, channels, and reservoirs. A great beast of burden, the Spokane River has been domesticated to make our lives more comfortable by powering our lights, air conditioners, and laptops. Over the past century, we have straightened and channeled the once-meandering river and dumped industrial waste and sewage into it. In 2004 the heavy metals and PCBs landed it among the top ten endangered rivers named by the American Rivers organization. The slack water is now home to exotic (nonnative) fish, while numerous invasive plants line the riverbank, providing cover for trash and homeless people's camps. And yet . . .

When the Bitterroot Mountains release their grip on winter and the cherished snowpack makes a hurried exit, the Spokane River swells to eighteen thousand cubic feet per second (cfs) and more. As the river hurls itself over the falls and you stand on the bridge suspended over this mad rush of water, it's hard not to feel a sense of wild, untamed power. A subtler wildness lies in the surprise when a great blue heron hidden in backwater shadows lifts off with a few powerful strokes of its improbably long wings. You get the sense that this river might just have a will of its own, despite our efforts to corral and tame it.

But is it really "wild"? *Merriam-Webster's* gives us a fairly straightforward definition of *wild*: "living in a state of nature and not ordinarily tame or domesticated . . . ; growing or produced without human aid or care . . . ; not subject to restraint or regulation." Things get more complicated when we begin peeling back the layers and applying the concept of wildness to a

McGoldrick Lumber Mill and millpond (bottom left), 1931, a sign of the industrial manipulation of the Spokane River since white settlement. After the mill burned down in 1945, Gonzaga University converted the millpond into Lake Arthur as part of a decades-long campus beautification effort. Photo courtesy of University Archives and Special Collections, Gonzaga University.

river. Does the Spokane River exist in a state of nature, or is it domesticated? Can it "grow," or exist and thrive, without human aid? To what degree do we restrain and regulate the river? Can we consider the river undomesticated, free, or self-willed?

Discussion over the meaning of wildness and wilderness peaked during the great wilderness debate of the 1990s. Some ecologists settled on the parameters of "naturalness" and "freedom." Other thinkers, notably the poet Gary Snyder, harked back to the tectonic definition of "self-willed land." Historians pointed out that humans have manipulated landscapes for tens of thousands of years, if not longer. Even parts of the Amazon, it turns out, might actually be products of human artifice. Wildness isn't a black-and-white concept: it is a continuum.

Part of our challenge when defining wildness in a river is that, even more than land, we see the river as a resource, as a blue reflective pool, as H2O moving under the force of gravity, but not as really alive. We tend to view rivers as conduits of water, not as living beings or self-contained ecosystems. But try imagining a river as you might a forest: salmon as deer, crawfish as mice, aquatic invertebrates as insects, trout flying through the water as birds swim through the air. Imagine motorboats as ATVs and dams as clear-cuts.

In his brief but influential book, Richard White coined the phrase *organic machine* to describe the Columbia River, a hybrid of human and natural systems. This view is particularly apt in the Anthropocene, the current geological epoch. Geologists view the Anthropocene as a new and distinct era in which humans are the primary geological force, largely as a result of our releasing the Earth's carbon stores into the atmosphere and consequently changing the planet's climate, with cascading effects on weather patterns, ecosystems, and sea levels—all with potentially devastating effects. In such a world, can any place on earth now be considered truly natural and wild?

But the Anthropocene isn't just about degradation. While the impact of our species on the planetary system is undeniable, we can also restore ecosystems and, in the process, perhaps "re-story" ourselves. We still have the chance to rewrite our narrative, in which we can appear not as a destructive species but as a creative one. This possibility is most apparent in our rivers and streams, where restoration efforts are both repairing old ecosystems and creating new ones.

Thus far, the Elwha River on the Olympic Peninsula in Washington State serves as the poster child for successful river restoration, with the salmon runs returning after the removal of two dams, the Glines Canyon and the Elwha. Other high-profile restoration projects are better characterized by the term *renaturalizing*. Although less poetic, *renaturalizing* is a more accurate description, as *restoration* implies a return to a previous state, presumably pristine and unsullied by Western civilization. In most urban environments, such restoration simply isn't possible. For example, full restoration of the Spokane River would require massive infrastructure changes, including the removal of dams and bridges, recontouring the channel, and aggressively eliminating scores of exotic species.

Perhaps the best example of renaturalizing is the Los Angeles River. Envisioned nearly thirty years ago, the project of converting the LA River from a concrete viaduct into some semblance of a free-flowing river has recently made significant progress. In 2014, the city and the Army Corps of Engineers developed an extensive restoration plan for an eleven-mile stretch. The plan, now projected to cost more than $1.6 billion, would replace the concrete retaining walls with terraces, wetlands, and parks. The plan also includes bike paths, pedestrian bridges, public art installations, riverfront restaurants, and retail businesses.

But is this what we want for the Spokane River? Although landscaped greenways might be aesthetically pleasing and economically beneficial, they lack significant ecological value. Riverfront Park in downtown Spokane is a prime example of urban green space. While it is certainly an improvement over the pre-1974 rail yards and warehouses, functionally it remains ecologically depauperate, requiring continual human maintenance: it is what ecologists refer to as a "designer ecosystem."

The rest of the river can be considered a "novel ecosystem," one that is so much a product of human artifice that a return to its former state is unlikely, even impossible, yet one that functions in a self-sustaining manner. Geographers estimate that about one-third of the world's ice-free land mass now consists of such novel ecosystems. Echoing the concept of the organic machine, the geographer Erle Ellis notes, "Nature is now essentially a part of human systems."

Novel ecosystems are often "urban regions with heavily altered abiotic conditions and large numbers of exotic species." By all accounts, a dammed river constitutes a novel ecosystem. On rivers like the Spokane we have not only changed the abiotic environment and hydrology of the river but also eliminated the Lower Spokane River's keystone species, salmon. As a result, much of the Spokane watershed is biologically landlocked, its ecology greatly altered. Above Spokane Falls, the redband trout is in serious decline because of rising water temperatures, habitat loss, and competition from hatchery rainbow trout. The introduction of fifteen species of exotic fish and dozens of plants in the riparian zone has also reshaped the aquatic ecosystem in significant and unpredictable ways.

Novel ecosystems are characterized by a significant shift from native to exotic species. In ecological restoration projects, land managers expend considerable time and energy attempting to eliminate exotic species under the assumption that they outcompete and replace native species. For decades we've been warned about the hazards of invasive species: water hyacinth, zebra mussels, knapweed, and carp. We equate any nonnative species with ecosystem degradation and collapse. Yet we have forgotten that the vast majority of exotics do not become invasive. Many ecologists, such as Mark Davis, the author of the textbook *Invasion Biology*, suggest that we dispense with the distinction between alien and native species, arguing that it is more appropriate to examine what a species is doing within a given ecosystem than it is to worry about its origins. In fact, native species can sometimes become aggressive invaders, while exotic species can function as "proxies" to re-create ecosystem processes once performed by now-rare or extinct species. Russian olive, for example, considered an invasive species throughout the arid West, provides ecosystem services by stabilizing banks and providing food and habitat for native birds and nectar for nonnative honeybees.

We should consider invasive species as symptoms rather than causes of a problem. After all, invasive species rarely flourish in intact, undisturbed ecosystems: rather, they exploit an open niche, usually created by significant human changes. Driven by climate change, plants and animals are moving in and out of what we once considered stable ecological communities, becoming more like haphazard assemblages of native and exotic species. Ecosystems are starting to resemble an international airport, with a diversity of beings of many shapes, sizes, and colors; each snapshot in time captures only one set of organisms and their particular interactions. While this observation might cause apoplexy among some environmentalists, invasive species are really good at what they do: they are extraordinarily well adapted to rapidly changing ecosystems and human disturbances. I can't help but wonder if by eradicating alien species, we are eliminating those best adapted to negotiating the Anthropocene. In other words, might we be hindering the evolutionary process of adaptation and survival of the fittest?

If we accept that returning the Spokane River to its historical condition through the removal of dams and exotic species may be impossible, how are we to think about "restoring" the river? If we consider that novel ecosystems like the Spokane River might actually be self-sustaining ecosystems capable of adapting to change without human manipulation and interference, we might also consider *rewilding* as a more realistic and even a more desirable approach than restoration. Rewilding is less about re-creating a historical ecosystem and more about generating the conditions in which a self-willed ecosystem can evolve and flourish, even if its evolution takes unexpected and unpredictable directions.

Unlike a farm, garden, park, or fishing pond, the Spokane River doesn't require continual intervention or maintenance. Even if we did nothing— whether we released more hatchery trout or stopped releasing them, controlled weeds or not—the river would still sort itself into a suite of old and new species. Nutrients would continue to cycle through the system. But the key to rewilding is *resilience*, which may be defined as a capacity to grasp and adapt to disruption or change while maintaining key functions. In an urban environment in the Anthropocene, ecosystem resilience is more important than whether or not a species is native.

So why bother? If nature is capable of reorganizing itself after human disruption, why should we worry about taking an active role in rewilding? Wouldn't benign neglect be a suitable and low-cost strategy? In some cases, yes, but it might take a few nudges here and there and even some serious intervention before we could step back and let nature do its thing. We also need to consider human needs and desires. What do we want the Spokane River to be? Can we envision a vibrant ecosystem that sustains and invigorates both human and natural communities?

What would rewilding the Spokane River entail? The first step in facilitating any recovery is to quit pummeling the patient. In many ways, we've taken that first step. The gorge and the falls provide scenic amenities and connect people to the river. Riverside State Park protects the riparian zones and river. The Little Spokane, apart from the fish hatchery, is an outstanding example of public-private cooperation in watershed protection. We've added access points, we have reduced pollution from PCBs and stormwater runoff, and we conduct well-organized annual river cleanups. But all of these efforts have been piecemeal. We lack a strategic conservation plan for the Spokane River watershed, a comprehensive approach that focuses on ecological resilience and rewilding. Our goal should be a resilient, self-sustaining ecosystem that is capable of evolving and adapting to changes and provides benefits to humans and other residents of the watershed. After all, we need the river more than it needs us.

## A Brief Prescription for Our River Patient

*Maintain instream flows.* Although the dams have created an organic machine out of the Spokane River, we can alleviate the extreme drops in the river flow that occur each summer as the result of climate change and increased human demands. While complex, the problem is political and social, not technological. In other words, making consistent flows a priority would require "only" better cooperation between Avista Utilities (the company that manages most of the dams), Idaho, Washington, and the federal government.

*Quit raising hatchery rainbow trout.* This one is even easier. Redband trout are resilient and well adapted to our watershed. If we give them half a chance and minimize their hybridization with hatchery rainbow trout, redband numbers will rebound, and the river will once again host a vibrant native fishery.

*Consider salmon.* Restoring salmon runs is much more complicated than restoring native trout populations. Getting salmon over the dams on the Columbia and Lower Spokane Rivers to spawn is a major but not impossible challenge, especially now that the Spokane Tribe is making salmon restoration a priority. How amazing would it be to have thirty-pound chinook salmon running up the Spokane River once again?

*Slow the flow.* Along much of its course, the Spokane River is deeply chan-neled and acts more like a sluice box than a river. A healthy river requires a variable flow. Fish need deep pools and riffles, sloughs and backwaters, islands and braided channels, logs and woody debris. Some of these vari-ations can easily be created, using heavy equipment to push some of the concrete and basalt into the river to create breakwaters and peninsulas.

*Stabilize river banks.* The Spokane Conservation District and other organ-izations, along with legions of volunteers, have planted willows and upland species along the steep, eroding banks of the river. We can continue and expand this effort. Not only is it relatively inexpensive and enduring in its results, but such efforts also connect people to the river and provide a sense of purpose and ownership.

*Focus human use.* Currently we have a rather haphazard pattern of access along the river, involving public green space, bike paths, lawns, boat launches, and extensive informal access. While manicured green space and paved bike paths might be appropriate in some locations, these sterile environments diminish overall biodiversity and provide no ecosystem services. Such designer systems are the antithesis of wildness. A comprehensive manage-ment plan would highlight the areas most appropriate for recreation and those best suited for ecological services and rewilding efforts.

*Manage homeless camps.* These camps generate trash and human waste along the river banks. While increased vegetation can discourage informal use, it doesn't address the societal problems of which homelessness is a symptom. One way to improve both the riparian environment and quality of life would be for the city to establish a formal camping area with ablution facilities, security, food, and clothing distribution. Spokane could turn to corporations, as Seattle has done, to ease pressure on the river. A new Ama-zon building in Seattle, for example, will contain a homeless shelter. New Spokane construction might follow suit.

*Continue to improve water quality.* More than a century of mining and heavy industry has left a legacy of heavy metals and toxins, including PCBs. Thanks to a concerted effort by local, state, and federal governments, the Spokane Tribe, and environmental organizations, the water quality is slowly improving. Unfortunately, agricultural and storm-water runoff continue to pollute the river. Two key improvements would be to diminish allotments or draws from the river and to clean up the dirty flows from Hangman Creek.

*Restrict streamside development.* Residential and urban development along the banks is the largest potential threat to the river. Such development presents us with a conundrum: as we improve the river environment and increase access, we increase the property values and desirability of housing along the river. Although many of the river banks are private property, we need to recognize the river as a public resource and improve cooperation between landowners and state agencies to adopt and enforce regulations that restrict streamside development.

*Remove the dams.* Sooner or later the seven dams on the Spokane will have to come down, as they have a finite life span. Replacing the old hydroelectric dams with innovative power projects that provide both electricity and a free-flowing river will usher in a more sustainable future in which the Spokane River becomes more "organic" than "machine" and we acknowledge the intertwined needs of humans and nature. One innovation being explored is "standard modular hydropower," which scales capacity to smaller sites.

*Let nature do the rest.* We humans have a penchant for meddling. In rewilding, the goal is a resilient, self-sustaining ecosystem that functions with little to no human manipulation. Even if we accomplish only some of this prescription, nature can heal itself, so long as we cease polluting the water, paving the land, replacing empty lots and shorelines with manicured lawns and houses, spraying herbicides and other poisons, and killing off wildlife. Nature will return, and it will be as wild, unpredictable, strong, and adaptable as we let it be.

*Heal the river and heal ourselves.* As Henry David Thoreau pointed out, "We require an infusion of hemlock-spruce or arbor-vitae in our tea." In other words, humans have a psychological need for wildness. Thanks to Richard Louv, we even have a new term—*nature-deficit disorder*—to describe the loss of contact with the natural world. Increased exposure of urban dwellers to biodiversity enhances our psychological well-being, fosters ecological literacy, and reorients our interior landscape. But providing opportunities to connect to nature in an urban environment requires a mental shift away from imprisoning nature, confining it to national parks and designated wilderness areas, and toward allowing it to flourish within the city.

Ultimately, rewilding the Spokane River can be part of a larger conservation strategy. Rewilding the river would create a vibrant ecological corridor that connects core wildlife habitats in the Mount Spokane and Riverside State Parks with the Dishman Hills, the Little Spokane River, and other county conservation lands, providing a network of natural habitats within a matrix of human development. In the process, we would reconnect ourselves with our community and to the place where we live. Nearly half a million people live in the Spokane watershed, but we do not have to dominate it: with the help of a rewilded river, we can infuse our urban and suburban existence with a wild nature. In the Anthropocene, we might need to modify Aldo Leopold's dictum: "A thing is right when it tends to preserve the integrity, stability, and beauty of the biotic community. It is wrong when it tends otherwise." Adding *resilience* to the dictum requires us to embrace unplanned diversity and accidental rewilding, so that we can develop a tough new ecosystem capable of adapting to the massive changes humans have wrought.

# Further Reading

Alexie, Sherman. *The Lone Ranger and Tonto Fistfight in Heaven.*
New York: New Grove Press, 1993.
———. *The Summer of Black Widows.* New York: Hanging Loose
Press, 1996.
Bean, Margaret. "Discovery at Spokane House: Jaco Finlay and His
Grave." *Spokesman-Review*, October 21, 1951.
Bowers, Dawn. *Expo '74 World's Fair Spokane.* Spokane: Expo '74
Corporation, 1974.
Brown, William Compton. *The Indian Side of the Story.* Spokane:
C. W. Hill, 1916.
Bullard, Oral. *Crisis on the Columbia.* Portland, OR: Touchstone
Press, 1968.
Cox, Ross. *Adventures on the Columbia River.* London: Colburn and
Bentley, 1832.
Cronin, John, and Robert F. Kennedy Jr. *The Riverkeepers: Two Activists
Fight to Reclaim Our Environment as a Basic Human Right.* New York:
Simon and Schuster, 1999.
Cronon, William, ed. *Uncommon Ground: Rethinking the Human Place
in Nature.* New York: Norton, 1996.
Deloria, Philip. *Playing Indian.* New Haven, CT: Yale University
Press, 1998.
Fahey, John. "Power Plays: The Enigma of Little Falls." *Pacific Northwest
Quarterly* 82, no. 4 (October 1991): 122–31.
———. *The Spokane River: Its History and Miles.* Spokane: Centennial
Trail Committee, 1988.

Glover, James N. *Reminiscences of James Glover.* Fairfield, WA: Ye Galleon, 1985.

Harmon, Alexandra. *Indians in the Making: Ethnic Relations and Indian Identities around Puget Sound.* Berkeley: University of California Press, 1998.

Hearne, Joanna. "Remembering Smoke Signals: Interviews with Chris Eyre and Sherman Alexie." *Post Script* 29, no. 3 (Summer 2010). www.freepatentsonline.com/article/Post-Script/247034914.html.

Hill, Kip. "Name for New Era." *Spokesman-Review*, September 19, 2016.

Jensen, Derrick, and George Draffan. *Railroads and Clearcuts: Legacy of Congress's 1864 Northern Pacific Railroad Land Grant.* Spokane: Inland Empire Public Lands Council, 1995.

Jonckers, Jon. "Centennial Trail Grows with Trail Extension." *Out There Monthly*, August 15, 2016. www.outtheremonthly.com/centennial-trail-grows-with-trail-extension.

Judson, Katharine Berry. *Myths and Legends of the Pacific Northwest.* Lincoln: University of Nebraska Press, 1997.

Kershner, Jim. "Olmsted Parks in Spokane." HistoryLink.org, July 18, 2007.

Knight, A. P. *Sawdust and Fish Life.* Toronto: Murray Printing Co., 1903.

Kramer, Becky. "Spokane Falls Will Flow Full Time." *Spokesman-Review*, May 6, 2009.

Limerick, Patricia. *The Legacy of Conquest: The Unbroken Past of the American West.* New York: W. W. Norton, 1987.

Lindholdt, Paul. "Lokout (1834–1913)." HistoryLink.org, October 27, 2013.

———. "Portrait of Yakama Indian Lokout Adds to History of Brother Qualchan." *Spokesman-Review*, December 1, 2013.

Louv, Richard. *Last Child in the Woods: Saving Our Children from Nature-Deficit Disorder.* Chapel Hill, NC: Algonquin Books, 2008.

Molenaar, Dee. *The Spokane Aquifer, Washington.* USGS Water-Supply Paper 2265. Washington, DC: Government Printing Office, 1988. https://pubs.usgs.gov/wsp/2265/report.pdf.

Morrissey, Katherine G. *Mental Territories: Mapping the Inland Empire.* Ithaca, NY: Cornell University Press, 1997.

Nash, Roderick. *Wilderness and the American Mind.* 3rd ed. New Haven, CT: Yale University Press, 1982.

Neuberger, Richard L. *Our Promised Land.* New York: Macmillan, 1938.

Nisbet, Jack. *Sources of the River: Tracking David Thompson across Western North America.* Seattle: Sasquatch Books, 2007.

———. *Visible Bones: Journeys across Time in the Columbia River Country.* Seattle: Sasquatch Books, 2003.

Nixon, Edgar B., ed. *Franklin D. Roosevelt and Conservation, 1911–1945.* 2 vols. Washington, DC: Government Printing Office, 1957.

Peterson, Nancy J., ed. *Conversations with Sherman Alexie.* Jackson: University Press of Mississippi, 2009.

Pettit, Stephanie. "Spiral of Alexie Poem a Visual Monument." *Spokesman-Review*, February 7, 2008.

Prager, Mike. "Centennial Trail Gets Grand Addition." *Spokesman-Review*, September 28, 2013.

Reisner, Marc. *Cadillac Desert: The American West and Its Disappearing Water.* New York: Penguin, 1993.

Roosevelt, Franklin D. "Remarks at Grand Coulee Dam." October 2, 1937. The American Presidency Project, edited by Gerhard Peters and John T. Wooley. www.presidency.ucsb.edu/ws/?pid=15472.

———. "Remarks at the Site of the Grand Coulee Dam, Washington." August 4, 1934. The American Presidency Project, edited by Gerhard Peters and John T. Wooley. www.presidency.ucsb.edu/ws/?pid=14732.

Ruby, Robert H., and John Arthur Brown. *The Spokane Indians: Children of the Sun.* Norman: University of Oklahoma Press, [1970] 2006.

Runte, Alfred. *National Parks: The American Experience.* Lincoln: University of Nebraska Press, 1997.

Splawn, A. J. *Ka-Mi-Akin: Last Hero of the Yakimas.* Portland, OR: Kilham Printing, 1917.

*The Spokane River.* Directed by R. L. Pryor. Narrated by Stanley J. Witter Jr. Northwest Film Productions, 1970.

Stegner, Wallace. *The American West as Living Space.* Ann Arbor: University of Michigan Press, 1994.

Stimson, William. *Spokane: A View of the Falls: An Illustrated History*. Sun Valley, CA: American Historical Press, 1999.

Strand, Ginger. "The Crying Indian." *Orion*, November 20, 2008.

Stratton, David H., ed. *Spokane and the Inland Empire: An Interior Pacific Northwest Anthology*. Pullman: Washington State University Press, 2005.

Thayer, Robert L. Jr. *LifePlace: Bioregional Thought and Practice*. Berkeley: University of California Press, 2003.

Thompson, David. *Columbia Journals*. Edited by Barbara Belyea. Montreal: McGill-Queen's University Press, 2007.

Thompson, Terry, and Steven M. Egesdal, eds. *Salish Myths and Legends: One People's Stories*. Lincoln: University of Nebraska Press, 2008.

Tinsley, Jesse. "Photos Then and Now: Banks by Bridge Once 'Shacktown.'" *Spokesman-Review,* October 28, 2013.

Todd, Ally. "That Place Where Ghosts of Salmon Jump: Spokane Falls." Spokane Historical Society. www.spokanehistorical.org/items/show/149, accessed August 29, 2017.

US Bureau of Fisheries. *Report of the Commissioner of Fish and Fisheries on Investigations in the Columbia River Basin in Regard to the Salmon Fisheries*. Washington, DC: Government Printing Office, 1894.

Valtin, Tom. "Landmark Agreement Restores Flows in Spokane Falls." Grassroots Scrapbook, July 23, 2009. http://sierraclub.typepad.com/scrapbook/2009/07/landmark-agreement-restores-flows-in-spokane-falls.html.

White, Richard. "Environmentalism and Indian Peoples." In *Earth, Air, Fire, Water*, edited by Jill Kerr Conway, Kenneth Keniston, and Leo Marx, 125–44. Amherst: University of Massachusetts Press, 1999.

———. *The Organic Machine*. New York: Hill and Wang, 1995.

Wilma, David. "Archaeologists Unearth Artifacts Beginning on June 7, 2005, Which Indicate That Spokane Is the Oldest Continually Occupied Human Habitation in Washington." HistoryLink.org, October 8, 2016.

———. "U.S. Army Colonel George Wright Hangs Yakama and Palouse Prisoners at the Ned-Whauld River Beginning on September 25, 1858." HistoryLink.org, September 24, 2016.

Winthrop, Theodore. *The Canoe and the Saddle: A Critical Edition*. Edited by Paul J. Lindholdt. Lincoln: University of Nebraska Press, 2006.

Worster, Donald. *Nature's Economy: A History of Ecological Ideas*. New York: Cambridge University Press, 1994.

———. *Under Western Skies: Nature and History in the American West*. New York: Oxford University Press, 1992.

Wriglesworth, Chad. "The Poetics of Water: Currents of Reclamation in the Columbia River Basin." In *The Bioregional Imagination: Literature, Ecology, and Place*, edited by Tom Lynch, Cheryll Glotfelty, and Karla Armbruster, 86–99. Athens: University of Georgia Press, 2012.

Young, Frederick G., ed. *Correspondence and Journals of Captain Nathaniel J. Wyeth, 1831–6*. New York: Arno Press, 1973.

Youngs, J. William T. *The Fair and the Falls*. Cheney: Eastern Washington University Press, 1996.

# Contributors

**Sherman Alexie** is a poet, writer, and filmmaker with ancestry in several tribes. He grew up on the Spokane Indian Reservation and now lives in Seattle. His first young-adult novel, *The Absolutely True Diary of a Part-Time Indian*, won the 2007 US National Book Award for Young People's Literature.

**Bob Bartlett** is a senior lecturer in Sociology and Justice Studies at Eastern Washington University. A passionate outdoorsman, fly fisherman, and lover of rivers, he has fished and walked the banks of the Spokane River for nearly thirty years.

**Tim Connor,** best known for his reporting on complex environmental and legal issues, is the recipient of three national Sigma Delta Chi Awards from the Society of Professional Journalists, which recognize distinguished service to the American people and journalism.

**Rick Eichstaedt** is the executive director of the Center for Justice (CFJ) in Spokane. He became the first Spokane riverkeeper in 2009, after five years as staff attorney at the CFJ in environmental and land-use litigation. He began his legal career protecting natural resources and treaty rights for the Nez Perce Tribe.

**Don Fels** is a visual artist and writer who works on the relationship of natural resources around the world to place and culture. He has created artworks around several bodies of water, including the Bay of Naples; Lake Sammamish; and the Duwamish, Willamette, Mississippi, and Marne Rivers.

**Guadalupe Flores,** born and raised in Spokane, has a BA in literary studies and an MA in technical writing from Eastern Washington University. In 2000, after working for environmental nonprofit organizations for ten years, he founded KYRS–Thin Air Community Radio, a nonprofit, noncommercial community radio station based in Spokane.

**Jerry R. Galm** is emeritus professor of anthropology and Fulbright Fellow in the Department of Geography and Anthropology, Eastern Washington University. His research has included investigations in Ghana, West Africa, Kazakhstan, and Uzbekistan, in addition to the Pacific Northwest and other parts of the United States.

**Greg Gordon** lives a short walk from the confluence of Latah (Hangman) Creek and the Spokane River. He is an associate professor of environmental studies at Gonzaga University and is writing a book about urban rewilding.

**Stan Gough,** emeritus director of Archaeological and Historical Services and Distinguished Fellow of Archaeology at Eastern Washington University, has conducted archaeological investigations in Oklahoma, the US Virgin Islands, and the Pacific Northwest since 1980.

**Margo Hill** teaches planning classes, including American Indian law, at Eastern Washington University. A member of the Spokane Tribe who was raised on the Spokane Indian reservation, she is a semifluent speaker of the Spokane Indian (Salish) language. She has served as a Spokane tribal attorney and Coeur d'Alene tribal court judge.

**Chris Kopczynski,** a lifelong resident of Spokane and an avid climber, was the ninth American to summit Mount Everest and the twelfth climber in the world to summit the highest peak on every continent. Past president of the Inland Empire Associated General Contractors of America, and currently vice president of the Dishman Hills Conservancy, he has four children and three grandchildren.

**Becky Kramer** is a reporter for the *Spokesman-Review* newspaper in Spokane, where she writes about natural resources, energy, and health. Her favorite reporting assignments involve tagging along with scientists on their fieldwork.

**Beatrice Lackaff,** a transplant from Portland, Oregon, has lived in west-central Spokane for more than thirty years. After obtaining a degree in geography from Eastern Washington University and retiring from a career in geographic information systems, she took up journalism and now writes frequently for *Out There Monthly*.

**Paul Lindholdt** teaches at Eastern Washington University. His ecological memoir, *In Earshot of Water: Notes from the Columbia Plateau*, won the 2012 Washington State Book Award.

**Tod Marshall** teaches at Gonzaga University. His 2014 collection of poems, *Bugle*, won the Washington State Book Award. He is the Washington State poet laureate for 2016–18.

**Camille McNeely** is an associate professor of biology at Eastern Washington University. She received a PhD in integrative biology from the University of California, Berkeley, in 2004. She first met the giant salmonfly in the Eel River of northern California during her PhD research on stream food webs.

**Bart Mihailovich** works for Waterkeeper Alliance as the affiliate coordinator, charged with recruiting and supporting new Waterkeeper affiliates around the world. He spent 2010–14 as the Spokane riverkeeper. A graduate of Eastern Washington University, he now lives in Missoula, Montana.

**Stan Miller** managed Spokane County's water resources program for twenty years. During that time he oversaw the plans for regulations and facilities to protect water quality in the Spokane Valley–Rathdrum Prairie aquifer. Later Stan began recreating on the river and learned better how to protect it as a citizen.

**Barry G. Moses (Sulustu),** a tenured faculty member at Spokane Community College, earned a master's degree in education from Whitworth University. An enrolled member of the Spokane Tribe of Indians, he has studied the Spokane language for twenty years and has a personal commitment to promoting cultural awareness and understanding.

**Carmen A. Nezat,** associate professor in geology and environmental science at Eastern Washington University, focuses her research on soil and water quality. She received her BS from the University of Southwestern Louisiana, MS from the University of Alabama, and PhD in geology from the University of Michigan.

**Jack Nisbet** has written biographies of the fur agent David Thompson and the naturalist David Douglas, who provided some of the first written descriptions of the Spokane River. Nisbet's most recent book, *Ancient Places*, is a cycle of stories about people and phenomena that helped shape the landscape of the greater Northwest.

**Rachael Paschal Osborn** is a public-interest lawyer who received a BA in environmental studies and a JD from the University of Washington. She writes, litigates, and has taught water law at Gonzaga University Law School. Her recent publications include "Hydraulic Continuity in Washington Water Law" and "Climate Change and the Columbia River Treaty."

**John Roskelley** earned a degree in geology from Washington State University and has written three adventure books and a paddler's guide to the Columbia River. A former Spokane County commissioner, he served on multiple state boards. He and his wife, Joyce, have been married forty-four years and have three children.

**Allan T. Scholz** received a PhD in 1980 from the University of Wisconsin, Madison, where he investigated olfactory imprinting and homing in salmon.

Professor emeritus at Eastern Washington University, he has published multiple books on regional fishes and is working on a new book that investigates Indian uses of the salmon.

**William S. Skylstad,** former president of the US Conference of Catholic Bishops, chaired the steering committee of the Columbia River pastoral letter project. He is bishop emeritus of the ninety-thousand-member Diocese of Spokane.

**William Stimson,** a former reporter who covered Spokane city government, holds a PhD in American history and is author of *Spokane: A View of the Falls* (1999). He is currently a professor of journalism at Eastern Washington University.

**Julie Titone** now serves as communications and marketing manager for Sno-Isle Libraries in northwestern Washington State, following a career in journalism and university communications.

**Nance Van Winckel's** sixth book of poems, *Pacific Walkers*, and fourth collection of stories, *Boneland*, were published in 2013. Professor emerita at Eastern Washington University, she now teaches in the low-residency MFA in Writing Program at the Vermont College of Fine Arts.

**Sara L. Walker,** with Archaeological and Historical Services, Eastern Washington University, specializes in Plateau and Northwest Coast archaeology, material culture studies, and household archaeology. She earned a master's degree in archaeology from the University College London Institute of Archaeology.

**Jess Walter** is the author of eight books. His novel *The Zero* was a finalist for the National Book Award, and his novel *Beautiful Ruins* was a *New York Times* best seller. He is a lifelong resident of Spokane.

**Jerry White** has been the Spokane riverkeeper since 2014. He has a long history of working to protect rivers in the Inland Northwest. As a former staff member of Save our Wild Salmon, Jerry advocated for the restoration and protection of native Snake River salmon and steelhead.

**Chad Wriglesworth** is associate professor of English at St. Jerome's University, Waterloo, Ontario. He received his doctorate from the University of Iowa, where he specialized in twentieth-century American literature with an emphasis in religious thought, environmental studies, and the literature and culture of the Columbia River basin.

**J. William T. Youngs,** a graduate of Harvard (BA) and the University of California, Berkeley (PhD), is professor of history at Eastern Washington University. He has published five books, including *The Fair and the Falls: Spokane's Expo '74,* which won a Washington State Governor's Award.

# Index